THE FIRST WAVE

ALSO BY ALEX KERSHAW

THE FIRST
WAVE

The D-Day Warriors Who
Led the Way to Victory
in World War II

ALEX KERSHAW

CALIBER

Dutton Caliber
An imprint of Penguin Random House LLC
penguinrandomhouse.com

Copyright © 2019 by Alex Kershaw
Penguin supports copyright. Copyright fuels creativity, encourages diverse voices,
promotes free speech, and creates a vibrant culture. Thank you for buying
an authorized edition of this book and for complying with copyright laws
by not reproducing, scanning, or distributing any part of it in any form
without permission. You are supporting writers and allowing
Penguin to continue to publish books for every reader.

DUTTON CALIBER and the D colophon are registered
trademarks of Penguin Random House LLC.

Maps by Storystudio

LIBRARY OF CONGRESS CATALOGING-IN-PUBLICATION DATA
Names: Kershaw, Alex, author.
Title: The first wave : the D-Day warriors who led the way to
victory in World War II / by Alex Kershaw.
Description: New York : Dutton Caliber, [2019] |
Includes bibliographical references and index.
Identifiers: LCCN 2018057388 (print) | LCCN 2019002021 (ebook) |
ISBN 9780451490063 (ebook) | ISBN 9780451490056 (hardcover)
Subjects: LCSH: World War, 1939–1945—Campaigns—France—Normandy. |
World War, 1939–1945—Commando operations. | Soldiers—Biography. |
Commando troops—Biography. | Allied Powers (1919–)—Armed Forces—Biography.
Classification: LCC D756.5.N6 (ebook) | LCC D756.5.N6 K4694 2019 (print) |
DDC 940.54/21421—dc23
LC record available at https://lccn.loc.gov/2018057388

Printed in the United States of America
1   3   5   7   9   10   8   6   4   2

While the author has made every effort to provide accurate telephone numbers,
internet addresses, and other contact information at the time of publication,
neither the publisher nor the author assumes any responsibility for errors
or for changes that occur after publication. Further, the publisher does not
have any control over and does not assume any responsibility for
author or third-party websites or their content.

For John Snowdon

CONTENTS

THE FIRST WAVE

PART ONE

Twilight of the Idols

When you talk about combat leadership under fire on the beach at Normandy, I don't see how the credit can go to anyone other than the company-grade officers and senior NCOs who led the way. It is good to be reminded that there are such men, that there always have been, and always will be. We sometimes forget, I think, that you can manufacture weapons, and you can purchase ammunition, but you can't buy valor and you can't pull heroes off an assembly line.[1]

—SERGEANT JOHN ELLERY,
16th Infantry Regiment, US 1st Infantry Division

CHAPTER 1

June 5, 1944

THE CLOCK IN THE WAR room at Southwick House showed 4 A.M. The nine men gathered in the twenty-five-by-fifty-foot former library, its walls lined with empty bookshelves, were anxiously sipping cups of coffee, their minds dwelling on the Allies' most important decision of World War II. Outside in the darkness, a gale was blowing, angry rain lashing against the windows. "The weather was terrible," recalled fifty-three-year-old Supreme Allied Commander Dwight Eisenhower. "Southwick House was shaking. Oh, it was really storming."[1] Given the atrocious conditions, would Eisenhower give the final go-ahead or postpone? He had left it until now, the very last possible moment, to decide whether or not to launch the greatest invasion in history.

Seated before Eisenhower in upholstered chairs at a long table covered in a green cloth were the commanders of Overlord: the no-nonsense Missourian, General Omar Bradley, commander of US ground forces; the British General Bernard

Law Montgomery, commander of the 21st Army Group, casually attired in his trademark roll-top sweater and corduroy
slacks; Admiral Sir Bertram Ramsay, the naval commander
who had orchestrated the "miracle of Dunkirk"—the evacuation of more than 300,000 troops from France in May 1940;
the pipe-smoking Air Chief Arthur Tedder, also British; Air
Chief Marshal Sir Trafford Leigh-Mallory, whose blunt pes-
simism had caused Eisenhower considerable anguish; and
Major General Walter Bedell Smith, Eisenhower's chief of
staff.

A dour and tall Scotsman, forty-three-year-old Group Captain James Stagg, Eisenhower's chief meteorologist, entered the
library and stood on the polished wood floor before Overlord's
commanders. He had briefed Eisenhower and his generals every
twelve hours, predicting the storm that was now rattling the
windows of the library, which had already led Eisenhower to
postpone the invasion from June 5 to June 6. Then, to Eisenhower's great relief, he had forecast that there would, as he had
put it with a slight smile, "be rather fair conditions" beginning
that afternoon and lasting for thirty-six hours.

Once more, Stagg gave an update. The storm would indeed
start to abate later that day.[2]

Eisenhower got to his feet and began to pace back and forth,
hands clasped behind him, chin resting on his chest, tension
etched on his face.

What if Stagg was wrong? The consequences were beyond
bearable. But to postpone again would mean that secrecy would
be lost. Furthermore, the logistics of men and supplies, as well
as the tides, dictated that another attempt could not be made for

weeks, giving the Germans more time to prepare their already formidable coastal defenses.

Since January, when he had arrived in England to command Overlord, Eisenhower had been under crushing, ever greater strain. Now it had all boiled down to this decision. Eisenhower alone—not Roosevelt, not Churchill—had the authority to give the final command to go, to "enter the continent of Europe," as his orders from on high had stated, and "undertake operations aimed at the heart of Germany and the destruction of her armed forces."[3] He alone could pull the trigger.

Marshaling the greatest invasion in the history of war had been, at times, as terrifying as the very real prospect of failure. The last time there had been a successful cross-Channel attack was 1066, almost a millennium ago. The scale of this operation had been almost too much to grasp. More than 700,000 separate items had formed the inventory of what was required to launch the assault. Dismissed by some British officers as merely a "coordinator, a good mixer," the blue-eyed Eisenhower, celebrated for his broad grin and easy charm, had nevertheless imposed his will, working eighteen-hour days, reviewing and tweaking plans to launch some seven thousand vessels, twelve thousand planes, and 160,000 troops to hostile shores.

Eisenhower had overseen vital changes to the Overlord plan. A third more troops had been added to the invasion forces, of whom fewer than 15 percent had actually experienced combat. Heeding General Montgomery's concerns, Eisenhower had ensured that the front was broadened to almost sixty miles of coast, with a beach code-named Utah added at the base of the Cotentin Peninsula, farthest to the west. It had been agreed, after Eisenhower had carefully managed the "bunch of prima donnas," most of them British, who made up his high command—the men gathered now before him—that the attack by night should benefit from the rays of a late-rising moon.

In addition, it was decided that the first wave of seaborne troops would land at low tide to avoid being ripped apart by beach obstacles. An elaborate campaign of counterintelligence and outright deception, Operation Fortitude, had hopefully kept the Germans guessing as to where and when the Allies would land, providing the critical element of surprise. Hopefully, Erwin Rommel, the field marshal in charge of German forces in Normandy, had not succeeded in fortifying the coast to the extent that he had demanded. Hopefully, the Allies' greatest advantage—their overwhelming superiority in air power—would make all the difference. Hopefully.

Not even Eisenhower was confident of success. "We are not merely risking a tactical defeat," he had recently confided to an old friend back in Washington. "We are putting the whole works on one number."[4] Among Eisenhower's most senior generals, even now, at the eleventh hour, there was precious little optimism.

Still pacing, Eisenhower thrust his chin in the direction of Montgomery. He was all for going. So was Tedder. Leigh-Mallory, ever cautious, thought the heavy cloud cover might prove disastrous.

Stagg left the library and its cloud of pipe and cigarette smoke. There was an intense silence; each man knew how immense this moment was in history. The stakes could not be higher. There was no plan B. Nazism and its attendant evils— barbarism, unprecedented genocide, the enslavement of tens of millions of Europeans—might yet prevail. The one man in the room whom Eisenhower genuinely liked, Omar Bradley, believed that Overlord was Hitler's "greatest danger and his greatest opportunity. If the Overlord forces could be repulsed and trounced decisively on the beaches, Hitler knew it would be a very long time indeed before the Allies tried again—if ever."

Six weeks before, V Corps commander General Leonard Gerow had written to Eisenhower outlining grave doubts, even though it was too late to do much to alter the overall Overlord plan. It was distressingly clear, after the 4th Division had lost an incredible 749 men—killed in a single practice exercise on April 28 on Slapton Sands—that the Royal Navy and American troops were not working well together. Apart from the appallingly chaotic practice landings—the woeful yet final dress rehearsals—the defensive obstacles sown all along the beaches in Normandy were especially concerning.

Eisenhower had chided Gerow for his skepticism. Gerow had shot back that he was not being "pessimistic" but simply "realistic."[5] And what of the ten missing officers from the disaster at Slapton Sands who had detailed knowledge of the D-Day operations, the most important secret in modern history? They knew about "Hobart's Funnies," the assortment of tanks specially designed to cut through Rommel's defenses—including flail tanks that cleared mines with chains, and DUKWs, the six-wheeled amphibious trucks that would take Rangers to within yards of the steep Norman cliffs—and they knew exactly where and when the Allies were landing. Was it really credible to assume that the Germans had not been tipped off, that so many thousands of planes and ships had gone unseen?

Even Winston Churchill, usually so ebullient and optimistic, was filled with misgivings, having cautioned Eisenhower to "take care that the waves do not become red with the blood of American and British youth."[6] The prime minister had recently told a senior Pentagon official, John J. McCloy, that it would have been best to have had "Turkey on our side, the Danube under threat as well as Norway cleaned up before we undertook [Overlord]." The British Field Marshal Sir Alan Brooke, chief of the Imperial General Staff, had fought in Normandy in 1940 before the British Expeditionary Force's narrow escape at Dunkirk. Just a few hours earlier, he had written in his diary that he was "very uneasy about the whole operation. At the best it will fall so very, very far short of the expectation of the bulk of the people, namely all those who know nothing about its difficulties. At the worst it may well be the most ghastly disaster of the whole war!"

No wonder Eisenhower had complained of a constant ringing in his right ear. He was almost frantic with nervous exhaustion, but he dared not show it as he continued now to pace back and forth, lost in thought, listening to the crackle and hiss of logs burning in the fireplace. He could not betray his true feelings, his dread and anxiety.

The minute hand on the clock moved slowly, for as long as five minutes according to one account.[7] Walter Bedell Smith recalled, "I never realized before the loneliness and isolation of a commander at a time when such a momentous decision has to be taken, with the full knowledge that failure or success rests on his judgment alone."[8]

Eisenhower finally stopped pacing and then looked calmly at his lieutenants.[9]

"OK. We'll go."[10]

THE FIRST WAVE – JUNE 6, 1944

US
4th
Division

US
29th and 1st
Divisions

US
British
50th
Division

Canadian
3rd
Division

British
3rd
Division

Valognes

Lillyman

Sainte-Mère-Église

82nd & 101st
Airborne Divisions

Carentan

Schroeder

Utah

Kerchner

Omaha

Spalding

Hollis

Gold

The Daltons

Juno

Lovat and Gautier

Sword

Otway

6th Airborne
Division

Howard

Caen

NORMANDY

Saint-Lô

N

5 miles

THE SHADOWS WERE LENGTHENING at North Witham airfield when an officer stepped down from a C-47 plane, a small case attached to his right wrist. Armed guards who usually patrolled the airfield, which lay a hundred miles north of London, accompanied the officer into a building where he was met by twenty-eight-year-old Captain Frank Lillyman, a slightly built New Yorker who could often be found with a wry smile and an impish glint in his eye but was now all business.

The officer opened the small case and pulled out a message and handed it to Lillyman, who since December 1943 had commanded the 101st Airborne's pathfinders. At last, after weeks of growing tension and restless anticipation, the top-secret orders from the division commander, General Maxwell Taylor, had arrived—D-Day was on. The drop was a go. "Get the men ready," Lillyman told a sergeant, and then the message was burnt.[11]

Lillyman's men assembled at a flight line where they began to strap on their silk parachutes. Having watched a 1939 film about the legendary Apache warrior Geronimo, some had shaved their scalps, leaving an unruly strip of hair across their heads. They were all volunteers, many of them cocky misfits busted down the ranks for bad behavior, or, as one of them put it, "a bunch of good guys who had screwed up one way or another."[12] For all their past faults, none doubted that they now belonged to an elite group that had been superbly trained; Lillyman had rejected three out of four applicants, disappointing some unit commanders who thought they had gotten rid of troublemakers.[13]

Out of nowhere, it seemed, there appeared grinning Red Cross girls with hot coffee, a gaggle of cooing press photographers, a Signal Corps cameraman using rare color film, and several members of the 101st Airborne's top brass, all present to witness the departure of the very first Americans to fight on D-Day, the spearhead of the Allied invasion.

There was playacting for the cameras, followed by nonchalant waves and friendly punches to buddies' shoulders. A paratrooper riding a children's bicycle did circles in front of a plane to much laughter. Then a medic gave Lillyman's chain-smoking pathfinders "puke" pills in small cardboard boxes to combat airsickness, and bags to vomit into. Some threw the pills away, not trusting them, wanting to be sharp, clearheaded, the moment they touched the ground in France.

There was the guttural coughing of engines as the C-47s started warming up, and the horsing around came to an end. Lillyman's men clambered or were helped aboard the twin-propped aircraft, which had been hastily daubed with black and white "invasion" stripes—the colors of Operation Overlord. Brown masking paper covered some areas of the fuselage to prevent damage from the still drying paint.[14] To preserve secrecy, the stripes had been added to thousands of planes in a matter of hours, consuming a hundred thousand gallons of precious paint and twenty thousand paintbrushes.[15]

Captain Lillyman took his place beside the door of one C-47, his customary stogie between his lips, wearing white leather gloves, a tommy gun strapped to his left leg just above the M3 trench knife (useful for slitting throats) attached to his shin. He would be the first American to leap into the darkness over

Normandy—if he made it to the drop zone. None of the path-finder aircraft were armed, and none had any protection against anti-aircraft fire, and there would be no escort to defend against enemy fighters. Once airborne, Lillyman and his men would be all on their own.

IT WAS EARLY evening as thirty-one-year-old Major John How-ard and his men from D Company of the Oxford and Bucking-hamshire Light Infantry arrived at RAF Tarrant Rushton, in Dorset, where six Horsa gliders awaited them, chalk-marked with the numbers 91 to 96. Howard noticed the wind was up and there was some rain, but the sky seemed to be clearing in parts. A half-moon was just visible in the gathering gloom. The trucks carrying him and his 140 men rolled along a runway and were greeted by women belonging to the Women's Auxiliary Air Force, who wished them luck, some with tears dripping down their cheeks.

A sprightly, dark-haired Londoner with a wisp of a mustache, armed with a pistol and a Sten gun, Howard was a rarity among field commanders of Britain's elite forces on D-Day: He was dyed-in-the-wool working class. The eldest of nine children, the son of a barrel maker who had fought in the trenches in Flan-ders in World War I, he'd joined the army to escape unemploy-ment during the Great Depression. Cruelly turned down for a commission, he'd left His Majesty's armed forces, angry and dejected, to become a police officer before rejoining upon the outbreak of war.

Howard still felt the sting of rejection from a decade before.

Even though he had risen steadily through the ranks since 1939, he was still acutely aware of his lowly status in the British caste system, at its most hierarchical in the military. And although he had drawn high praise from superiors, he had yet to prove himself as a leader in combat. He had never killed or even been shot at. In just a couple of hours' time, he'd have the perfect opportunity to show his mettle under extreme duress.

Howard was pleased to see the Horsa pilots awaiting him and his men.[16] Before long, the pilots were chatting away with his troops, using first names, casually sharing cigarettes. Hot tea was passed around, and Howard watched as his men, their faces blackened with burnt coke, checked their weapons and gear. Some had coal-black hands, having stuck them into truck exhaust pipes and smeared the soot on their pale cheeks.

"Your face isn't black enough," Howard told one man. "You've got to get more on."[17]

Just two days earlier, the commander of all Allied ground forces on D-Day, General Bernard Montgomery, had visited Howard. "Get as many of the chaps back as you can," he told the major. Montgomery asked if Howard thought he could pull off Operation Deadstick. Could his men seize a bridge across the Caen Canal, code-named Pegasus Bridge, and one across the Orne River, four hundred yards farther east, in just a few minutes? Both bridges were crucial objectives, essential to securing the eastern flank of the D-Day landings; were German tanks able to cross those bridges, the consequences for the Allied landings could be devastating. The bridges had to be taken in a bold coup de main operation—so quickly that the Germans would be left stunned, flat-footed and unable to react in time.[18]

That was the easy part. The bridges then had to be held until commandos under Brigadier Lord Lovat arrived from Sword Beach. Only then could Howard and his men move to their final objective: higher ground a few miles even farther east, running from the village of Le Hauger to Escoville. This ridge had to be held with other 6th Airborne troops and then defended against what were bound to be fierce counterattacks by German armored forces. If the high ground remained in German hands, Rommel's panzer forces and artillery would be able to fire down relentlessly on exposed British positions.

The plan for Operation Deadstick, rehearsed a total of forty-three times in the previous few months, had been approved on high, but it was essentially Howard's own design. He'd assured Montgomery that it would succeed, but of course there was no way of knowing. In war, as the famous Prussian general Helmuth von Moltke had once declared, and as Montgomery himself had learnt in North Africa, no battle plan survives first contact with the enemy.

THE COMMANDOS of the 1st Special Service Brigade gathered their kit in a field near Southampton. Their commanding officer, Lord Lovat, watched as they packed Bren and Sten gun ammunition and stuffed their Bergen rucksacks full, "belting up amid the dust." Some men wore their green berets at jaunty angles.

Lovat had no time for any kind of slacking or ineptitude, and as a result his commandos were "probably as perfect a fighting force as could be found anywhere," recalled one officer.[19] Those who served under him remembered a debonair and romantic leader. Lovat had a neat mustache, dark, curly hair, and "long, tapering hands."[20] He was a masterful battle planner, utterly "at ease under fire," and at times a "terrifying" disciplinarian. Known to friends as "Shimi" Lovat, the thirty-two-year-old Oxford graduate had spent just three days in combat since March 1941, but such was the drama, panache, and success of the three commando raids he had conducted that he was already a legend among his troops.

Standing before men from 45 Commando Royal Marines and Commandos number 3, 4, and 6, Lovat addressed his troops for the last time. "I weighed each word," he later remembered, "then drove it home, concentrating on the task ahead and simple facts."[21]

Among the men were 177 Frenchmen belonging to the Kieffer Commando.[22] Twenty-one-year-old Léon Gautier looked on as Lovat, "wearing the gilet of a gentleman farmer," hands in his trouser pockets, began to speak.[23] Slim and wiry and several inches shorter than Lovat, Gautier had served in the French navy before joining Charles de Gaulle's Free French in July 1940. He now belonged to Troop 8, attached for D-Day to Number 4 Commando, whose mission was to seize the seaside resort of Ouistreham, at the eastern end of Sword Beach.[24]

At last, Lovat addressed Gautier and his fellow countrymen directly in colloquial French, and they yelled their approval.[25]

"You are going home," he stressed in French. "You will be the first French soldiers to fight the [German] bastards in France itself. Each of you will have his own Boche. You're going to show us what you can do. Tomorrow morning we'll have them."[26]

Switching to English, Lovat congratulated all of his men for being "a proper striking force, the fine cutting edge" of the British Army in the invasion. He knew they would face stiffer opposition than ever before. Described by Winston Churchill as his "steel hand from the sea," they would land where enemy fire would be heaviest in the British sector.[27]

"The bigger the challenge," Lovat told his men, "the better we play."[28]

Three regular infantry battalions would land on Sword before Lovat's first wave of commandos, helping to eliminate German defenses. This would hopefully allow the commandos to exit the beaches quickly. Lovat's lads would then cross minefields and move inland, passing through several villages, not stopping until they had linked up with airborne troops holding key bridges some six miles from Sword.

Lovat finished with critical advice that many men would thankfully remember.

"If you wish to live to a ripe old age—keep moving tomorrow."[29]

"It was truly inspiring," remembered a British officer who listened to Lovat's address. "There was no nonsense, no cheap appeal to patriotism. He spoke simply but he imbued each man with the spirit of the same task."[30]

Lovat's speech took all of two minutes. Then his men boarded trucks and were on their way to war. As the vehicles rolled through the countryside toward the coast, every field they passed, it seemed, had become a massive stockpile of supplies and weapons, more than two million tons of them, hopefully enough to sate an Allied army two and a half million men strong.[31] "England has become one vast ordnance dump and field park," one newsman observed. "In the whole history of the world, there never has been such a concentration of all the paraphernalia of war in so small a place."[32]

It was early evening when Lovat and his commandos started to board landing craft. Some were in a jubilant mood, eager to get back to France. Among the more fearsome was a shady character who Lovat suspected had seen the inside of several French jails—tattooed on his forehead were the words PAS DE CHANCE. *Tough luck.*[33]

As for Léon Gautier, he wasn't thinking about what he'd do to the Germans in just a few hours' time. In a pocket of his dark green uniform he kept a portrait of a young Englishwoman called Dorothy. They'd met the previous fall while he was on guard duty. He'd heard strange noises and been surprised to find her installing a telephone in a high-security area, and he rather rudely questioned her. She was no spy, she replied defiantly, just an eighteen-year-old local girl trying to make a bit of money to support her family.

In clumsy English, Gautier apologized. They chatted, and he became smitten. Would she like to go dancing sometime? A second date followed, and then magical, precious evenings when the two jived late into the night, behind blackout curtains, oblivious to the war that would inevitably pull them apart.[34] He promised he would marry her that coming October—if he lived.

It was now his turn to board his boat, Landing Ship Infantry 523, or LSI 523.

His name was called and he replied.

Gautier.

"No return ticket, please," he added.[35]

It was a beautiful evening, in spite of gloomy forecasts.[36] One British naval officer remembered that there was "a grotesque gala atmosphere more like a regatta than a page of history, with gay music from ships' loud hailers and more than the usual quota of jocular farewells bandied between friends."[37]

As far as Gautier could see, there were all manner of boats, hundreds and hundreds, many already heading out to sea, led by minesweepers that would clear lanes toward Overlord's five landing beaches. Never had such a large force gathered to wage war. Gautier knew he was part of something truly colossal, the likes of which would never be seen again.[38]

DWIGHT EISENHOWER could do nothing more to determine the outcome of D-Day. But he could not rest his mind, even for a minute. There was no distraction in any of the things he usually turned to for relaxation, not even the cheap western novels piled beside his bed, near the overflowing ashtray, in the spartan trailer on the grounds of the stately, whitewashed Southwick House, near Portsmouth.[39]

The Supreme Allied Commander had to be with his troops, so he left the Georgian splendor of Southwick House, with its colonnade of paired Ionic columns, and ordered his chauffeur to drive him to Greenham Common, midway between Portsmouth and Oxford, where the 101st Airborne, the first US troops to go into action, were readying themselves for combat.

Eisenhower was driven by the raven-haired thirty-five-year-old Captain Kay Summersby, who hailed from County Cork,

Ireland, and was the daughter of a "black Irish" lieutenant colonel in the Royal Munster Fusiliers.[40] With her high cheekbones and slim figure, she'd found work as a model before the war. During the London Blitz she drove an ambulance with courage and skill. She knew the cost of war, having lost her American fiancé early on when he was killed while clearing a minefield in North Africa. Since being assigned to Eisenhower as his driver in May 1942, she had become utterly devoted to the plainspoken, surprisingly humble general.[41] Some whispered that she was more than simply a driver, that she was, in fact, his lover. Regardless, she knew more than anyone how great the strain of preparing for D-Day had been on Eisenhower. She had seen his bloodshot eyes, his shaking hands when he lit a cigarette.

"If it goes all right," Summersby had told him, "dozens of people will claim the credit. But if it goes wrong, you'll be the only one to blame."[42]

It was too late now to call off the whole affair. A vast fleet and an army of 200,000 invasion troops had finally been set in motion. A "great human spring," coiled and tense for so many months, recalled Eisenhower, had finally been released.[43] Would the airborne operations herald the start of a successful crusade to liberate Europe? Or would Leigh-Mallory be proved right, and the "greatest amphibious assault ever attempted" be remembered instead as Eisenhower's tragic failure?

Eisenhower had already written what would be his final words as Supreme Allied Commander should the invasion fail. He had scribbled a few sentences on a plain sheet of paper, using a soft lead pencil because his hand was weak after dashing off so many orders and memos.[44] The note now in his pocket read: "Our landings in the Cherbourg-Havre area have failed to gain a satisfactory foothold and I have withdrawn the troops. My decision to attack at this time and place was based upon the best information available. The troops, the air, and the Navy did all that bravery and devotion to duty could do. If any blame or fault attaches to the attempt it is mine alone."[45]

When they arrived at Greenham Common, Kay Summersby watched as Eisenhower moved casually toward a group of paratroopers, a broad grin on his face radiating what appeared to be easy confidence. "There was no military pomp about his visit," she remembered. "Ike shook hands with as many men as he could. He spoke a few words to every man and he looked the man in the eye as he wished him success. 'It's very hard really to look a soldier in the eye,' he told me later, 'when you fear you are sending him to his death.'"[46]

Corporal Bill Hayes was busy smearing a foul mixture of cooking oil and cocoa powder onto his face. Others from his company in the 101st Airborne's 2nd Battalion did the same, knowing that those with pale faces in close combat in the hedgerow country of Normandy wouldn't last long. They were scheduled to jump onto Drop Zone A, which Captain Lillyman and his fellow pathfinders would mark with lights and radar beacons.

Twenty-two-year-old Hayes, who had sold paint and wallpaper in a Sears store in Wisconsin before being called up, wondered if he had packed his seventy pounds of kit correctly.

Armament: three knives, a machete, .45 pistol, rifle, nine grenades, a Hawkins anti-tank mine, four blocks of TNT.

Check.

Rations: 200 cigarettes, five days' K rations, fresh water in a canteen.

Check.

Change of underwear and socks.

Check.

Focused on his pack, Hayes heard a voice.

"Well, are you ready?"

"Yeah," said Hayes. "I guess so."[47]

Hayes looked up and was astonished to see Eisenhower standing before him. The pair exchanged a few pleasantries. Eisenhower showed no sign of the overbearing stress that caused him to chain-smoke sixty filterless cigarettes a day.

It seemed to Hayes that his supreme commander was asking him if he was scared but was being careful not to use the exact words.

"You're damn right I'm scared," said Hayes.[48]

Eisenhower wished him luck and moved on. Hayes refocused on his kit. He was among the smallest men in his unit, at five feet nine inches and 160 pounds. He had fifteen training jumps to his credit but only one at night. It didn't take long for his mind to settle once more on what he was going to do when the Germans tried to kill him.

Eisenhower began to talk with yet another "stick," or plane-load, of paratroopers.

"Quit worrying, General," someone called out. "We'll take care of this thing for you."

The time had come. All around Eisenhower, men started to put on their parachute backpacks. Each soldier was heavily burdened, some carrying almost half their body weight in extra equipment.

"Load up!"

Men began to board planes, and there was a final handshake between Eisenhower and General Maxwell Taylor, commander of the 101st Airborne.[49] Then Taylor's plane's engines growled, and it crept down the runway, with others lined up behind, noses into the wind.

Eisenhower saluted every plane as it passed him, bound for France. "I stayed with them until the last of them were in the air," he remembered.[50] The general then walked slowly back to his jeep. Kay Summersby later recalled that her boss had tears in his eyes as she drove him away.

"Well," said Eisenhower softly. "It's on."[51]

AROUND 9:30 P.M., boats holding the fifteen-hundred-odd elite troops of the 1st Special Service Brigade[52] slipped their moorings and set sail, heading for the Channel, first crossing Stokes Bay, with its shingle beaches, near Gosport on the south coast.[53] The bay was calm, the wind having died down, and on a nearby boat a New Zealand naval officer played "Heart of Oak," the marching song of the Royal Navy, on a gramophone.[54] The music carried across the water to the commandos sipping self-heating soup and chewing on biscuits, their final supper before action.

> Come, cheer up, my lads, 'tis to glory we steer,
> To add something more to this wonderful year;
> To honor we call you, as freemen not slaves,
> For who are so free as the sons of the waves?[55]

Lord Lovat stood on the deck of his LSI, surveying the waters around him. In the bow was a twenty-one-year-old bagpiper called Bill Millin, who held the distinction of being the only man among the Allied invasion's 150,000 soldiers to wear a kilt—the same Cameron tartan his father, a Glasgow policeman, had worn in the trenches of World War I. Lovat had selected Millin to be his personal piper, having breezily dismissed the young man's concerns about the army regulation that forbade pipers from being in the front lines: "Ah, but that's the English War Office, Millin. You and I are both Scottish so that doesn't apply."[56]

Lovat had assured Millin he would be a part of the "greatest invasion in the history of warfare." And there was no way in hell that he, Lord Lovat, the twenty-fourth chieftain of Clan Fraser, was going to wade ashore without the whining skirl of bagpipes. They were essential to men's morale, as impactful as any weapon Millin might otherwise carry.

Now, in their LSI, steadily chugging in the direction of battle, Lovat ordered Millin to play his bagpipes.[57] "It was exhilarating," recalled one of Lovat's men, "glorious, and heartbreaking when the crews and troops began to cheer. The cheers came faintly across the water gradually taken up by ship after ship . . . I never loved England so truly as at that moment."[58]

Night was falling. Many of the commandos welcomed it, for they had operated after dark mostly with greatest success. The folds of night made them feel less tense. By contrast, countless invaders scheduled to go in with the first wave were, in the words of journalist Alan Moorehead, "oppressed by a sense of strangeness and insecurity. In the darkness the dangers of the voyage became magnified and unbearable, and the rising sea alone seemed sufficient terror, without the unthinkable climax of the assault at the other end."[59]

As his boat entered the English Channel, Lovat started to relax. "Immediate worries were over," he recalled, "with time to unwind before touch-down. Now the parcel was in the post and out of my hands." An officer had found a bottle of gin, which Lovat and others quickly passed around. Another man pulled out a paperback he had found belowdecks—Dr. Marie Stopes's *Married Love*. Giddy with gin and anticipation, Lovat and other officers laughed hard at the advice for nervous young lovers, full of performance anxiety, setting out to discover the naked truth on a honeymoon. "Soft beds and hard battles have something in common after all!" Lovat would later quip. After finishing the gin, Lovat's officers returned to their units, "hopping across lengthening shadows on the gently heaving decks."[60]

Lovat went belowdecks to rest before battle. The last time he had led men into combat—"wearing corduroy slacks, a rifle hung rakishly from the crook of his arm," as one man recalled—was on a commando raid during the Dieppe operation of August 1942. Unlike the rest of the failed assault on the Channel port, Lovat's attack on a six-gun battery to the west of the main landing beaches had been an unqualified success. He had stubbornly demanded that the raid be done his way, despite opposition from more senior figures, and had, according to a fellow officer, "led and controlled it perfectly,"[61] earning him high praise as "probably the best military brain on either side in the Second World War."[62]

Lovat was a brutally efficient marauder. Winston Churchill described him to Joseph Stalin as "the mildest-mannered man that ever scuttled a ship or cut a throat," but at Dieppe there had been nothing good-natured about his or his men's actions. At one point, a German sniper had shot one of Lovat's lads and then stamped on his face as he lay wounded, incensing other commandos who saw this as a gross violation of an unspoken code of honor. The German was shot down beside Lovat's man. A commando was quickly at his mate's side, providing morphine, while another Green Beret bayoneted the German to death. There was, remembered one man, no "gloating, no pity for an enemy who knew no code and had no compassion."

As his men destroyed the battery's guns, Lovat had gestured to others and pointed to buildings nearby.

"Set them on fire," he ordered. "Burn the lot."

One of Lovat's men, a junior officer, remembered that "these were not the words of a commanding officer in the British Army. They were the order of a Highland Chief bent on the total destruction of the enemy."[63]

Lovat's raid went like clockwork. "Every one of the gun crews finished with the bayonet," Lovat nonchalantly notified his most senior commanding officer, a fellow aristocrat called Lord Mountbatten.[64] But a thousand patriotic Canadians, who had been so eager to show what Canada could do in the war, lay dead. To justify this unforgivable loss, it would be argued that critical lessons were learnt from the raid, ones that would prove invaluable on D-Day: *Do not make a direct attack on a heavily defended port. Ensure that supporting tanks can actually move across landing beaches—the large, round stones at Dieppe had stopped many in their tracks. Make certain that naval and air support is close and carefully coordinated with the first wave of invasion troops.*

The Dieppe operation had been, in Lovat's words, a "first-class blunder."[65] Returning to England after the failed attack, utterly exhausted, his uniform soiled, his pale face grimy, Lovat had tried to find a bed in London, without luck, and had fallen asleep in the bathtub of his officers' club. He then spent a terrible night, swaddled in towels, lying on the floor of a library, shivering, jolted awake by a nightmare "where tracer bullets probed the darkness, and leaden feet pounded desperately on slopes of slippery [pebbles] that rolled back, like shifting walnut shells." At dawn he had realized that he faced a greater anguish: having to inform the families of his eighteen dead men that they would not be coming home.[66]

Now, bobbing in darkness in the middle of the stormy English Channel, Lovat was returning to France for the first time since August 1942, when so much had gone so badly for the Allies. He felt confident that he had done everything possible to ensure that his part in Operation Overlord would be a success. His men were in superb fighting condition, having already left targets in smoking ruins along Hitler's vaunted coastal defenses—the so-called Atlantic Wall. They had been guaranteed massive, unprecedented naval and air support. And there was no need to take a major port like Dieppe in the first days of this invasion; the Allies had performed a miracle of engineering and secretly built huge concrete caissons that would be pulled across the Channel and then linked to form two large

Mulberry floating harbors. They would bring their own port with them.

Lovat removed his boots and lay down on a bunk. Before long, he was sound asleep. "I can snore through any form of disturbance," he remembered, "provided I go to bed with a quiet mind."[67] Meanwhile, up on deck, listening to the wind growl and shivering in the spray of a spiteful sea, many of his lads were not nearly so nonchalant. Sword Beach had been described as a "hot potato" with a reinforced German garrison to contend with. And some of those who had barely escaped Dieppe two years before could not help but wonder if this time they would share the fate of those poor bloody Canadians, mown down in their scores before even setting foot ashore.

ABOARD THE USS *SAMUEL CHASE*, Captain Edward Wozenski and Lieutenant John Spalding were hunched over a rubber carpet, examining a mock-up of the Normandy beach defenses, complete with miniature houses and trees laid out in loving detail, all based on the most recent reconnaissance photos. Of most interest to Spalding was Easy Red, one of eight sectors on the five-mile-long Omaha Beach, which, in turn, was one of the two landing beaches assigned to US troops. "They'd set up that model of Omaha with little flags," remembered one soldier. "Easy Red. Fox Green. Colleville-sur-Mer. We knew it like we knew our cocks in the dark."[68] There was just one exit—a draw leading through hundred-foot-high bluffs—from Easy Red, where Spalding would land at H-Hour, 6:32 A.M. It was code-named E-1 and was heavily defended by two German strongpoints.

Captain Wozenski was the commander of E Company of the 16th Infantry Regiment of the 1st Division—the storied "Big Red One."[69] Of the three American seaborne divisions to hit the beaches on D-Day, the Big Red One was the only unit to have seen previous combat. Some stalwarts had fought since 1942, first in North Africa and then in Sicily, and they resented being sent into the breach yet again.

Yet there was no choice in the matter—if men and especially tanks were to get off the beach, the E-1 draw had to be taken. Doing so was a formidable challenge, even for the most experienced of combat commanders. Unlike at Utah, steep green bluffs lay beyond a crescent-shaped beach that was studded with defensive obstacles. No fewer than eighty-five pre-sighted machine guns would sweep every inch of that beach from east to west. Just one MG42, capable of firing an extraordinary twelve hundred rounds per minute, could pump bullets three times faster than any American weapon across three hundred yards of waterfront. Powerful artillery had been aimed to fire along the beach, not out to sea, thereby inflicting maximum carnage among those who somehow managed to get past the mines and stakes that skirted the hard sands, more than three hundred yards wide at low tide.

Asked to lay money on Lieutenant Spalding, even the wild gamblers squatting around craps games on the top deck would have snorted derisively. He had joined E Company after its move to England to prepare for D-Day, and only recently had he been made a section leader, in charge of thirty-two men in one landing craft. He was not exactly raring to fight. According to a medical report, he had been deeply troubled in recent months, "nervous, irritable," his fitful sleep plagued by "battle dreams."[70] Appearances were also less than convincing. A former sports-writer from Kentucky, with a strained marriage due to his absence and a young son he barely knew, Spalding, with his boyish face, thin frame, and unruly mop of thick black hair, looked much younger than his twenty-nine years. He had not been drafted but had decided to join the army in any case, kissing his wife and son good-bye almost a year before the Japanese bombed Pearl Harbor.[71]

Thankfully, E Company had its share of combat veterans, and they were lucky to be commanded by Captain Edward Wozenski, a big bear of a man from Connecticut who had won the Distinguished Service Cross in Sicily. Having previously led Company G in combat, Wozenski was highly respected, regarded as the calmest officer under fire in the entire 16th Infantry Regiment. His words carried weight. From experience, he knew only too well that it didn't matter how well planned the invasion was, how accurate the reconstruction of the beach was on the sand table—there would inevitably be great chaos and confusion. Things were bound to go wrong. The best way for those in the first wave to survive was to stay on their feet and keep going—to attack and kill the enemy.[72]

In the belly of the *Samuel Chase,* the soldiers of E Company were gathered in a large hallway, listening intently to a final briefing, their faces illuminated by the glow of red lights. The celebrated war photographer Robert Capa, having brilliantly covered the war in Europe for *Life* magazine, had chosen to land with the first wave, and he later recalled the pervading mood on the ship. "We were all suffering from that strange sickness known as 'amphibia,'" he wrote. "Being amphibious troops had only one meaning for us: We would have to be unhappy in the water before we could be unhappy on the shore."[73]

When the briefing concluded, many men returned to their quarters. Some stared, deep in thought, at the bunk above them. Many penned last letters. Green officers like Spalding worried, above all, about how they would perform in just a few hours' time. They were more afraid of failing their men, of losing their nerve, than they were of the Germans. As with so many other junior officers in the first wave, Spalding had no idea what leadership in combat truly entailed. Hopefully, the predictions of minimal resistance would come true—and if not? Earlier that evening, he'd given his home address in Owensboro, Kentucky, to a fellow officer, just in case.

ON A RUNWAY at RAF Tarrant Rushton, Major John Howard chatted briefly with some of the pilots of the Halifax bombers set to tug his force of six Horsa gliders.

"I've got to hand it to you boys," said one pilot. "We've flown on some sticky jobs in our time, but what you lot are going to do—well, that takes some guts."

Howard did not want to dwell on the danger—not now, just before takeoff.

He looked at his watch and called out to his men—time to synchronize watches.

It was exactly 10:40 P.M., June 5, 1944.

"Now!" said Howard.

Watches were set.

Just a few weeks earlier, attempting to cut his force to 180 soldiers, Howard had watched grown men cry as they pleaded with him not to leave them behind. They didn't want to abandon their mates or, no doubt, miss out on the honor of being the first British troops to fight on D-Day.

"Good luck!" one soldier shouted to a friend boarding another glider.

"See you over the other side!"[74]

Howard had just enough time to go from glider to glider, shaking each man's hand. "I am a sentimental man at heart," he later confessed, "for which reason I don't think I am a good soldier. I found offering my thanks to these chaps a devil of a job. My voice just wasn't my own."[75]

Howard repeated three words over and over: *Ham and jam.* "Those were code words and they meant a terrible lot to us," he recalled. "They were the success-signal code words for the capture of the bridges intact. The success-signal for the canal bridge was 'ham,' and for the river bridge, 'jam.' And it was a goodwill wish for everyone—ham and jam. I then took my seat in the number 1 glider. I could look through to the cockpit and see Staff Sergeant Jim Wallwork, the pilot, quite clearly."[76] Many of Howard's men had loaded up with extra ammunition and grenades, knowing they would need all they could get. They'd be alone for quite some time until reinforcements arrived. A couple of extra magazines for the Bren and the Sten, a couple of extra Mills bombs in a pocket—any last-minute grabbed item might come in handy.[77] They were, in fact, so weighed down with kit that they had to be helped up the ladders into the Horsa gliders. They staggered to their places. If they fell over, they had to be hauled back to their feet.

As Howard watched the last of the men in his glider sit down, he had a lump in his throat "as big as a damn football."

A private nearby looked at a clearly emotional Howard and felt sorry for him.[78] Whatever lay ahead would not be pretty. Their glider was about to be towed across the Channel and then set loose at five thousand feet. They would then crash-land at around one hundred miles per hour, aiming for a narrow landing strip in the dead of night with no protection against enemy flak. Survival depended completely on the glider's pilot, Jim Wallwork. In training, he'd practiced by literally flying blindfolded, reaching a target with a co-pilot calling out times on a stopwatch and readings on a compass. Even so, tonight's mission, he knew only too well, would require luck as much as skill.

There was a problem.

Howard's Horsa was overweight. Too many men, packets of English cigarettes stuffed down their elasticized sleeves, had brought along too many phosphorus grenades and bandoliers of .303 ammo, too many Hawkins anti-tank mines. "The German is like a June bride," they'd been told of the enemy. "He knows he is going to get it, but he doesn't know how big it is going to be."[79] If Howard's lads had their way, it would be very big indeed.

Howard looked at his troops, many still teenagers.

"One of you has got to drop out . . . I need one volunteer."

No one answered his call, and so it was decided that some equipment would be jettisoned instead. Finally, the doors to the gliders were shut and the pilots of the Halifax bombers, which would tow them to Normandy, prepared to take off. Before long, some of Howard's men began to feel euphoric. "Germany hadn't a chance," one remembered.[80] Then someone said, "We're off." The towrope took the strain and Howard's glider began to shift. Then men felt the glider leave the ground and Howard checked his watch—they were on schedule, in the air "right on the dot" at 10:56 P.M. Now he and his men "were cut off from the rest of the world," he recalled, "except for Jim Wallwork's ability to talk to the Halifax. Through the portholes we could see lots of other bombers, and we knew they must have been going to bomb the invasion front."[81]

It was hard to discern other men's blackened faces, and therefore their emotions, in the darkened interiors. Here and there, cigarettes glowed. Everyone was tense, and the usual banter heard in training was absent. But as the minutes passed and they headed toward the English Channel, the men seated nervously behind Jim Wallwork on hard benches began to ease up.[82]

A man at the back of the glider called out to Howard.

"Has the Major laid his kit yet?"[83]

Had Howard been sick?

On every previous flight, Howard had vomited. He had not taken the anti-sickness tablets offered before takeoff and now realized he was so pumped up on adrenaline, so tense with nerves, that he did not feel the least bit queasy.

Twenty-two-year-old Corporal Wally Parr, an aggressive and quick-witted cockney, was seated near John Howard. Parr had chalked the words LADY IRENE on the nose of the Horsa for good luck—his wife was called Irene.[84] He looked at Howard, his commander, his "gaffer." At times he'd thought the major was a "mad bastard" during their training in Exeter, where they'd practiced day and night, seizing a bridge over a canal, annoying the locals by fishing in the River Exe with powerful fragmentation grenades. "Slog! Slog! Slog!" That's what life under Howard had become, a constant quest to be better, faster, sharper. "Got to be better than the chap next door. Always better."[85]

Someone began to sing.[86] Others joined in. Parr began belting out the chorus to "A-Be My Boy," a music hall classic, popular in particular with the many cockneys on board.[87]

> A-be, A-be, A-be my boy . . .
> What are you waiting for now?
> You promised to marry me one day in June.

In the cockpit, Jim Wallwork checked his gauges. They were at six thousand feet. The towline bowed gently, leading through the darkness to the lumbering hulk of the Halifax bomber ahead.

> It's never too late and it's never too soon
> All the family keep asking me, "Which day? What day?" . . .
> A-be, A-be, A-be my boy,
> What are you waiting for now?[88]

Nineteen-year-old Private Bill Gray, Number 1 Platoon's Bren gunner, was less vocal than his mates—having gulped down too much rum-infused tea before takeoff, he now badly needed to urinate. Gray looked at his fellow cockneys singing at the tops of their voices. "If they could have got up and danced they would have," he remembered. "The vast majority of us were

Londoners and they were mostly London songs—'Roll Out the Barrel' and 'I'm Forever Blowing Bubbles.'"[89]

Seated to the right of Major Howard was twenty-eight-year-old Lieutenant Herbert Denham "Den" Brotheridge, a talented soccer player from a region in Britain's industrial heartland known as the Black Country. Just before takeoff, he'd made a bet with Howard as to who would be the first to put his feet on the ground in France.[90] Despite their difference in rank, the leader of Number 1 Platoon, with his curly dark hair and thick Midlands accent, was a close friend of Howard's. He had a young wife who was about to give birth, and in recent days he had at times become maudlin, reciting out loud the fateful lines from a famous Rupert Brooke poem:

> If I should die, think only this of me:
> That there's some corner of a foreign field
> That is for ever England.[91]

Howard himself had two young children with his wife, Joy, "a very pretty girl with pale green eyes, slender figure and light brown hair." She'd been worried about Howard's meager social pedigree, or rather what her snobbish mother might think, when they became engaged, in 1939—surely she was marrying beneath her station?[92] Fortunately, things had worked out just grand with Howard, who only occasionally reverted to his Camden Town rhyming slang.[93] Howard's mother-in-law could now boast that her grandchildren's father was a dashing major, a bona fide member of the officer class.

Every now and again, as his men belted out cockney classics,

Howard glanced in the direction of Jim Wallwork, unrecognizable in his flying mask and goggles. Known to his rugby chums at grammar school as "Handsome Jim," Wallwork had joined the army before the outbreak of the war, because he could, as he put it, "smell it coming" and wanted to cover himself "in glory and medals and [drink] free beer for the duration, surrounded by adoring females."[94] Unlike Howard, Wallwork, all of twenty-four years old, had since seen plenty of action. The only child of a World War I artillery sergeant, he'd already survived a major disaster during the invasion of Sicily in July 1943, in which a quarter of his fellow glider pilots had ditched in the sea and drowned.[95]

During training a few weeks back, Howard had shown Wallwork photos from aerial reconnaissance of poles newly placed in fields near Pegasus Bridge. Dubbed "Rommel's asparagus," the wooden poles were up to sixteen feet long and had been planted upright around seventy-five to a hundred feet apart. Rommel had ordered that mines and grenades be attached to the tip of every third pole, and then connected to other poles with trip wires, turning many fields in Normandy into infernal mazes, a veritable "Devil's Garden."[96]

Howard had been disheartened by the aerial shots.

The Germans were going to spoil the fun.

"That's just what we need," Wallwork had told Howard. "You remember that embankment where we end up by the road?"

Of course Howard remembered.

"Well," Wallwork added, "we've always been worried about piling into that if we overshot the landing zone. A heavy landing and one grenade going off by accident and—woof—up goes the lot. Now these stakes are just right. They're spaced so as to take a foot or two off each wing and pull us up just right."[97]

Howard burst out laughing.

Surely Wallwork was joking?

Like the other glider pilots in Operation Deadstick, Wallwork had been "petrified" upon seeing the photos of the stakes.[98] But what good would have come of showing his concern? The mission was not about to be abandoned. To Wallwork's surprise, Howard had appeared to accept his highly optimistic assessment, no doubt because he wanted to believe it.

Now the French coast was approaching, a white line just visible, surf breaking on the Normandy beaches.

Before long, the Halifax bomber ahead would set them free. Then their lives would depend entirely on Wallwork.

Howard could see the tensed muscles on the pilot's neck.[99]

Had Wallwork been right about those damned stakes?

In just a few minutes, he would find out.

At North Witham airfield,[100] co-pilot Captain Vito Pedone, seated in the cockpit of his C-47, prepared for takeoff, waiting for the order to go.[101] A veteran of twenty-five bomber raids over enemy territory, he knew tonight's mission would be the most important he'd ever carry out, no matter how long he lived.[102] He checked the gauges on the instrument panel, listening to the growl of the engines. He regarded his plane as the best weapon of World War II, a "sweet-flying, rugged, dependable ship," the "point of the lance" for every major operation in Europe. If he survived the next few hours, he'd celebrate his twenty-third birthday in three weeks' time, hopefully with his wife,[103] an attractive and high-spirited first lieutenant flight nurse named Geraldine Curtis,[104] who would also be on active duty on D-Day.[105]

Beside Pedone was the lead pilot, thirty-three-year-old Lieutenant Colonel Joel Crouch, the most experienced and highly regarded officer in IX Troop Carrier Command. In fact, he was considered the best in his business, having been the lead pathfinder pilot for the invasion of Sicily and then of mainland Italy a few months later.[106]

All that spring and early summer, he'd honed the skills of fellow pilots such as Pedone, sending them on three missions a day, rewarding some flight crews with forty-eight-hour passes if they could drop a dummy attached to a parachute within fifty yards of a target on the ground. On Crouch's uniform was a pair of jump wings, a sign that he was not just any old pilot—he'd actually made nine jumps himself, and he expected all his fliers to leap at least once from a C-47 so they would appreciate what the men they were dropping were up against. There'd been broken bones and more than a few bruised egos, and his bosses in the Ninth Air Force had disapproved of the risks to valuable pilots, so Crouch had written up reports explaining that so many had sprained ankles because they'd jumped out of moving trucks, not C-47s at a thousand feet. He couldn't have cared less what the top brass thought, so long as his men were prepared for the most critical pathfinder mission of World War II.

In just a few minutes, he'd begin to taxi along the runway and then take to the air, carrying eighteen paratroopers, pathfinders who would be the first Americans to drop into enemy-occupied France.[107] In radio silence and bad weather, he'd lead two other planes in his flight in a V formation at low altitude. Other flights, carrying two hundred more pathfinders, would follow Crouch's lead. Once safely on the ground, the pathfinders would set up radar and lights to guide the planes that would deliver an entire division of airborne troops—6,600 "Screaming Eagles." If the pathfinders failed, the whole invasion would, too.

It was 9:50 P.M., and the light was fading fast as Crouch's C-47 hurtled down the runway and then lifted into the air.[108] Exactly four minutes later, the commander of the IX Troop Carrier Command Pathfinder Unit reported to ground control that he was on his way to France,[109] flying southwest, making for the English Channel[110] at three thousand feet.[111] The former pilot for United Airlines, who before the war had mostly flown along the West Coast, from Seattle to Los Angeles, was now officially "the spearhead of the spearhead of the spearhead" of the D-Day invasion.[112]

Crouch then steered directly south, toward a major landmark, the Bill of Portland, a spur of land that juts into the wind-lashed English Channel.[113] A private seated nervously on a bench in Crouch's plane, tail number 23098, was after an hour growing impatient, wondering why Crouch was flying "around England for what seemed like hours." An officer nearby gave a lame excuse: Crouch was trying to "confuse the enemy."[114]

It was around 11:30 P.M. when Crouch saw the English Channel below, the cue, recalled co-pilot Pedone, to turn off the plane's lights. They would stay dark until the pathfinders had "hit the drop zones and were headed back over England."[115] It was a sobering moment. Crouch knew that he and three-quarters of his fellow fliers could be killed or wounded over the next sixty minutes.[116] That had been the prediction in planning.

The C-47 swooped toward the gray waves and leveled out in radio silence below a hundred feet, engines throbbing as it flew undetected toward France, passing above dozens of ships, flying so low it seemed to sailors below that it might actually clip the masts of their vessels. Crouch's only guides were two Royal Navy boats, positioned at prearranged spots in the Channel, shining green lights. After passing the second boat, Crouch turned his C-47 ninety degrees to the left. The two other planes in his flight duly followed. Crouch spotted German searchlights, stabbing the stormy skies from positions on the islands of Alderney and Guernsey, the sole British territory occupied since 1940 by the Germans.

The eighteen pathfinders on his plane were soon belting out drinking songs as if they were headed to London for a wild weekend with some saucy "Piccadilly commandos," not toward enemy territory. Certain to be among the loudest, Crouch knew from experience, was their commanding officer, the suave, fast-talking Captain Frank Lillyman, once described by a superior as an "arrogant smart-ass," now standing with a black cigar clenched between his teeth in an open door at the rear of the shuddering plane.

Tonight, this night of nights, Lillyman's stick would mark out Drop Zone A with seven amber lights, which would be turned on when Lillyman gave the order, some thirty minutes after they had dropped from around five hundred feet. The amber lights would be placed in a T. The tail of the T would indicate to later waves of pilots when to turn on the green jump light. Others in Lillyman's stick carried Eureka radar sets, which would send out signals to be picked up by the aircraft bringing in the main body of the 101st Airborne.

Lillyman was in pain, having torn leg ligaments in a training jump four days prior. Not wanting to miss D-Day, he'd tried his best to hide the injury. At least he had his cigar to chew on, to help take his mind off the goddamn leg. The cigar was, in his words, a "pet superstition."[117] Uncle Sam had thoughtfully issued him twelve a week, and he'd never jumped without one stuck between his lips. Whenever he risked running low, his wife, Jane, a wavy-haired beauty back home in Skaneateles, in the Finger Lakes region of upstate New York, had sent him extras along with her almost daily letters, many of them about their three-year-old daughter, Susan.

In his previous forty-seven jumps, Lillyman had burnt himself only once, when he accidentally swallowed a glowing cigar butt. And just one time he had forgotten to chew on a stogie before leaping from a plane—he would always remember the glum look on his men's faces as they approached a drop zone over England.

"Hey," he had asked, "what's the trouble with you fellas?"

"The captain hasn't got his cigar," a man replied.

Lillyman quickly pulled a cigar from a pocket and stuck it in his mouth for all to see. The jump went off without a hitch.

Tonight would be different. For the first time, he'd be in a proper fight. He'd finally get the chance to show that he could handle himself in combat, just like his father, Major Frank Lillyman. "Dad didn't like it much when I went into the paratroopers,"

Lillyman had recently told a reporter. "That was back in April of 1942 at Ft. Benning. He was an old horse cavalry man in the regular army." Sadly, he had passed away in March 1943, a wizened and highly decorated warrior who'd also served time as a mercenary. "Dad was an honest to goodness soldier of fortune," remembered Lillyman. "He served in the Argentine navy, the Brazilian cavalry and the U.S. navy and army."[118]

Lillyman looked down at the white-capped waves of the English Channel. Crouch was now flying so low that cold water sprayed through the open door, soaking Lillyman's combat jacket.

In a C-47 following Crouch's plane, another paratrooper also stood at an open door. He had drunk too much coffee before takeoff and now unzipped his fly to urinate into the sea. Unfortunately, the back draft from the plane's propellers blew his efforts into his blacked-up face and showered some of his comrades, who swore loudly in protest.

"You guys are gonna have a lot more to worry about than a little pee!" the paratrooper replied.

A cigarette perched between his lips, the paratrooper began to sing:

> *I'm smokin' my last cig-a-rette,*
> *Sing that cowboy song—*
> *I ne-ver will for-get . . .*
> *I'm smokin' my last cig-a-rette.*

No one needed reminding that they might soon be dead. "Shut up, you bastard!" someone shouted.[119]

Standing at the open door of his C-47, Captain Frank

Lillyman could see his men hunched over on folding seats, loaded down with equipment, waiting calmly for the green light. Just a few hours earlier, before boarding Crouch's plane, Lilly-man had waxed lyrical to a reporter about them, describing Private Frank "the Rock" Rocca as being "knee-high to a jug of cider and as hard as a keg of nails. He can hold that Tommy gun at his hip weaving like a hula dancer and splinter silhouette targets. [Private John] McFarlen—he's a fighting son of a gun. He likes to fight for the fun of it. It is all I can do to keep him out of the guard house. Wilhelm and Williams—our scouts—can't lose those guys. Mangoni and 'Zamanakes the Greek'—what they can't do with dynamite. Give those guys the credit, not me."

The impressed reporter had noted, just before a "nerveless" Lillyman climbed up into Crouch's plane, that the wisecracking captain's "brow was knit in furrows as if he was worried . . . Then I noticed what it was—an obstinate wrapper on a slim cigar."[120]

Again Lillyman peered into the distance.

A coastline appeared, and then the plane entered thick clouds.[121]

They were over enemy territory.

La Belle France.

CHAPTER 2

Ham and Jam

MAJOR JOHN HOWARD looked through a small round window of his Horsa glider. The Channel below was dotted with boats, their arrowhead wakes all pointed toward the white, gently arcing shore of Nazi-occupied France. The gray seas were rough and choppy. Howard's thoughts turned to the seaborne soldiers in the first wave, packed into hundreds of landing craft. What a terrible crossing. They must be puking their guts up, what with the fear, the nerves, and the high seas.

Poor devils.

Better to go to war this way—an hour's flight, a good old sing-along, and then smack bang into the enemy's lap. A fast, clean entry into battle, with little time to dwell on dark thoughts, to be afraid, unlike with those poor buggers far below.[1]

Pilot Jim Wallwork heard the calm voice of a Halifax pilot in his headset.

"Weather's good. The clouds are at six hundred feet, a couple of minutes before we cast off. And we all wish you the best of luck."

It was past midnight.[2] D-Day had arrived.

Wallwork looked out of the cockpit and saw surf breaking on beaches.

"Two minutes from cast-off!" Wallwork shouted to Howard and his men.

The Halifax pilot gave last details of wind speed and height.

"Prepare for cast-off!" yelled Wallwork.

The glider was past the coast now, the Merville Gun Battery below. Howard called for silence and his men stopped singing and tightened their safety belts, waiting for the familiar jerk as the glider was released.[3]

Wallwork reached for the control that would unleash his "flying coffin," as some men called the Horsa glider, from the Halifax bomber.

They were on time and on target.[4]

"Cast off!" said Wallwork.[5]

There was a distinct *twang* as the towrope was released.

Howard felt the Horsa jerk slightly and then the Halifax bomber disappeared, headed back to England,[6] and with it went the reassuring sound of its engines. "The silence was uncanny," recalled Howard, "and all we could hear was the air swishing past the sides of the glider; it was a sound that none of us would ever forget." Howard thought of his wife and his two young children, fast asleep back in Oxfordshire, and then felt for a lump in his breast pocket—a small red leather shoe, the first his son Terry had ever worn.

———

CAPTAIN FRANK LILLYMAN stared at a patchwork of Norman fields framed by hedgerows and speckled with old stone farm buildings, all bathed in bright moonlight.[7] Crouch was following a narrow road Lillyman could see below, heading for the 101st Airborne's northernmost drop zone, "A," between the town of Sainte-Mère-Église and the village of Saint-Martin-de-Varreville.

Lillyman checked his kit. His folding-stock M1 carbine was handy for spraying Germans up close, and his M2 switchblade in his chest pocket could be useful if he dropped into an apple tree and had to cut himself free of his harness. He then crouched down on one knee, looking out the open door, trying to identify landmarks he'd examined so many times so carefully in aerial reconnaissance photos.

A red light flashed on.

Four minutes to go.

The pathfinders glanced at one another. Tension showed in their taut features, some painfully aware of what a staff sergeant had told them in a last briefing back in England when asked about their chances of getting out alive. *Not good, not good at all.* Hopefully the Germans lay sleeping soundly below.

Lillyman stood and ordered his men to their feet. To shed weight, many had dispensed with their reserve chutes, leaving them stuffed under their seats.

"Snap up!" called Lillyman.

They attached their cords to a cable that ran above their heads along the length of the cabin, then quickly checked each other's packs and equipment. Lillyman stepped down the row of men, making sure each had snapped his line to the cable. There was no kettledrum roll of anti-aircraft fire. No searchlight. They'd not been spotted. Thick fog now shrouded the landscape below as Lillyman waited the last few seconds for the light to turn green. He was the very tip of the Allied airborne spearhead, the first man who would jump from the first US plane over Normandy on D-Day.[8] It was an honor, a great privilege, to be number one, entrusted with arguably the most important task of any officer who belonged to the American first wave—those who would encounter a startled and trigger-happy enemy first.[9]

When the newspapers and radios blare out the news, remember that your pappy led the way.

Those were the words he'd written to his three-year-old daughter a couple of weeks earlier, after learning of his mission.

In the cockpit with Crouch and Pedone was a radio operator who announced that they were close to the hamlet of Saint-Germain-de-Varreville.[10] Dark fields rushed past below. Crouch pulled back on the throttle, slowing the plane, cutting prop blast.

A green light flashed a few seconds later.

"Let's go!" shouted Lillyman, and he stepped out into the prop blast, followed by seventeen other Americans.

Crouch noted the time as he dived low, heading back toward the English Channel.

It was 12:15 A.M., June 6, 1944. The most important day of the twentieth century.

The first Americans had arrived in France.[11]

IT WAS TIME TO OPEN the doors on Major John Howard's Horsa glider. "This could be a fairly perilous task," remembered Howard. "Den Brotheridge released his safety belt and, as I gripped his left hand in a double wrist-grip, and his platoon stretcher bearer held onto his straps and equipment, he leaned forward and heaved the door upwards. The other man and I then yanked him backward and he sank back into his seat with a sigh of relief and refastened his safety belt. Suddenly, we were all aware of the sweet, damp night air over the Normandy countryside as it filled the glider and we all breathed in, for the first time, the smell of France."[12]

Pegasus Bridge was just a couple of miles away.

In training, Wallwork had asked Howard where he wanted him to place the glider.

"Ideally, Jim," Howard had answered, "right through the wire defenses of the bridge."

"Right-ho, sir!" Wallwork had replied.

He never expected Wallwork to take the request seriously. It would require a tremendous feat of flying, especially in a flimsy glider.

Beside Wallwork was his co-pilot, John Ainsworth, holding a stopwatch.

Wallwork checked the compass on the control panel.

Ainsworth monitored the glider's airspeed.

The seconds ticked by on the stopwatch.

Almost time to make the critical turn toward the target.

Below, on Pegasus Bridge, Private Helmut Romer, a thin-faced eighteen-year-old with blond hair, walked across the structure's planking. Tracer fire lit up the sky over Caen, several miles away. The city was being bombed, as it had been on many nights in recent weeks. A gun crew was asleep in a nearby bunker. Some of Romer's comrades were at a late-night bar in Bénouville, no doubt drinking cheap plonk with stolid, milk-fed Norman farm girls.

Seven thousand feet above Romer, Wallwork could now see nothing but cloud from his large Perspex window. He was flying blind, relying on Ainsworth, whose eyes were glued to his stopwatch.

Wallwork glanced at the indicators just in front of his left knee.

Airspeed: 160 miles per hour.

Ainsworth stared at his stopwatch.

Three minutes and thirty-nine seconds . . . forty seconds . . . forty-one . . . forty-two.

"Now!" said Ainsworth.

Wallwork put the glider into a full turn.

Still full cloud cover. Nothing but gray through the large cockpit window.

Where were the damn bridges? The large area of woods shown on the maps?

"I can't see the Bois de Bavent," said Wallwork, referring to the forest indicated on his maps.

"For God's sake, Jim, it's the biggest place in Normandy," replied Ainsworth. "Pay attention."[13]

"It's not there."

"Well, we're on course anyway."

Ainsworth looked at his stopwatch and again began to count down.

"Five. Four. Three. Two. One. Bingo! Turn to starboard onto course."

Wallwork again turned the glider, this time to the north, making for the eastern bank of the Caen Canal, as planned. In his mind, he could picture the bridge, the defenses . . .

The altimeter near his left knee showed he was losing height fast.

Still just gray skies. Cloud cover. But behind him, over his shoulder, were red flashes from bomb explosions near Caen. Searchlights stabbed the black sky above the city.

They'd be lucky to survive in one piece. At best, a broken leg or two. That was what Wallwork and Ainsworth had agreed.

The glider's speed was slowing, but Wallwork knew he would still be touching down at ninety miles per hour on rough ground, and if he hit a defensive obstacle or a tree . . . The cockpit was as flimsy as a paper bag in rain, all Perspex window and wooden struts. Wallwork could deploy a parachute to slow the glider on landing, but using it could send the craft's nose into the ground, killing him instantly.

At last, Wallwork was below the clouds, and at once he could see flooded fields, thick hedgerows, small villages. In the bright moonlight, the Orne River and the Caen Canal sparkled like "strips of silver." There they were—the bridges.

Wallwork saw all the key landmarks, all the places that had

been etched into his memory from months of practice, that had been mocked up in the models he had examined endlessly.

To hell with the course.

He knew the distance to the target and how high he was. He'd fly by instinct and experience from now on, "by guess and by God."

He headed down toward the bridge.

Throughout the glider, there was no more singing—the men heard only the sound of the cold wind rushing against the glider's wings.

"Hold tight!" yelled Ainsworth.

Howard prayed, *Please God, please God . . .* [14]

"Link arms!" cried Wallwork.[15]

AN UNLIT BLACK cigar between his lips, Captain Frank Lillyman drifted down at sixteen feet per second from 450 feet, trying to spot a clearing as the earth rushed up to meet him. He pulled on his forward risers and a few seconds later touched down in a small field near Saint-Germain-de-Varreville.[16] He freed himself of his parachute and looked around. He thought he could see something moving in the shadows cast in the moonlight by tall poplar trees. Germans? He loaded a clip into his tommy gun. There were shapes moving. Friend or foe? He used his "cricket," a small metal signaling clacker.

Click, clack . . .

Click, clack . . .

He was about to open fire when one of the shapes made a

sound: a loud *moo*. The shapes were cows, and he laughed to himself and felt a little less nervous.

Click, clack . . .

Click, clack . . .

Some men replied with their crickets, and within a few minutes Lillyman had connected with seven of his stick. He'd ordered them not to open fire unless absolutely necessary, as it would attract the enemy, and now they silently examined maps and scouted the immediate vicinity in pairs. Lillyman realized he was more than a mile north of where he should be, but there was no time to get to the planned position for setting up lights. They had less than thirty minutes before the main body of troops would arrive, so Lillyman decided to use the nearest suitable fields.

The silence was broken by the rattle of machine gun fire, and Lillyman took cover as Germans, hidden in a hedgerow, fired several more bursts. He sent two men to "convince these Krauts of the errors of their ways," he recalled, and then he "heard a grenade go off with a 'whumf,'" and everything was "lovely and quiet."[17] But then Lillyman apparently learned that two more Germans, riding bicycles, were heading his way, no doubt alerted by the machine gun fire.

A couple of pathfinders acted fast, it would later be claimed, stretching a "length of piano wire" across a road, "at neck level to a standing man, and secured tautly to a pair of large trees. Soon the pair of Germans came along on their bicycles, and they flipped over backward [as] the piano wire caught their necks. Nearly decapitated, the two died instantly."[18]

Lillyman could make out a church less than a hundred yards away, at the center of the village of Saint-Germain-de-Varreville, and before long he and his men had gathered in its graveyard. The church steeple would be an excellent spot for a Eureka radar set.

A priest came to the heavy wooden door at the main entrance. He looked afraid. One of Lillyman's men, a young lieutenant, could speak French.

"Bonsoir, padre," he said. "You've just been liberated."[19]

The lieutenant explained what they were doing, and a Eureka set was placed in the steeple, as were three others along a hedgerow near the church. Lights forming the tail of a T were laid out two hundred yards east of the church, in a field beside a narrow lane. Then two men climbed a tree and put another Eureka set in the branches to help guide the planes scheduled to drop hundreds of Screaming Eagles on Drop Zone A, one of six landing areas for American airborne troops.[20] Lillyman's men turned on the first Eureka set at 12:30 A.M., just fifteen minutes after arriving on the ground.[21]

All they could do now was wait. But then Lillyman discovered from a scout that there was a large farmhouse, seemingly occupied by Germans, close to a 22-millimeter anti-aircraft gun position that could wreak considerable havoc. "Two others and myself went to the house where we met a Frenchman smoking a pipe," remembered Lillyman. "He was standing in the doorway. He jerked his thumb toward the stairs and said, 'Boche.' We caught one German, in a nice pair of white pajamas, in bed. We disposed of him and expropriated the bottle of champagne beside the bed."[22]

———

WITHIN MOMENTS of Captain Lillyman's arrival in France, Major John Howard and the men in his Horsa glider lifted their knees and held hands, locking fingers together in a "butcher's grip." In his last seconds in the air, Howard wondered "what the strength of the enemy would be . . . I was worried about a machine gun wiping us all out before we could have a chance to fight back." The glider was carrying explosives. Would they detonate if they crashed badly? How fast were they going? More than one hundred miles per hour?

Howard looked at Jim Wallwork, a few feet away, the back of his neck sweaty from tension.[23]

Wallwork knew he was approaching too fast. "There was a feeling," he recalled, "of the land rushing up and I landed probably at about ninety-five instead of at eighty-five."

Wallwork called out, "Stream."

His co-pilot, John Ainsworth, flicked a switch.

The parachute brake opened. The glider's nose went down, but not too much, and the parachute worked, slowing them abruptly.

One second.

Two.[24]

"Jettison."

Ainsworth pressed another switch and the parachute fell away.[25]

It seemed for a moment as if the glider might come to a halt with little damage. But then the wheels fell off and the undercarriage skidded along the stony ground, sparks showering everywhere. "There followed a sound like a giant canvas sheet being viciously ripped apart," recalled Howard, "then a mighty crash like a clap of thunder and my body seemed to be moving in several directions at once." The glider slid to a halt. Inside, men and equipment were jumbled up in a tangle of limbs and kit.

God help me, thought Howard, *we must all be dead.*[26]

"For a frightful second," he recalled, "I really believed that I might have been blinded, and then just as quickly realized that my helmet had rammed down over my eyes as I hit the roof or the side of the glider."[27] He could see "a misty blue and greyish haze," then, from "somewhere out in endless space there zoomed towards me a long tracer-like stream of multi-colored lights, like a host of shooting stars" zipping toward him at great speed. A moment later, he knew he was not a target, not being shot at yet: "I was simply concussed and seeing stars!"

He pulled up his helmet and looked at his watch. It had stopped, the minute hand frozen at 12:16.[28] A few men stirred, emerging from shock. In a few moments, others were fully alert, snapping into action, their training kicking in as they instinctively freed themselves of canvas straps and reached in the darkness for ammunition, Sten guns, and grenades. In training, Howard had drummed into them that every second counted if they were to retain the element of surprise. It was their deadliest weapon. Every moment wasted now could cost a life.

The glider's smashed exit door was blocked by ripped canvas and splintered wooden struts. Howard and others quickly broke through with the butts of their rifles and climbed out. Wallwork had, in Howard's words, done "a fantastic job in bringing the slithering, bouncing and crippled glider to a halt with its nose buried into the canal bank and within seventy-five yards of the bridge."[29]

Lieutenant Den Brotheridge emerged from the wreckage.

"Gun out!" he ordered.[30]

A man carrying a Bren gun climbed out.

Howard noticed that Brotheridge was limping.

"You all right, Den?" he asked.

Yes, he was fine.

"Get cracking with your first section."[31]

Brotheridge moved quickly toward the bridge. Howard followed, glancing back at the stricken glider. Its nose had been smashed in on impact, pushed back almost to the wings. Had the pilots survived? It seemed unlikely, given the wreckage. "I had been very lucky," recalled Howard, "but I thought that those who were forward of me must have been badly smashed up or killed."[32]

In fact, Wallwork had been thrown through the glider's Perspex windscreen and now lay flat on his stomach a few yards away, stunned and badly bruised. He was in shock but able to move all his limbs, and he called to Ainsworth, still trapped under the collapsed cockpit.

"Can you crawl?"

"No," answered Ainsworth.

Forcing himself up, Wallwork tried to lift the nose of the glider so he could free his co-pilot.

Could Ainsworth get out of the wreckage, he asked, if the weight was taken off him?

"I'll try."[33]

Wallwork felt as if he were lifting the "whole bloody glider," but the adrenaline coursing through him gave him extra strength and Ainsworth was able to crawl free of the wreckage.

Meanwhile, John Howard crouched down. Thirty men were gathered near him, ready to rush the drawbridge, its iron superstructure towering above them in the moonlight, before the Germans could blow it up. There were trenches nearby and a pillbox, but no sign of Germans. For a few seconds, they all stared at their objective, then Howard stood up.

"Charge!"

A private carrying a Bren gun spotted a German to his right and opened up, hitting the man, then kept firing as he ran toward the bridge. He saw a blockhouse and threw a grenade inside, then pressed his trigger again, emptying his magazine, spraying bullets inside.[34]

Germans began shooting from trenches to his right.

Howard's men returned fire, calling out the code words for their platoons to avoid hitting one another.

"Dog, dog, dog!"

"Sapper, sapper, sapper!"[35]

Howard heard a crash as a glider landed, followed by another. Both gliders skidded to a halt less than fifty yards away, narrowly missing a pond.

On the west side of the bridge, Georges Gondrée, a café owner, was sleeping soundly beside his wife in his bedroom in the small brick building that served as both his home and his business. His wife had been awoken by the sound of the gliders crashing and she tried to stir her husband to action.

"Get up. Don't you hear what's happening? Open the window."

A sleepy Gondrée didn't understand.

"Get up. Listen. It sounds like wood breaking."[36]

Gondrée climbed out of bed and went to the window. The bridge lay only yards from his café, and he could see a German soldier nearby in the moonlight. "His features were working," recalled Gondrée, "his eyes wide with fear. For a moment he did not speak, and I then saw that he was literally struck dumb by terror. At last he stammered out one word, 'Parachutists!'"[37]

Private Helmut Romer may have been the soldier Gondrée spotted. He was certainly among the first Germans to confront the Allied invasion.[38] "As far as I was concerned," Romer recalled, "I was on a fairly boring bridge in the middle of rural France and was just very glad to be there and not on the Russian front." He had been on watch for two hours, waiting, impatiently, to be relieved. "One minute it was a duty like any other. The next there was this swishing noise, followed by a bang and we thought it was part of an Allied plane that had been shot down. But the sound kept getting nearer to us, accompanied by a huge shadow and we froze. Then some soldiers, their faces smeared all in black, started coming towards us and in the half-moonlight we saw they were British. In a split second, we realised what the story was."

Romer was terrified.

He fired a flare that flooded the bridge with bright white light.

"Achtung!" he screamed.

Bullets cut through the air, and Romer and two other Germans ran for their lives, throwing themselves into the nearest cover, an elderberry bush.

A German sergeant emerged from a pillbox on the eastern side of the bridge.

"What's wrong?"[39]

The sergeant was quickly shot and killed.

Around a hundred yards west of Pegasus Bridge, another German sergeant, Heinz Hickman, was leading four of his men from the German 6th Fallschirmjäger Regiment toward the bridge, having heard the clatter of Sten and Bren guns. He had "no great respect whatever for the American soldier," but the British were a different case altogether.[40] As he neared, he saw figures moving across the canal—Howard's troops.

"Come on, come on," Hickman urged his men. "Don't start firing before I fire, wait for me."

Hickman was soon blasting away at Howard's lead platoon—and quickly running out of ammunition. "I'm not a coward," he later stated, "but at that moment I got frightened. If you see a Para platoon in full cry, they frighten the daylights out of you—the way they charge, the way they fire, the way they ran across the bridge . . . Then I gave the order to pull back. What [could] I do with four men who had never been in action?"[41]

Lieutenant Brotheridge ran ahead of his platoon.

"Come on 25!" shouted Brotheridge. "Come on 25!"[42]

Other men followed, moving west across the bridge. Twenty-two-year-old Lieutenant Richard Smith had injured his knee upon landing, and now he hobbled toward the Café Gondrée, leading Number 3 platoon. A German threw a stick grenade at Smith and it exploded, a piece of shrapnel hitting Smith in the wrist. The German ran for cover and was climbing a wall when Smith's weapon answered. "I gave him quite a lot of rounds, firing from the hip—it was very close range."

A corporal approached Smith.

"Are you all right, sir?"

Smith looked at his wrist. Skin and muscle had been ripped off, exposing bone. *Christ! No more cricket,* thought the lieutenant, who had been a keen sportsman at Cambridge University.

Smith heard a sound from the café and saw Georges Gondrée peering from a window. "I wasn't messing around, having just had this bloody German, and I just put my Sten gun up and fired." A bullet just missed Gondrée's head, hitting the stone ceiling of his bedroom and ricocheting down into his bed.[43]

Across the canal, Jim Wallwork had meanwhile pulled Ainsworth into a ditch, out of the line of fire. Blood seeped from a wound to Wallwork's head, so much that he wondered if he'd lost an eye. Yet his overriding emotion was of satisfaction, "glad to have done the job and delivered the boys." It had been some job indeed. Air Chief Marshal Sir Trafford Leigh-Mallory, head of the Allied air forces on D-Day, would later describe Wallwork's landing as "one of the greatest feats of flying of the second world war."[44]

Major Howard ordered his men to clear trenches and dugouts nearest the downed gliders. Corporal Wally Parr and another man had a running start, fifteen yards ahead of the others. Parr's mouth was dry, his tongue glued to the roof of his mouth. He thought he was going to choke, so he took a deep breath, then let out a piercing scream. He didn't know why—he just screamed. Two years of training for this moment, five years of war, of Hitler's bombs killing so many innocents in the East End of London, where he'd grown up. Time to get even.

"Come out and fight, you squirrelly little bastards."

Parr reached a blockhouse on the eastern side of the draw-bridge, opened the door, and made ready with a hand grenade. Another man covered him with a Bren gun as he pulled the gre-nade's pin, threw it inside, and shut the door. A few seconds later, there was a loud explosion.

"Get in!" he shouted to the soldier with the Bren, who promptly opened the door and sprayed the inside with bullets. Then it was on to the next strongpoint, where Parr again pulled out a phosphorus grenade and threw it inside. He ran back to-ward Howard, near the bridge.

"You cleared those?" asked Howard.

"Yes, cleared, sir."

"Run, run, run. Get across that bridge!"

Parr and another soldier began to sprint across.

"Ham and jam!" shouted Parr.

"You know you're not supposed to shout ham and jam," the soldier told Parr.

Parr was so excited, he'd used the code name to be employed only once the bridges had been secured, not before. They were the only words he could find, and saying something—anything—in English had meant he'd been recognized and therefore not shot by mistake. When he reached the other side of the bridge, he saw a Belgian belonging to Howard's unit gesturing with his left thumb at a window in the Café Gondrée, about to throw a smoke grenade through it.

Parr grabbed the Belgian's arm.

"What the hell are you going to do with that thing?"

"I'm going to smoke the bastards out."

"We're going to need that café tomorrow, for more reasons than one."

Parr moved closer to the café. "There was a dead German. He had no equipment, no uniform, just trousers and what appeared to be a jumper, or possibly a shirt. He was lying in the middle of the road. A big stout chap. I checked him. He was dead." He couldn't see any sign of Lieutenant Brotheridge, his platoon leader.

"Where's Denny Brotheridge?" he shouted. "Where's Brotheridge?"

The plan was for Parr to meet up with Brotheridge thirty yards beyond the café, in a ditch. As he made his way there, he passed another body lying in the road. "It was Lieutenant Brotheridge. I knelt down beside him. I put my rifle down, put my hand behind his head and lifted him up. He was conscious and he said something."[45]

Parr leaned closer.

"I'm sorry, sir, I can't hear you."

Brotheridge started to speak again but then closed his eyes, exhaled, and slumped back to the ground.

Parr looked at his hand, which had been supporting the lieutenant's head. It was covered in blood.

My God.

All the years of training had come down to this.

What a waste.

One of Parr's comrades ran over.

"What the hell's going on?"

"It's Denny," said Parr. "He's had it."

"Christ almighty."

Brotheridge died not long after, becoming the first Allied soldier killed in combat on D-Day. A medical officer later found him "lying near a low stone wall . . . He was looking at the stars, bewilderment on his face and a bullet hole in the middle of his neck below his chin."[46]

Parr turned back to the Café Gondrée and tried to find a sergeant to tell him he was now platoon leader. Then he sprinted back across the bridge toward Major Howard, who had taken up position near the bridge on the eastern side.

"Where you going, Parr?" asked Howard.

"Sir, I'm afraid Mr. Brotheridge has been killed."

Howard looked at Parr and then stared across the bridge.

"What do you mean?"

"I'm sorry, he's dead."

Shaken by the news of his good friend's death, it was several seconds before Howard was able to issue further orders. "Top of my mind," recalled Howard, "was the fact that I knew Margaret, his wife, was expecting a baby almost any time."[47] She would in fact give birth to a girl seventeen days later.

At twenty-five minutes past midnight, Howard learnt that there were no explosives under Pegasus Bridge. Then still more good news: The bridge over the Orne had also been captured. So long as both could be held, the British would control the flow of troops and armor to the eastern flank of the Allied bridgehead. Howard peered through the gun smoke across Pegasus Bridge. The shooting had died down. His men were in control. The attack had lasted just ten minutes.

He turned to his radioman.

"Send it out," said Howard. "Ham and Jam. Ham and Jam. Keep it up until you get acknowledgment."[48]

It was the first message of success on D-Day.

Ham and jam . . . Ham and jam.

FIFTY MILES AWAY, at Drop Zone A, beside the old stone church in Saint-Germain-de-Varreville, Captain Frank Lillyman waited anxiously for the sound of engines.[49] Never had time passed so slowly—these were by far the "longest minutes" of his life. At 12:40 A.M., he finally heard it—the steady drone of hundreds of planes to the north—and ordered his men to turn on the drop zone's lights. "Those lights never looked so bright in training," he recalled, "but that night they looked like searchlights. One light went out, and we had to rig an emergency connection. We were silhouetted against it for a few minutes."[50]

Meanwhile, among the swarm of fast-approaching C-47s carrying the US Army's 101st Airborne, a BBC reporter observed the callow young men, grim-faced, "burdened like pack-horses so that they could hardly stand unaided . . . So young they looked, on the edge of the unknown. And somehow so sad.

Most sat with eyes closed as the seconds ticked by. They seemed to be asleep, but I could see lips moving wordlessly."[51]

The first aircraft flew over the T that Lillyman's men had placed on the ground. It was three minutes before one o'clock. The main body of American airborne troops had arrived.[52]

CHAPTER 3

The Cruel Seas

ABOARD THE USS *BARNETT*, in the middle of the English Channel, twenty-five-year-old Captain Leonard Schroeder ate steak and eggs, served by a British marine in an immaculate uniform. Some of his fellow officers from the US Army's 8th Infantry Regiment of the 4th Division could not help but think they might be tasting their last suppers.[1] "If you fellows ever want to get home," their division commander, Major General Raymond Barton, had told them a few hours before, "you have to be the meanest, dirtiest son-of-a-bitches the world has ever seen." The division's acting deputy commander, Brigadier General Theodore Roosevelt Jr., had added, for good measure, "Don't you ever think for one minute that the [Germans] won't shoot to kill you."[2]

Schroeder considered several of his fellow officers to be close friends, having served with them in the 4th Infantry "Ivy" Division since 1942. He had memorized the names of all 219 men in

F Company, which he led, and could recognize each man in the dark by the sound of his voice. Many were from the South and were described by a fellow officer as "country boys from Florida, Alabama and Georgia . . . squirrel-shooters who weren't afraid of the dark, who could find their way home in woods and feel at home."[3] Born just below the Mason-Dixon Line himself, Schroeder was no backwoods boy, having been a star soccer player at the University of Maryland, where he had enjoyed a full scholarship.[4]

It was almost time to board the landing craft, but before doing so, Schroeder and other company commanders slated for the first wave were called to a meeting with the 2nd Battalion commander, Lieutenant Colonel Carlton MacNeely, and General Roosevelt, the eldest son of the twenty-sixth president of the United States. The arthritic Roosevelt, who at fifty-six sported a bad heart and a bum leg, had begged his superiors repeatedly to allow him to go in with the first wave. "I personally know both officers and men of these advance units," he had stressed, "and believe that it will steady them to know that I am with them."[5]

"The general was reading western stories when we arrived," Schroeder later recalled as he and the other officers assembled in Roosevelt's quarters. Schroeder and Roosevelt were on good terms—Roosevelt called the thickset athlete "Moose" because of his muscular build, and Schroeder was proud of the nickname. Several days prior, Schroeder had come down with a high fever and had been sent to the sick bay. He had quickly given up hope of being released in time to lead his men on D-Day, but then, to his surprise, he had found Roosevelt standing before him.

"Moose, get dressed and come with me," ordered Roosevelt.

Schroeder had done as he was told. He followed the general past guards, keeping a poker face, and rejoined his company.

One last time, Schroeder listened as his commanders went through the invasion plan for the 2nd Battalion. They would be the first seaborne forces to fight on D-Day, landing in the first wave, supported by amphibious tanks, and would break through a seawall before securing vital causeways leading off Utah Beach. "All commanders reported everything was ready," recalled Schroeder. "All we wanted was to get going."

As the meeting broke up, officers wished each other the best of luck and shook hands. MacNeely put his arm around Schroeder's broad shoulders.

"Well, Moose, this is it. Give 'em hell!"

MacNeely was emotional, all "choked up," as was Schroeder.

"Well, Colonel," Schroeder blurted, "I'll see you on the beach!"[6]

That night, aboard the *Barnett*, Roosevelt penned a letter to his wife, Eleanor. "We are starting out on the great venture of this war," he wrote, "and by the time you get this letter, for better or for worse, it will be history. We are attacking in daylight the most heavily fortified shore in history, a shore held by excellent troops . . . The men are crowded below or lounging on deck. Very few have seen action. They talk of many things, but rarely of the action that lies ahead. If they speak of it at all it is to wisecrack."[7]

It was after midnight when Captain Schroeder stepped onto the *Barnett*'s deck. Hundreds of men stood in the darkness, waiting to form boat teams and then be called to the landing craft that hung, ominously, from davits along the sides of the former British passenger steamer. The sky was black. The wind howled above the thrum of the ship's engines. Then a loudspeaker blared and Schroeder heard a recording of Eisenhower's final message to the Allied forces: "You are about to embark upon the Great Crusade . . . The eyes of the world are upon you. The hopes and prayers of liberty-loving people everywhere march with you. In company with our brave Allies and brothers-in-arms on other Fronts, you will bring about the destruction of the German war machine, the elimination of Nazi tyranny over the oppressed peoples of Europe, and security for ourselves in a free world."[8]

Deeply moved by Eisenhower's words, Schroeder returned to his quarters. For half an hour, he wrote a last letter to his wife, Margaret, his high school sweetheart to whom he'd been married since December 1941 and with whom he had a two-year-old son. "I told her where I was," recalled Schroeder, "what I was about to do, and how much I loved her."[9]

ABOARD THE HMS *Amsterdam* stood twenty-six-year-old Lieutenant George Kerchner, waiting for the order to clamber down the ship's side netting and take his place in a flimsy landing craft with other men from D Company of the 2nd Ranger Battalion.[10] A platoon leader with dark hair, a broad, handsome face, and bright eyes, he was inordinately proud of the yellow diamond on the back of his helmet, his unit's insignia. He had never worked so hard, never endured so much, to belong to the elite, all-volunteer Rangers—only one in four men who had applied to join the five-hundred-strong battalion had made the grade.

A devout Catholic, Kerchner had left high school in the eleventh grade to help feed his family, working as a soda jerk at the Arundel Ice Cream Company and as a railroad security guard in his native Baltimore. He enlisted a year after Pearl Harbor, before volunteering for the Rangers in 1943.[11] He'd spent a brutally cold and wet winter in Scotland, practicing how to kill swiftly in silence and how to scale cliffs, driven hard by merciless British commandos.[12] Like so many men braced for combat on D-Day, he was anxious to prove himself, to get the job done and go home to his wife, Violet, whom he had dated in high school and married a year before the war in Europe began.

Kerchner had a great deal on his mind, so many concerns it was impossible to prioritize what he should worry about most. The previous afternoon, the *Amsterdam*'s British captain had admitted to Kerchner that his crew was "running out of food and fuel" after circling near the Isle of Wight for several hours, impatiently awaiting the final order to head to France. "The British food wasn't all that good," remembered Kerchner, "so that didn't worry us too much, but the fuel did."[13] Would the pre-invasion bombardment work? He had been told that fighter aircraft would attack Pointe du Hoc, a headland midway between Utah and Omaha Beaches, just three minutes before he and his men from D Company were to land. This would ensure that the Germans were kept back from the cliffs and would not be able to cut the Rangers' ropes as they climbed. But what if the Germans were well dug in on top of the cliffs, able to withstand rocketing and strafing?

To make matters worse, there had also been a recent, disconcerting change in command. A few days before, some of Kerchner's fellow officers had held a "little party." After having perhaps one too many slugs of gin, Major Cleveland Lytle, usually all "spit and polish," had gotten into a violent argument with other officers. Lytle was in command of D, E, and F Companies of the 2nd Ranger Battalion—"Force A"—assigned to attack a battery of guns at Pointe du Hoc, above hundred-foot cliffs. Intelligence reports had indicated that the Germans had placed six 155-millimeter guns atop the sheer cliffs.[14] The guns could fire as far as fifteen miles, hitting both American invasion beaches and Allied ships in the Channel. They had to be destroyed, but doing so would be one of the most formidable challenges of D-Day—"the toughest of any task," according to General Omar Bradley.[15]

Lytle had studied the most recent intelligence reports and concluded that the Rangers were being sent on a pointless mission. "We're all going to be killed," Lytle had protested. "There's not going to be one man left and it's all going to be for nothing."[16]

What was the point in dying if they didn't achieve any objective?

"Look at your maps, for chrissakes. What does it say?" Lytle continued, pulling out a map.

"Read it!"

Lytle pointed at the map. Two guns, numbers 4 and 5 on his map, had a comment scrawled beside them: "Guns dismantled."

"Whether you guys know it or not, intelligence says the guns aren't there," Lytle had stressed. "Our new orders simply state: 'The mission of the Rangers remains unchanged.' It's suicide, I tell you. And what for chrissake for?"[17]

Kerchner's fellow officers had tried to calm Lytle, but he punched the battalion surgeon, the much respected Captain

Walter Block.[18] It had required several men to hold Lytle down and then take him to his quarters.[19] As soon as the 2nd Battalion's commanding officer, Lieutenant Colonel James Rudder, was informed of the incident, he had decided that Lytle was in no fit state to command men, let alone inspire their confidence, so he had taken charge of Lytle's force at the eleventh hour. Rudder himself would lead men up the cliffs of Pointe du Hoc.[20]

While his men steeled themselves for combat, Colonel Rudder reported to Major General Clarence Huebner, the 1st Division's commander, aboard the USS *Ancon*. He told Huebner what had happened with Lytle, and of his intention to join the assault on Pointe du Hoc. He would not be staying on the *Ancon,* the headquarters ship.

"I can't let you do that," Huebner had said. "I need you here to oversee the entire Ranger operation. We may have Rangers spread over a four- or five-mile stretch of beach. You can't risk getting knocked out in the very first round."

"I'm sorry, sir, but I'm going to have to disobey you," Rudder replied. "If I don't take it—it may not go."[21]

Rudder had then left the *Ancon* and taken a motorboat across the dark, swelling waters to the HMS *Ben Machree,* where he formally relieved Lytle, who had to be removed, screaming and kicking, from a stairwell. "The process of arresting and leading off the former commander of the operation was a noisy one," remembered one bystander. "I opened the door to find out what was going on, only to see a group of struggling and shouting uniforms, and was immediately ordered back inside by Colonel Rudder."

Rudder had first learnt about Pointe du Hoc five months

before, in a second-floor room, blackout curtains drawn, in General Omar Bradley's headquarters in a stately London home. An officer had explained the mission in detail to Rudder and Lieutenant Colonel Max Schneider, who had trained the 1st Ranger Battalion. "When we first got a look at a photo of Pointe du Hoc," recalled Rudder, "Max just whistled through his teeth. He had a way of doing that. He'd made three landings already, but I was just a country boy coaching football a year and a half before."[22]

A naval officer had dismissed Rudder's chances, saying that "three old women with brooms could keep the Rangers from climbing that cliff."[23]

The plan had looked just as crazy to Rudder. General Bradley, commander of the US First Army, couldn't be serious?

It had been no joke, and now, past midnight on June 6, 1944, it was abundantly clear to his men that Rudder was under enormous stress. "He knew where we were going and what we were going to do," recalled one Ranger. "He knew we were going to lose eight out of every ten men. That means only two guys out of ten weren't going to get hurt. I looked at it this way—I wasn't going to get hurt; who would the other one be? That's the way I think most everybody looked at it."[24]

Tension mounted as the ships carrying the Rangers steamed closer to France.[25] After a meager breakfast of coffee and flapjacks at 2 A.M., in order to kill time, many men lost themselves, their worries, and their savings in intense gambling sessions. Few truly cared about winning or losing, so long as they didn't have to think about fighting and dying.

Belowdecks on the HMS *Amsterdam,* Staff Sergeant Jack

Kuhn, a whippet-thin twenty-four-year-old who belonged to Lieutenant Kerchner's platoon in D Company, watched as a fellow Ranger dealt out cards for what he knew might be his last-ever poker game.[26] Kuhn had held a special role in the run-up to the invasion. Faced with the daunting task of mounting a sheer wall of rock while under fire, Colonel Rudder had chosen Kuhn to liaise with a British company called Merryweather, which supplied ladders to the London Fire Brigade. Sworn to complete secrecy, Kuhn had explained to designers at Merryweather & Sons the extraordinary challenge facing the Rangers, and the firm had designed a one-hundred-foot extension ladder to be mounted in the base of an amphibious truck, a DUKW. Once beached, the truck could drive to the base of a cliff and the ladder could be placed against the cliff. Successful trials had followed at cliffs near Swanage, on England's south coast. Now, in just a few hours' time, some of Kuhn's fellow Rangers would dash up the made-to-order ladder, scaling Pointe du Hoc as if it were a tall building during an air raid.[27]

Kuhn studied the cards dealt to him—he had a hot hand at last. Then someone announced that Father Lacy was holding a final service up top.

"We gotta go and do a little praying," said one devout gambler. "Maybe we'll get some protection for tomorrow."

Three men cashed out and headed to the main deck to listen to Lacy and pray.

Father Joe Lacy was a plump Catholic priest from Hartford, Connecticut. At forty years of age, he cut an almost comical figure among the young, lean bodies of the Rangers, men who had been trained to reach peak fitness, like racehorses for a hard steeplechase. He was thirty pounds overweight, wore thick glasses, and was six long inches short of six feet, even in his jump boots—"a small, fat old Irishman," as one Ranger described him.[28]

"When you land on the beach and you get in there," Lacy told the Rangers gathered around him, "I don't want to see anybody kneeling down and praying. If I do I'm gonna come up and boot you in the tail. You leave the praying to me and you do the fighting."[29]

Meanwhile, Jack Kuhn had stayed behind to play out his hand.[30] None of the men who quit the game to pray would survive D-Day.

LIEUTENANT COLONEL TERENCE OTWAY, commanding officer of the 9th Battalion, Parachute Regiment, stood in the open door of a shaking plane as it approached the English Channel. With a lean and sensitive face, Otway looked more like an introspective academic than the leader of 750 of the toughest men in the entire British invasion force. Otway and his battalion had been tasked with seizing the heavily defended Merville Battery, whose guns pointed at the British invasion beach, Sword, where 29,000 men were scheduled to land on D-Day. Destroying the battery was so crucial, yet so difficult, that only the finest unit in the British 6th Airborne had been considered for the job.

Having studied the battery's formidable defenses, Otway had decided that sixty men from his battalion—average age just twenty—would crash-land in three gliders on top of the battery itself, thereby avoiding a fifteen-foot-thick perimeter of barbed wire and a surrounding minefield that was a hundred yards wide.[31] "Our plan was . . . to have three glider-loads of troops land inside the battery," recalled Otway, "stopping themselves by knocking their wings off the [gun] casemates and taking the garrison entirely by surprise. The last part of the gliders' journey would be lit up by mortar flares laid by us."[32]

When Otway had asked for volunteers to go in with the gliders, every man in one company had stepped forward. He had been forced to select fewer than a third, each of them unmarried, knowing that most would be lucky to come home alive, "such was the nut to be cracked."[33] It was indeed "a Grade A stinker of a job," as one senior officer had put it. In his last address to Otway and his men, the 6th Airborne's commander, General Sir Richard Nelson "Windy" Gale, had hardly inspired confidence. "The Hun thinks only a bloody fool will go there," Gale had said. "That's why we're going."[34]

So stressed had Otway been before leaving his final base in England, after months of obsessive preparation, that he had spent a sleepless night pacing back and forth, hiding his anxiety from his officers and men, turning over every detail of his complicated assault plan. Thankfully, he had slept well the previous night, having been so exhausted from lack of rest and worry. Now he felt calm, utterly focused.[35]

Otway was not one to go easy on any man, friend or foe.[36] His father had been killed in the last war against the Germans, and his youth was overshadowed by the loss. There were bitter memories of his mother struggling to make ends meet on a war widow's pension, thanks to the bloody Hun. After graduating from Royal Military College, Sandhurst, he had been posted to the Far East and, based in heavily bombed Shanghai, had witnessed the carnage and horror of the Sino-Japanese War. He had also served on the North-West Frontier in India, where his men had frequently fought hand to hand with swords against local tribesmen.

Otway was a fastidious, unrelenting perfectionist, the second-oldest officer in the battalion and one of only two who had, as he put it, "ever actually been on the wrong end of artillery or rifle fire."[37] In training, he had made his men march fifty miles with sixty-pound packs on their backs. Some had suffered such bad blisters and their feet had bled so badly that their socks, encrusted with mud and blood, had to be cut away from their toes.[38] An experienced sergeant described Otway as "a man that you couldn't get through to. He was a very hard man, very standoffish, as you would expect a commanding officer to be. No tolerance for a fool whatsoever. You could not make a single mistake. He was a man I must say in all honesty I hated intensely as our commanding officer."

Otway didn't waste his time wondering what his men thought of him. "I may sound pompous and conceited," he retorted, "but I don't think a senior officer's job is to work on being liked. He should be respected. Yes, I wanted to be respected and I wanted to be considered a fair person but I wouldn't go out of my way to get popularity. I wanted an efficient, well-run, happy battalion and I reckon I had it."[39] To make sure his lads were in tip-top shape, he'd banned them from drinking for the past forty-eight hours.

Now Otway and his men were nearing the coast of France.[40]

"Twenty minutes to go, lads!" a man shouted. "Equipment check!"[41]

None of us is going to die, one of those lads thought. *We're all brave men. We're not going to die.*

Another of Otway's men, an eighteen-year-old, worried about his Sten gun. How many rounds were in each magazine? Would he run out of bullets when it mattered most? One of the most common fears among the first-wave troops on D-Day, and indeed all troops, was running out of ammunition in a firefight. Many paratroopers, knowing they might well need every bullet they could carry, were overloaded with extra magazines.

"We're approaching the coast!"[42]

Anti-aircraft fire opened up, becoming a steady bark as 22-millimeter shells exploded in black smudges among the clouds. Otway and his men could also see tracer bullets glowing, the color of amber, as they probed the sky. Any second now, the jump light would turn green and it would be time to drop, helplessly, dangling beneath a silk parachute, onto the enemy below.

IT WAS 12:50 A.M. At Pegasus Bridge, John Howard heard the steady drone of Stirling bombers, bringing in the 3rd and 5th Parachute Brigades of the 6th Airborne Division.[43] Searchlights illuminated the drop, showing white chutes falling like silken confetti as far as the eye could see. Tracer fire—green, orange, red—spat skyward. Howard could not help but stand and stare at the heavens: "It really was the most awe-inspiring sight."

Then Howard blew on his whistle.

Dat, dat, dat . . . Daaaa . . .

The bridges were in British hands.

The sound of the whistle carried for hundreds of yards, lifting the spirits of teenagers who were lost and alone in the darkness. "Paras who had landed in a tree or a bog, in a farmyard and away from their own friends," recalled Howard, "could hear that whistle. It not only meant that the bridges had been captured, but it also gave them an orientation." The question now was whether the men hearing the whistle, and others from the widely dispersed 6th Airborne, would be able to reinforce Howard before the 21st Panzer Division, based near Caen, could attack. If German armor arrived anytime soon, Howard would be in serious trouble without adequate anti-tank weaponry. His men could be massacred.

While Howard blew his whistle, his pilot, Jim Wallwork, was busy ferrying ammunition from his downed glider to Howard's command post, near Pegasus Bridge. "There was Howard, tooting on his bloody whistle and making all sorts of silly noises," recalled Wallwork, who had been ordered to bring hand-thrown explosives, called Gammon bombs, from the smashed glider to Howard's position.

"Gammon bombs!" Howard stressed. "Gammon bombs! Gammon bombs!" The major knew his men would need all the firepower they could find, but Wallwork reported that he had already searched the glider and found none.

"I put those Gammon bombs on the glider," Howard insisted. "Get those bloody Gammon bombs."

Wallwork did as instructed, returning to the glider to look once more, crawling inside its broken shell. But then he made a stupid mistake, deciding to use his flashlight to search for the elusive Gammon bombs. There was the metallic rip of machine gun fire—the enemy had spotted his light. He quickly flicked it off.

Back near Pegasus Bridge, less than thirty yards away, Howard's radio operator continued to send out the code words for the successful taking of the bridges. Howard was sure he heard a word of frustration added to the message, to which he had yet to get a reply from higher up in the division. "HAM AND JAM. HAM AND BLOODY JAM."

Around 12:52, paratroopers from the 5th Parachute Brigade of the 6th Airborne were spotted approaching Pegasus Bridge.[44] In the lead was thirty-six-year-old Brigadier Nigel Poett, who had jumped with pathfinders and landed not long after Howard and his men. "John Howard's Platoon Commander had not told him of my arrival," recalled Poett, "nor that I was on my way to see him. He was surprised, and a little put out, as I walked un- expectedly into his position. But he was so thrilled with his suc- cess, and with my very warm congratulations, that his Platoon Commander was quickly forgiven."[45]

Poett stood beside Howard, scanning the bridge and the landing area.

"Well, everything seems all right, John."

Poett had spoken too soon. Not long after came the sound of enemy tanks in the distance, drawing closer. A sergeant was told to get ready with a PIAT, an anti-tank weapon, the only one that could be found. Then a Panzerkampfwagen IV, with a black cross just below its turret, lumbered into view, tracks clanking louder and louder. Another followed behind, protected by three- inch-thick armor and boasting powerful 7.5-millimeter guns.

"Hold your fire!" shouted one of Howard's men.

The soldiers waited for the first tank to lumber within range of the sergeant's PIAT. By now he was so nervous he was "shaking like a bloody leaf." "The lads behind me were only lightly armed with Bren guns, rifles and grenades," he recalled. "They knew I wouldn't stand a chance if I missed and the whole operation would be over."

The tank rolled closer.

"This is it!" the sergeant said to himself. "You mustn't miss."

He pulled the trigger on the PIAT and made a direct hit. In a couple of seconds, remembered the sergeant, the tank lit up like a "fire-work display," and then "machine-gun clips inside the tank set off grenades which set off shells. There was the most enormous explosion, with bits and pieces flying everywhere and lighting up the darkness . . . The other tank fled."[46]

Howard and his men had won an important reprieve. But how long would it be before the Germans struck again? Would reinforcements arrive, along with more vital anti-tank weapons, before Howard had to face a much more powerful counter-attack?

CHAPTER 4

A Grade-A Stinker

In Lieutenant Colonel Otway's plane, paratroopers stared at the red light, waiting for it to turn green. It was a few minutes before 1 a.m. They did not know it, but on the ground things had gone seriously wrong.[1] Strong winds and fierce German flak had caused pathfinders to be badly scattered, leaving no time to find their correct spots to set up lights and beacons.[2] Up ahead, 512 Squadron's Wing Commander B. A. Coventry, leading the thirty-three planes carrying Otway's men,[3] looked for signs of life on the screen of a Rebecca set, which was supposed to be receiving signals from a Eureka placed by pathfinders on the ground. With no signal, all Coventry could do was time his flight inland from the coast and make a rough estimate of when to drop the men aboard his plane.[4]

The Merville Battery had been bombed heavily twenty minutes earlier, but again fortune had not favored the Allies. The hundred heavy bombers, encountering low visibility, had inflicted considerable damage to the surrounding minefields, but the battery itself was still mostly intact. What was worse, confused Allied pathfinders trying to find their way to their drop zones had been hit by some of the bombs.[5] One hundred and fifty Germans, wide awake and primed to fight, manned more than a dozen machine guns with interlocking fire.[6]

Otway looked at his men, just seconds from jumping. After takeoff, he had managed to nap until his plane began to cross the English Channel, and then, as it had neared the French coast, he had handed around a bottle of whiskey. He now held the half-empty bottle—few men had taken more than a cursory swig. They needed luck, not Dutch courage.

Anti-aircraft fire intensified, puffs of smoke filling the sky, and the pilot began to throw the plane around, trying to avoid the flak, which sent Otway's men tumbling.

"Hold your course," shouted Otway. "You bloody fool."

"We've been hit in the tail."

"You can still fly straight, can't you?"

The green light came on, and an explosion from anti-aircraft fire sent one of Otway's men tumbling out the open door.[7]

Otway handed the bottle of whiskey to one of the plane's crew.

"You're going to need this."[8]

Otway leapt into the darkness and the cold, rushing air. There was the snap of his parachute's twenty-eight-foot canopy as it unfurled, then a jolt and he began to drift down. It was unnervingly quiet, but then Germans below spotted him and opened fire.[9] "There were incendiary bullets coming up at me," remembered Otway, "and actually going through my chute, which was disturbing. In fact, I was bloody angry about it . . . It had never occurred to me that my chute might catch on fire while I was in it."[10]

Would Otway drop to his death below a flaming canopy? He could see a farmhouse. On planning maps, he remembered, it had been ringed in blue, meaning it was an enemy headquarters.[11] His feet hit the ground at fifteen miles per hour, mere yards from the farmhouse, which was indeed occupied by Germans.[12] A corporal crashed into a nearby greenhouse, alerting Germans inside the farmhouse, and Otway heard shooting. The corporal, thankfully, was quick-witted and hurled a brick through a window, the Germans mistook it for a grenade, took cover, and allowed the corporal and Otway a few vital seconds to sprint clear of the farmhouse.

Where were his other men?[13] Accompanied by the corporal, he scrambled through hedgerows and began to cross a field, one of many that had been flooded on Erwin Rommel's orders that spring. The cold, muddy water rose to Otway's chest, but he kept on wading toward an agreed rendezvous point where his men would gather before attacking the Merville Battery. He saw two paratroopers, white parachutes above them, dropping into marshland. By the time Otway and the corporal reached the new arrivals, it was too late. "We tried to pull them out by their parachute harness but it was useless," recalled Otway. "With their sixty-pound kitbags they sank out of sight at once and were drowned in the mud and slush . . . The suction was unbelievable. We just couldn't get them out." He'd never forget the anguished cries of one man before he disappeared beneath the mud for good.

Not long after, Otway and the corporal came across two

middle-aged Germans on bicycles. To Otway's surprise, the men mistook him and the corporal for SS officers pretending to be British paratroopers.[14] Could they please be allowed back to their barracks? They'd had enough of the SS playing such games. Otway made them understand that he was indeed the real thing, threw their rifles away, and told them to get clear of the area.[15]

Otway and the corporal finally arrived at the assigned rendezvous point, near some woods.

An officer emerged from the darkness.

"Thank God you've come, sir."

"Why?"

"The drop's a bloody chaos. There's hardly anyone here."

Otway noticed that his aide was among the few who had reached the meeting point.

A professional boxer before the war, the aide held up a small flask.

"Shall we have our brandy now, sir?" asked the aide, offering him the flask.[16]

Otway turned to the corporal who had landed with him.

There was a rare moment of hesitancy.

"I don't know what I'm going to do . . ."

"There's only one thing to do, sir. No need to ask me."

"Yes, I know. Get the officers and NCOs. We'll move in five minutes."[17]

The corporal and Otway set off in the direction of the battery and before long came across a young lieutenant.

"You're commanding C Company," Otway told the lieutenant.

The young officer had no combat experience. Until now he had led a platoon of eighteen men, not a company of two hundred.

"Well, don't just stand there," snapped Otway. "Get on, go and see your company."

The lieutenant gathered men from C Company. There were just half a dozen of them. Clearly, things had gone badly wrong.[18] "The plan that Colonel Otway had devised was exceedingly complex," remembered the lieutenant, "so complex that it was like a multiple chain that depended on each individual link, and the links were all disappearing one by one before our eyes. Two of my men were in a dreadful state, one had lost his rifle and the other had lost his helmet and his rifle, and we'd been told—it was more of a threat than an intention—that any man losing his rifle would be court-martialled. A silly threat, because you can't have court-martials in battle, but it was sufficient to upset these two chaps very much."

The lieutenant told the men they could find some discarded German weapons. They shouldn't worry. Then a fellow officer from C Company, who outranked the lieutenant, showed up.

"Here's your company," said the lieutenant. "You can take it over now, you're senior to me."

The senior officer looked shocked. C Company now comprised all of ten soldiers, down from its full strength of more than 150 men.[19]

Otway waited for others to arrive, but he couldn't afford to do so for long. After twenty minutes, another fifty men had turned up and he briskly ordered his group to leave the rendezvous and head for the battery. "We heard a German anti-aircraft battery firing," remembered Otway, "not more than a hundred yards from us on our left and some of the soldiers wanted to go for that and I wouldn't let anybody do that—that wasn't our job."

Otway could hear the occasional bellowing of a startled cow. There was a farm halfway to the battery where Otway had planned to meet with one of his leading officers, Major George Smith. Thankfully, Smith arrived on time, but he had yet more bad news—Otway's force had landed without mine detectors and tape for marking paths through the minefield surrounding the battery. However, with extraordinary courage, an advance party had cut through a barbed-wire perimeter and crawled across the hundred-yard-wide minefield, disarming mines with their bare fingers in the dark. These men had then "sat on their backsides and dragged their heels on the ground, making a path through the minefield."

Smith added that there were now two gaps in the perimeter, not four, as planned. Otway quickly devised a new plan of attack and ordered his men on toward the battery, and before long they were weaving between mounds of earth and large craters. "There were a hundred [bombers] in support of my operation," recalled Otway, "each carrying a thousand-pound bomb, and they had missed the battery but they successfully bombed our route without knowing it, so we had to go in and out of these huge craters." Around halfway from the farm to the battery, Otway heard troops—a German patrol.[20] "They didn't seem to be making any effort to conceal themselves and we all lay down and they passed so close to us we could have reached out and caught them by the ankles, but they didn't see us or hear us. And we moved on."

Otway finally reached the battery's perimeter. A young

officer beside him looked up and saw the moon appear between clouds and then spotted the battery's casemates. They looked like "toads squatting there, somehow nasty." The churned ground was covered with gray, sticky earth, thrown in every direction by bombing.

The young officer gathered his few men.

"We're here, we've trained for it—we're ready for it. If we don't do it, imagine what will happen to your wives and daughters."

Precious minutes passed as Otway and his attack parties waited for the arrival of the three gliders that were scheduled to crash-land inside the battery itself. But then the first glider appeared in the night sky, making a whistling sound as it passed overhead before disappearing.

A few moments later, another glider was spotted.

An anti-aircraft gun inside the battery opened fire.

There were five bursts.

One of Otway's men looked up. For a second or so, the glider seemed to hang in the air, hesitant. Then it was hit. A shell exploded inside the glider and set fire to a man with a flamethrower.[21] Raging flames quickly engulfed him.

The glider swooped down like a harried bird.[22]

"There's the battery!" cried a man inside the glider.

Then the pilot spotted thick barbed wire and pulled on his control stick, and the glider crashed in an orchard some fifty yards from the battery, breaking in half and losing its wings.[23] Those alive inside got out as fast as they could. The man carrying the flamethrower had burnt to death.

The third glider failed to arrive.

Otway's overly elaborate plan now lay in tatters. Not one glider had landed on the battery. His men were dispersed for many miles. He had no mine detectors, no 3-inch mortars, no portable bridges to cross anti-tank ditches, no radio.[24] There was just one machine gun, a Vickers, and no explosives to destroy the battery guns.[25]

Surely it would be prudent to abandon the mission and save the lives of the few men he had left?

What should he do?

He was supposed to attack the Merville Battery with a battalion of more than six hundred men. He had only 150.

"Do I go with a hundred and fifty?" Otway asked himself. "Or do I pack it in?"[26]

Meanwhile, at an airfield near Earls Colne, a small village in Essex, northeast of London, the pilots of the 323rd Bombardment Group were awoken. According to Stars and Stripes reporter Bud Hutton, who would accompany them to France later that morning, the pilots were "sleepy, worn with the strain of two hauls a day almost every day for two months" as they walked through the "wet night" to a briefing.[27]

In the run-up to D-Day, their fellow Allied fliers had, since April 1, flown more than 200,000 combined sorties and dropped almost as many tons of bombs on road networks, railyards, and coastal batteries, destroying all the bridges across the Seine and Loire Rivers, thereby isolating Normandy. But such a gain came at a high cost: More than two thousand planes had failed to return, and some twelve thousand men had been lost, to ensure that the Luftwaffe would not pose a serious threat on D-Day. Fewer than four hundred German planes would be deployed against more than thirteen thousand Allied transport aircraft, fighters, and bombers.[28]

Bud Hutton watched as the young fliers assembled before twenty-five-year-old Colonel Wilson Wood, a tall and debonair Texan, for their final briefing at 2 A.M.[29] The pilots of the fifty-four "White Tailed" B-26 Marauders in the 323rd Bombardment Group may have been worn down after long weeks of "bridge bombing," but they were now "babbling" with excitement, eager to get into the air, as they waited for Colonel Wood to address them for the last time. Only now, after midnight on June 6, did they discover that they were to play a key role on D-Day. It would be their task, explained Wood, to destroy the defenses along Utah Beach, where the 4th Division was scheduled to land at 6:30 A.M.

"This morning's mission," said Wood calmly in his Texan drawl, "is the most important mission you've ever flown. Maybe the most important mission anyone has ever flown. This is the invasion. Our job is to bomb the beach, and right after our bombs go down, thousands of Americans just like us will be landing there from the sea. I don't care if any of your aircraft are not a hundred percent. You'll fly them this morning, and you'll take any risk to get right on your targets and give those boys in the boats every bit of help you can."[30]

The critical time was 6:17 A.M., when the airmen would begin to drop their bombs above Utah. Flying conditions would be poor, and "moderately heavy flak" could be expected.[31] Many of

Wood's pilots had been in action for almost a year, and some crews had completed more than fifty missions, often flying low to hit key targets in northern France.[32] Every one of them now knew that in a few hours' time, if they didn't do a damn fine job, Captain Schroeder and his battalion could be slaughtered before even getting their feet wet.

Wood congratulated his men on having destroyed so many vital targets that spring.

Now they had to finish the job.

Some would remember Wood's next words for the rest of their lives.

"Let's kick the hell out of everything Nazi that's left."

Wilson's men cheered.[33]

As WOOD FINISHED BRIEFING HIS MEN, thirty-one-year-old Sergeant Major Stanley Hollis, a six-foot-two-inch redhead with prominent front teeth,[34] awoke at reveille in the middle of the English Channel aboard the five-thousand-ton *Empire Lance*. It was around 2:30 A.M. as he joined his fellow Green Howards and made his way to breakfast, the medal ribbon worn just above his heart showing that he had seen more than his fair share of action. The *Empire Lance* was some six miles from Gold Beach, the center of the Allied landing zone,[35] and was rolling badly in the rough seas; not many men felt like eating.[36] Hollis then went on deck and watched as men from his company checked the tips of their bayonets, their Sten guns and 2-inch mortars, and the breeches of their Lee-Enfield rifles. Many hailed, as Hollis did, from Yorkshire, with a hard core coming from the large industrial town of Middlesbrough—solid blokes who wouldn't hesitate to do anything Hollis asked of them.[37] They were now, according to one soldier, "in high spirits and singing to the mouth organ. Whisky and rum [were] being passed round freely."[38]

The Green Howards would land with other elements of the British 50th Infantry Division on the five-mile-long Gold Beach, fight their way inland, and seize the port of Arromanches, to the west, before linking up with the Americans on Omaha Beach. Montgomery had wanted troops with combat experience to assault Gold, and so, among the first wave of British troops, he selected the Green Howards, some of the finest soldiers in the British Army, who had distinguished themselves during the Dunkirk evacuation, in 1940, and then in North Africa and Sicily.[39] "You wouldn't have expected there to be a rush to take part in the first wave," recalled the 6th Battalion commander, twenty-six-year-old Lieutenant Colonel Robin Hastings, an urbane Oxford University graduate, "but, in fact, everyone seemed to want to be there."[40]

For sheer guts and grit, none in the 6th Battalion could rival Stanley Hollis, who described himself in all sincerity as a "lower form of life" in the British Army. He had joined up in the early summer of 1939, before the Nazis had invaded Poland,[41] and had since been seriously wounded four times, first seeing action as an intrepid dispatch motorcycle rider in northern France in the spring of 1940. Hollis had been to sea before—he had run away from home several times as a youth and spent a number of years working on a steamship, mostly on voyages to West Africa, before enlisting with the 4th Battalion of the

Green Howards. Now, finally, he was returning to France, determined to avenge the humiliation of Dunkirk, burning with a fierce hatred of the Germans. Once, he had been captured in North Africa and beaten unconscious, his cheekbones broken, by his guards before he escaped back to British lines, consumed by thoughts of revenge. The only good German soldier, Hollis now believed, was a dead one, preferably one he himself had killed.

The last time he had been aboard a boat in the middle of the English Channel, he was delirious with pain, part of a defeated army, close to death after several weeks of chaos, humiliation, and terror. He had retreated with his fellow Green Howards before the lightning German advance, the blitzkrieg, that had erupted on May 10, 1940, with Hitler's attack on France and Belgium. He had given his all as a dispatch rider and was seen several times asleep while seated on his motorbike, his flaming red hair showing beneath his round helmet, after yet another grueling mission. He never failed to deliver his messages, no matter how intense the battle that raged around him. In the industrial city of Lille, he had seen why Hitler had to be defeated, coming across dozens of dead and dying French civilians, among them young women and children, who had been machine-gunned as they fled the German advance.[42]

Then, one day in May 1940, as the British Army fell back to the Channel port of Dunkirk, Hollis's luck ran out. As he weaved through a convoy of trucks, a German mortar exploded, the blast throwing Hollis from his motorbike and clear across a road where he lay stunned, much of his uniform stripped from him, his back peppered with red-hot shell splinters. Fortunately, some of his mates in the Green Howards had searched for him and then helped him to one of the beaches near Dunkirk.

A vast black cloud covered the doomed port's harbor, bombed day and night by the Luftwaffe's screaming Stukas. Tens of thousands of desperate soldiers filled the beaches, strafed by Messerschmitts as they waded out to yachts, dinghies, tugboats, and canal barges, all manner of craft summoned to cross the Channel and rescue what was left of British pride and a roundly defeated British Expeditionary Force. His mates still refused to abandon Hollis and helped him swim to a navy boat, where he was laid down on the crowded deck and wrapped in a blanket, one of an extraordinary 338,000 soldiers pulled off the fatal sands at Dunkirk in just eight days.

Hollis had escaped "by the skin of his teeth," he said, yet after a spell in the hospital he declined to be invalided out of the army and eagerly rejoined the Green Howards, who nicknamed him "the Man They Couldn't Kill."[43] Hollis had then been sent to fight Erwin Rommel's Afrika Korps in Egypt. Promoted to sergeant major in 1941, he had most recently served in Sicily under Lieutenant Colonel Robin Hastings and had then joined D Company of the 6th Battalion in time to train men for D-Day.[44] "I am sure he was older than he claimed to be so as to be allowed to enlist," recalled Hastings. "Apart from his natural aptitude for battle, he had a keen sense of humor and a great way with his men."[45] As did Hastings, an avid foxhunter who'd won the Military Cross at El Alamein and then been rapidly promoted by Montgomery, who preferred to have young men as field commanders.

The previous evening, June 5, Hastings had hailed a passing

landing craft and made a last-minute visit to a destroyer slated to provide fire support for the Green Howards' first wave. Over a drink with a naval officer, Hastings had explained that he had seen recent aerial photographs and noticed new diggings just inland, indicating a strengthening of the German defenses.

"I hear you are to support our landings," said Hastings. "What targets have you got?"

"Oh, just to shoot up the coast. We can do a lot of damage with these guns. Would you like to see them?"

"No, but if I showed you some weapon pits recently dug behind our beach, would you put them out of action?"

"Yes, of course, old boy. Anything to oblige."[46]

Hastings could now only hope that the destroyer would indeed oblige as he stood on the bridge beside the captain of the *Empire Lance,* urging him to speed up because he was slightly behind schedule.

The Green Howards were called to their embarkation areas. D Company's commanding officer, Major Ronnie Lofthouse, stood watching men gather in their platoons. Lofthouse was a good friend of Hollis's, despite their difference in rank.

He handed Hollis a small box.

"Give one of these to each of the men, Sergeant Major."

Hollis opened up the box and found condoms inside. They could be slipped over muzzles to keep them dry during the landing.

"Sir, are we going to fight or fuck them?"

Troops nearby laughed as Hollis began to distribute the condoms.[47]

―――――

As HOLLIS AND HIS MEN made last-minute preparations for combat, Captain Frank Lillyman and his stick of pathfinders gathered in the medieval stone church of Saint-Germain-de-Varreville. It was around 3:10 A.M. Black-faced Lillyman and his men had turned off their Eureka sets and the lights that had acted as guides to the 101st Airborne. The first, most important part of their D-Day mission was over. Between 12:48 and 1:40 A.M., almost seven thousand Screaming Eagles had been dropped as part of Mission Albany, whose Drop Zone A had been set up by Lillyman's men. At 1:51, around 6,500 men of the 82nd Airborne had followed the Screaming Eagles, part of Mission Boston. In just five hours, both divisions needed to secure an "airhead" of enemy territory, some seven miles wide by twelve long, including five narrow causeways leading through flooded fields to Utah Beach. The causeways connected the beach to a north–south road and had to be seized if 4th Division troops were to move inland and avoid being trapped on Utah and then shelled mercilessly by some 110 heavy guns from an estimated twenty-eight batteries.

Back in England, Supreme Allied Commander Dwight Eisenhower waited anxiously for news about the first wave. He was particularly concerned about the fate of Lillyman and his fellow paratroopers, the men he had wished good luck and looked in the eye at Greenham Common. During these first hours of D-Day, full of second guesses and excruciating tension, Eisenhower had chosen to be alone with Kay Summersby at his command post, code-named "Sharpener," deep in a wood a mile along muddy lanes from Southwick House.[48] "If Ike had wished," Summersby recalled, "he could have been surrounded by top brass, by Churchill and de Gaulle, by any of the important personages who were gathered just a few miles away in Portsmouth. But he preferred to wait in solitude."[49] Now and again, Summersby moved over to Eisenhower and tried to soothe him. "I would stand behind Ike and massage his shoulders but in those predawn hours, no matter how much strength I used, I could not undo the knots at the base of his neck."[50]

The first news of the first wave to reach Eisenhower in the early hours of June 6 may have been delivered by none other than Colonel Joel Crouch and his co-pilot, Vito Pedone, who had dropped Lillyman and his men into France. They had by 2 A.M. returned to England, crossing the Channel in darkness, the flame damper on their C-47's exhaust helping to conceal their path through the moonlit clouds. Only when Pedone was back on solid ground and had finally stopped worrying about the next thing that could go wrong had he allowed his real feelings to surface. Only back in England, wheels on runway, had he felt the fear he had controlled to get the job done. He could replay every minute in his mind.[51] They'd taken the Germans by surprise. There'd been no German fighters. Thank God. They'd have been sitting ducks with no armament or armored protection for their gas tanks, none of which were self-sealing.[52] One well-directed bullet and they would have been blown out of the sky.[53]

Pedone and Crouch, according to one report, had been ordered to provide a detailed account to Eisenhower, who had wanted "a first-hand assessment."[54] Pedone later remembered, "We reported to Eisenhower and told him the pathfinders did their job, and explained what we saw."[55] The pathfinders had indeed done their job, but it could hardly be described as a smashing success. It would later be revealed that fewer than a third of the pathfinders had landed in their drop zones. In some cases, pilots had panicked under heavy flak and dived too low and too fast, releasing their human cargoes too soon.[56] Crouch and Pedone had in fact dropped Lillyman and his stick more than a mile from the target zone.

The pathfinder operation had, however, been less chaotic than the main drops that followed. Dozens of men had landed in flooded fields and drowned. The 502nd Parachute Regiment's Corporal Bill Hayes, with whom Eisenhower had spoken the previous evening, had landed in a tree and, after "literally hanging in the wind," had cut himself down and spent ninety minutes all alone before finding a single comrade.[57] Thousands of his fellow paratroopers were still enduring a long, lonely night of confusion and sometimes terror, snapping their crickets, hearts thumping, wondering if the sudden rustle in a bush had been made by a comrade or a teenage Nazi pumped up on amphetamine, with dagger drawn. "Never in the history of military operations have so few been commanded by so many," recalled the 101st Airborne's General Maxwell Taylor, who had spent his first hour in France in charge of a single private.[58]

Amid the marshes and hedgerows of Normandy, Ike's paratroopers were displaying plenty of bravery and devotion to duty, but few were in any doubt that the airborne landings had gone badly awry. The 82nd Airborne's assistant division commander, Jim Gavin, watched with bitter frustration as a lieutenant stripped naked and stood "pale and white as a statue" before diving into "a vast expanse of water"—the flooded valley of the Merderet River—to rescue vital equipment.[59] It would be two days before either airborne division had gained any semblance of unit cohesion.[60]

Captain Frank Lillyman's own battalion had been scattered far and wide, some men landing with a sound, recalled one paratrooper, "like large ripe pumpkins being thrown down to burst."[61] Among those who had thudded down onto the pastures near Saint-Germain, some were too badly injured to be moved, and Lillyman had hidden them under the care of a medic in a nearby house. It was around 3:30 A.M. when Lillyman set off with the able-bodied men from his stick and more than a hundred other paratroopers from his battalion and headed for a small village a couple of miles to the south. He then left his force under the command of a fellow captain in the village while he scouted ahead with just a couple of men, searching for a battery near the coast.[62]

The battery had been "completely demolished" by Allied bombing, remembered Lillyman, the casemates smashed to smithereens and showered with earth and rock. For several minutes he filmed the damage with a small, clockwork cine camera, and then sent a radio report. Not long after, he made contact with twenty-nine-year-old Lieutenant Colonel Patrick Cassidy, who was leading a group of around seventy men.[63] The neatly mustached Cassidy, nicknamed "Hopalong" by his men, commanded the 1st Battalion of the 502nd Parachute Infantry Regiment.

"I've got news for you," Lillyman told Cassidy. "I scouted the coastal battery. It's thoroughly bombed out. No need to worry about that one."[64]

Cassidy was delighted and relieved—the battery could have caused major problems for the 4th Division, due to land on Utah at 6:28 A.M., in just a couple of hours' time. He told Lillyman to establish a roadblock and a command post two miles farther north, at the entrance to the village of Foucarville.[65] Before long, Lillyman had done so, setting up machine guns and a 60-millimeter mortar and ordering one man to climb into a nearby church steeple and keep his eyes peeled for Germans.[66] Hopefully, the observer would provide Lillyman and his men with plenty of advance warning. There was little they could do, however, if panzers came clanking their way. They had no effective anti-tank weapons. The 101st Airborne's artillery unit had suffered a truly disastrous drop, with just two of fifty-four loads landing on target and all but one howitzer lost. For Lillyman and his fellow paratroopers, a long night still lay ahead.

CHAPTER 5

Bloody Lucky

ABOVE THE ENGLISH CHANNEL, RAF bomber pilots flew through thick cloud and then broke through into an open sky and, looking down, marveled at the hundreds of minesweepers and other ships bathed in a faint moonlight. For thirty miles, the invasion fleet trailed across the dark waters: huge battleships such as the USS *Nevada*, sunk by the Japanese at Pearl Harbor but refloated and now armed with ten vengeful 14-inch guns; hospital ships painted an eerie bone white; command ships such as the USS *Augusta*, carrying General Omar Bradley, the eighteen-knot westerly wind whistling through its tangle of radio and radar antennae. On every ship's bridge there was a hushed quiet, but every captain, every admiral, and every signalman was wide awake, many of them exultant, waiting for the sound of eight bells, at 4 A.M., to mark the call to battle stations.

Aboard the USS *Barnett,* Brigadier General Theodore Roosevelt moved from one group of 4th Division soldiers to another, encouraging them in a soft voice. He had not slept that night and looked gray-faced and gaunt. For some months he had suffered from chest pains. He knew he had a bad heart, but he would rather breathe his last in Normandy, on the battlefield, than miss the greatest invasion in history.

The father whom he idolized, whose greatness no son could reasonably hope to emulate, had famously once said, "Believe you can and you're halfway there."[1] In his mind, Theodore Roosevelt Jr. was already halfway to Utah.

"Where in hell is my lifebelt?" he asked his aide.

"I've given you four already."

"Well, give me another. I've lost the whole damn lot."[2]

Amid the men gathered on deck nearby was F Company commander Leonard Schroeder, awaiting the final order to board landing craft, ready to lead his company in the first wave. "We all had our lucky charms," he recalled. "I carried a watch that my wife had given me on my right wrist and the one the army had given me on my left one. Everyone had a bracelet, given by his family, or wife. Under my helmet, I also had a photo of my wife."

They were fourteen miles from France when landing craft were lowered into the sea. As the men prepared to board, Roosevelt found Schroeder.

"Moose, have you got a place for me on your landing craft?"[3]

Schroeder could indeed take Roosevelt with him in the first wave. But as it turned out, Roosevelt chose to go in not with Schroeder but with Captain Howard Lees, leading E Company, scheduled to land around two hundred yards to Schroeder's right.

It was still dark on deck, and silent, other than the occasional rasp of wind. Schroeder knew there were hundreds of ships nearby. At 4:05 A.M., he and other men in the 4th Division's first wave began to board their landing craft, climbing or jumping five feet down into boats.

Roosevelt stood at the ship's rail, about to get into Captain Lees's craft. He was wearing a knit watch cap, not the regulation helmet, and looked more like "a frazzle-arsed old sergeant" than a general, as one man described him.[4]

A soldier held out his hand.

"Here, General, let me help you."

"Dammit," protested Roosevelt, "you know I can take it as well as any of you. Better than most."

Roosevelt boarded the landing craft unaided.

Up on deck, Roosevelt's aide turned to Lieutenant Colonel George Mabry, the 2nd Battalion's operations officer.

"Did you notice his armament?" the aide asked Mabry. "A pistol and seven rounds, and his cane. He says that's all he'll need."[5]

LIEUTENANT GEORGE KERCHNER, platoon leader in the 2nd Ranger Battalion's D Company, stood at the bow of his landing craft as it pulled away from the HMS *Amsterdam*.[6] He passed several battleships, ghostly hulks in the choppy seas. It was around 5 A.M. when one of the ships, the USS *Texas*, opened fire, bellowing with a deep bass, flames stabbing from its ten 14-inch guns. "It was a terrifying sound," Kerchner later recalled. "The

14-inch guns shot far over our heads, but were still close enough for us to hear and feel some of the muzzle blast."

Kerchner's platoon was seasick and looked tired. None, guessed Kerchner, had slept much the night before, and several shivered from the cold water that doused them every time the flimsy wooden craft crashed through a wave. They had spent months climbing ever higher and more rugged cliffs. On the Isle of Wight, they'd scaled the famous white chalk Needles, towering two hundred feet above the Solent, the channel of water separating the island from mainland England, and had also scampered up Tennyson Down, all 350 feet of coarse rock, named after the famous English poet who penned "Charge of the Light Brigade," with its immortal lines "Theirs not to make reply, / Theirs not to reason why, / Theirs but to do and die."[7] But at this moment, in the cold darkness, with the sound of angry waves slapping against the plywood hull, Kerchner's fellow Rangers didn't appear to be an elite unit, ready to kick the hell out of Hitler's best. They looked a forlorn, bedraggled, pathetic crew indeed, fit only to vomit and die.

They had trained so long and so hard. Kerchner could get up a hundred-foot cliff face, loaded down with full combat gear, in less than a minute. He could fire a rocket, with a grappling hook attached to it, with impressive accuracy. He'd seized pillboxes under live fire, crawled through barbed wire, bullets zipping just feet above his helmet. But never, not once, had he been launched with his men miles from an enemy-held coast in storm-tossed seas.

Kerchner was five miles from the French coast when a flotilla of craft appeared and fired hundreds of rockets at defenses on

Pointe du Hoc. "It was one continuous sheet of flame going up," remembered Kerchner, who then heard the drone of bombers overhead. "We couldn't see [the bombers] because there was a low overcast in a dull gray sky with clouds down to one or two thousand feet. But we could hear the bombs dropping and see them exploding as we came closer to the shore."[8]

The bombers were 115 Lancasters belonging to Number 9 Squadron RAF, which began their bombing runs at 4:53 A.M. and dropped 634.8 tons of bombs, more than twenty per acre, on Pointe du Hoc, killing dozens of Germans and deafening and paralyzing many others with terror. One shell-shocked machine gun crew ran for their lives. Another group of defenders found refuge in the wine cellar on a nearby farm and quickly got drunk.[9]

The Lancaster raid was not without casualties on the Allied side. Just after 5 A.M., in the first air battle of D-Day, fighter pilot Captain Helmut Eberspächer attacked the last bombers to hit the battery. In less than five minutes, the Luftwaffe ace downed three planes.[10]

Out at sea, Lieutenant Kerchner spotted amphibious Sherman tanks. They were struggling in the rough conditions, their canvas skirts swamped and battered. Then he saw a landing craft less than a hundred yards away. It was also in trouble, taking on water. It was in fact LCA 860, carrying other men from D Company, including company commander Captain Duke Slater, a good friend of Kerchner's. Then the craft disappeared beneath the waves.[11] D Company had lost its first men.[12] "That convinced me our landing craft were not unsinkable," recalled Kerchner. "We immediately began bailing with our helmets and

[that] managed to keep us afloat, even though we were taking on a lot of water."[13]

A *Stars and Stripes* reporter in a boat nearby saw Slater and his men trying to keep their heads above water. "There was nothing we could do to help those poor guys," he reported. "Just say a little prayer that they would be picked up before they froze to death. We all wanted to help but the success of our mission was too vital, and the Rangers knew they were expendable."[14]

Slater and twenty other men would eventually be rescued after surviving for several hours in the cold seas. "Give us some dry clothes, weapons and ammunition, and get us back in to the Pointe," implored Slater as he was fished out of the water. "We gotta get back!" His shivering and soaked men were, however, too numb from the water, a chilling 54 degrees Fahrenheit,[15] to be effective in combat and were ordered to return to England to recuperate instead.[16]

Slater's fate meant that George Kerchner, leader of his unit's first platoon, was now D Company commander.[17] It would be up to him, if his craft managed to reach France without sinking, to lead more than a hundred men up the sheer cliffs of Pointe du Hoc, towering a hundred feet above crashing surf.

LIEUTENANT COLONEL TERENCE Otway crouched down in the pitch darkness near rolls of barbed wire, fifteen feet thick and five feet high, that encircled the Merville Battery. He had finally reached his target, arguably the most heavily defended on D-Day. Beyond the jagged wire lay a minefield a hundred yards wide and then another belt of barbed wire, even denser and higher than the first. Some two hundred yards farther on stood four hulking casemates made of steel-reinforced six-foot-thick concrete, each housing Czech-made howitzers aimed toward Sword Beach that could also destroy Allied ships approaching the port of Ouistreham, at the mouth of the Orne River, marking the far eastern limit of the planned Allied beachhead.

Because Otway had so few men, two groups rather than four would attack, one through gaps that had to be blown through the wire and the other via the battery's main entrance. There were bound to be heavy casualties as Otway's men charged toward the casemates while others engaged 130 defenders manning a large blockhouse, fifteen machine gun nests, and an anti-aircraft gun position.

"Do not be daunted if chaos reigns. It undoubtedly will!" Those had been the parting words, before leaving England, of Otway's commanding officer. How true had been his prediction. Everything that could have gone wrong had done so.

The commander of A Company, Major Allen Parry, approached Otway.[18]

"Have you decided what to do, sir?" whispered Parry.

"Do?" snapped Otway. "Attack in three minutes, of course. Pass it on."[19]

A few minutes later came the haunting cry of a hunting horn, blown by one of Otway's lieutenants. The moment had come to take out the guns at Merville.

Otway turned to his men.

"Get ready."[20]

It was 4:30 A.M.[21]

Otway was not afraid of dying, but he was terrified of being mutilated.

"Everybody in! We're going to take this bloody battery!"[22]

Men dashed forward with Bangalore torpedoes, tubes that delivered an explosive charge that could clear paths several yards wide through barbed wire. Loud detonations followed. Otway's men took their cue and sprinted through the wreaths of smoke and the blown wire defenses, shouting like banshees, just as they had been trained.

A young officer was hit in the leg and fell to the ground, where he lay, like a "sheep on its back," and proudly watched his men fight their way toward one of the casemates.

A sergeant led eight men to a German gun position.[23]

"Paratruppen!" cried a German. "Paratruppen."[24]

Otway's men kept yelling, running, fighting hand to hand, gouging, stabbing, firing from the hip at shadows in the darkness, zigzagging through the battery to make themselves less of a target.

"Bastards!" shouted one man. "Bastards! Bastards!"[25]

The rips and whooshes of explosions were followed by the screams of men with legs blown to shreds.

"Mines!"[26]

Still Otway's men kept going, through a hail of bullets and brightly colored streams of tracers.

Lieutenant Raimund Steiner, the German commander of the Merville Battery, remembered the utter chaos of the combat: "There was artillery fire, machine gun fire, single shots everywhere. You couldn't tell who was shooting at whom, where the enemy was, where the fire was coming from."

A bullet tore through Otway's battle smock, just missing his chest. Another punctured his canteen. Unharmed, he ordered his men to take out several machine guns some fifty yards ahead. Bren guns blazed as grenades exploded and then volleys of MG42 machine gun fire stitched the darkness. Some paratroopers kept attacking even when severely wounded. One private, hit in the abdomen, was spotted holding in his insides with one hand while with the other he fired a Sten gun into a pillbox.

The assault appeared to Otway to be a "shambles . . . a mess . . . There was smoke about. There were German artilleries with shells firing on us . . . There were wounded lying about on the ground, getting wounded again by the German shells."[27]

The thick concrete casemates were covered in grass. Otway's men spotted air vents and were quickly hurling grenades down them. That did the trick, and in no time, it seemed, stunned and bloody defenders were staggering out of the casemates' iron doors.

"Kamerad! Kamerad! Kamerad!"[28]

Near one casemate, a man emerged with his hands in the air.

"Russki! Russki!" he shouted.

One of Otway's privates was confused.

What the hell is he on about?[29]

The man was a Russian who had been captured on the Eastern Front and forced to fight in Normandy.

The private watched as the last enemy soldier emerged from a casemate: a fat, ugly man, wearing spectacles, crawling on his hands and knees, in severe shock.[30] Most of the other defenders had by now been killed or wounded. In fact, only six men from 130 would survive unscathed and escape to fight another day.[31]

There was a heavy silence, broken every few seconds by the groans of the badly injured. A young sergeant would later remember a "most peculiar smell, from freshly turned earth, torn flesh, and blood and that sort of thing and it's a smell you never forget. Almost like [when] you go in for an operation in a hospital, and you smell ether for the first time—you never forget it."[32]

Otway was close to one casemate when a private approached and saluted.

"Battery taken as ordered, sir."

"Have you destroyed the guns?"

"I think so."

"Bloody well get back up there and make sure those guns are out of action."[33]

Otway soon learned that every one of the casemates had indeed been seized and the guns inside disabled.[34] It was around 5 A.M. when he gave the order to pull out and head to a prearranged meeting place. His battalion had succeeded against the odds, at great cost, in seizing the battery, thereby sparing the lives of many British troops due to land on Sword Beach in a couple of hours' time. Now Otway needed to get a message to the HMS *Arethusa*, offshore. In around thirty minutes, the British light cruiser was due to open up on the battery with her 6-inch guns. There was no need to do so, and the last thing he wanted was to get hit by friendly fire after already losing half of his men. "I had no radio to send a success signal," he recalled, "but I lit a yellow signal flare and an RAF plane went over, saw it, and waggled its wings. And my signals officer, unbeknown to me, had got a carrier pigeon with him, brought it all the way from England in his airborne smock, and he tied a victory message around its leg and sent it off."[35]

The RAF spotter plane radioed to the *Arethusa* with only minutes to spare.

As men began to move away from the battery and head for the rendezvous point, Otway spotted a guard dog, tied up beside a pillbox, and approached the animal. A wounded lieutenant lay nearby.

"Don't touch that, you bloody fool," the lieutenant cried. "It's a booby trap."[36]

Otway did as he was told and a few minutes later came to the edge of a minefield.

"How the hell do we get out of this place?" Otway asked one of his surviving officers. "The bloody mines are still there."

Otway's men had taken twenty-three Germans prisoner.

"Show me the way," Otway told the prisoners in fluent German.[37]

They refused.

"Well, okay," said an exasperated Otway, "we're going to make you walk forward and if you don't show us the way through the mines we're just going to start shooting the ground and you're going to lose your feet and maybe the mines will go up, too."[38]

They understood enough of Otway's threat to realize he was deadly serious and obediently began to lead Otway and his men through the minefield. They came across a young officer, Captain Havelock Hudson, a close friend of Otway's. He lay badly wounded in the minefield, blood soaking his wool uniform.

A soldier knelt beside Hudson and drew a breath in shock when he saw a gaping wound.

Otway approached.

"Are you all right?" he asked.

"I think so," said Hudson, clearly in agony.

"He's been hit in the stomach," said the soldier.

"Oh, bad luck," said Otway.

The good news, added Otway, was that they'd taken the battery.

"Fuck your bloody battery," replied Hudson.[39]

They continued through the minefield. One of Otway's men glanced back at the battery. "The area was strangely silent with men moving slowly out, some wounded and others quite still on the ground where they had fallen," he remembered. "The impression was of all passion spent but I personally felt strangely privileged and maybe a little satisfaction that I had been a member of this unit who had, I feel, achieved all that was asked of them."[40]

Otway needed to rest, to recuperate, before the fighting inevitably flared up again and killing and dying resumed. He made his way to the planned assembly point—a calvary with a bone-white effigy of Jesus Christ being crucified, atop a concrete square beside a crossroads almost a mile from the Merville Battery. He then told his men to set up a defensive perimeter nearby. But there was only so much they could do, given their depleted ranks. Of the 150 men with whom Otway had attacked the battery, there were just seventy-five who could now stand and fight.[41] What they had achieved would enter the annals of British military history as one of the greatest feats of arms of all time.[42]

Below the white stone figure of Jesus Christ hanging from the cross, Otway sat, exhausted, as around him dozens of wounded, many on stretchers, were attended to by medics.[43] Other men rested nearby, bleeding, battered, utterly spent. Some stood motionless, in a daze, no doubt replaying the fierce firefight and unnerving close calls in their heads. One lieutenant stared at his commanding officer, seated below the Christ, head in hands. Otway "had been through a tremendous amount," recalled the lieutenant. "To take what few men we had in to attack the battery was beyond human expectancy. What he'd put up with. Organizing the job and then to do it with so few tools, and knowing full well we had a full day in front of us . . ."[44]

A soldier pushed a wheelbarrow that carted an officer who'd been hit in the legs.

Otway's second in command, Major Allen Parry, pulled out a flask of brandy, swallowed a mouthful, and grinned.

"A jolly good battle, what?"[45]

Bewildered, grim-faced men finally managed to smile.

PART TWO

The Day

We were bound to one another—men on the same rope.[1]

—LORD LOVAT

CHAPTER 6

By Dawn's Faint Light

THE LONG-AWAITED DAWN. It was exactly 5:58 A.M. when daylight arrived.[1] The lean faces of young commandos, wearing green berets, were no longer cast in shadow but clear to see, whitened by the daylight, creased with fear and strain. On all the boats carrying Lord Lovat's two thousand commandos, each soldier had cleaned his boots, washed, and shaved—a regimen that never changed, whether they were in training in the misty glens of Scotland or about to launch a hit-and-run raid from a boat in some Norwegian fjord. Not once had Lovat's warriors fought with stubble on the chin.[2]

Now they waited, seated on benches. A few looked at their mates and tried to smile or crack a joke. They had waited to board trucks, waited to board ships, waited as they puked up their breakfasts, bouncing all the way across the bloody English Channel. They were sick to death of waiting. That was when their hearts and minds were weakest. Once they landed, they'd be too busy to worry, too focused to wonder if they'd die a virgin or ever down a pint again.[3]

Léon Gautier stood leaning against his eighty-pound rucksack, pressing against the metal side of LCI 523, one of two craft taking Number 4 Commando toward Sword Beach. He could feel every wave as it slapped against the boat.[4]

He had been drilled over and over—move fast, "split arse," as the Tommies said.

"Nip off a bit lively," an officer in Number 4 Commando had advised the previous evening. "Get off the beach a bit sharpish, and then go hell for leather for a place called Ouistreham to destroy the battery there."[5]

Stop for nothing and no one. Leave the wounded. Don't touch them, even if they're your best mates. Don't waste bullets. Don't stab and slash wildly. Creep up behind Jerry and slit his throat, or pull him firmly onto your sharpened Fairbairn-Sykes fighting knife, making sure its tapered "stiletto" blade slips between the ribs to the heart, like a surgeon's scalpel.

There would be no margin for error. Hitler had ordered that any man captured in a commando uniform be shot on the spot.[6] And the ever ruthless Lovat had made it known that any man who slipped up would never go into action with him again, a fate almost as painful as execution in the minds of Gautier and his comrades, bound together like blood brothers, "men on the same rope," in Lovat's words.[7]

Unlike most of his 176 French comrades in Number 4 Commando, Gautier was not seasick.[8] The smell of diesel fumes and the high seas were nothing new to him. It was now four long years since he had arrived in England to join de Gaulle's forces, having served aboard the French dreadnought *Courbet,* which had escaped France just two days before the armistice with the Nazis had been signed on June 22, 1940—what Gautier still regarded as the humiliation of his beloved France. It was hard to believe he was now nearing his homeland as one of Lovat's lads, a Frenchman wearing the green beret of the British commandos, his muscles hardened by months of speed-marching ten miles per day with an eighty-pound pack, his mind sharp, his hunger to avenge his countrymen's defeat greater than ever.[9]

Less than a mile behind Gautier, aboard his landing craft, Lord Lovat looked at the sea and noted that its color was changing to an oyster-shell gray with the dawn. Lovat was armed with a hunting rifle, dressed for a good day's walk on the moors: a white turtleneck sweater, suede vest, khaki corduroy pants, and a duffle coat, which he would leave behind when he went ashore.[10]

Lovat spotted the naval officer in command of his 105-foot boat, Lieutenant Commander Rupert Curtis, a steel helmet hiding his shock of red hair but not his "serious face." Curtis was in fact a flotilla commander, responsible for getting twenty-two pitching boats through swept minefields and to France on time.[11]

"Twenty miles from the coast and twelve to lowering point," shouted Curtis, who later recalled feeling exhilarated, glad to be alive, grateful to be able to play his part.[12] As he peered into the distance, straining his eyes, he imagined what it would be like back in England later that morning when Churchill announced the news of the invasion.[13]

A sailor aboard the HMS *Stork,* in the distance off Lovat's port bow, stood with an Aldis lamp and signaled: "GOOD MORNING, COMMANDOS, AND THE BEST OF BRITISH LUCK."

A fitting reply was sent from Lovat's boat.[14] "THANKS; THINK WE ARE GOING TO BLOODY WELL NEED IT."[15]

FIRST LIGHT. Dawn had stripped away the camouflage of the night. The lettering on a sign jutting from a brick building close to Pegasus Bridge was clear to see: HOTEL RESTAURANT GONDRÉE—TABLE RECOMMANDÉ. From a window, owner Georges Gondrée saw paratroopers digging foxholes in his vegetable garden. Were they British? They didn't sound like the short-tempered German officers who harangued the lazy Polish or Russian conscripts who formed most work details in Normandy. Not long after, he heard knocking on the front door of the café. Gondrée opened it and found two men, their faces blackened. They wanted to know if there were any Germans inside his café. He shook his head, but they weren't about to take his word for it, and before long he was showing them from room to room before leading them down to the cellar, where he had hidden his family.

"It's all right, chum," one of the soldiers reassured him.

The other soldier pulled out a bar of chocolate for Gondrée's children. Gondrée started to cry, so strong were his emotions. Of late, he had been living on his nerves, not knowing if the next knock on the door would herald a visit from the Gestapo, followed by torture, execution, or banishment into the *Nacht und Nebel*—night and fog—of the Third Reich's vast archipelago of concentration camps where more than eighty thousand French patriots had disappeared, never to return. He had fed important information about German defenses at Pegasus Bridge to the local Resistance, at great risk. His wife, Thérèse, had been born in a German-speaking region of France, Alsace, and had over-heard snippets of conversation among the Germans; this, too, had been reported and had in fact helped in the formation of Major John Howard's plan of attack.[16] Now Monsieur Gondrée watched as his wife embraced the soldiers, kissing them, the men's black face paint staining her pale cheeks.

Howard's men soon began using the café as an aid station. "I remember the casualties being brought into the café," recalled one of the Gondrées' daughters. "The tables had been pushed aside in the main room and the soldiers were laid out there. The kitchen was used as a reception area and the dining room as an operating theatre. Two officers operated at the dinner table. My mother was a trained nurse, and all her old skills came back."[17]

The Gondrées provided other favors for their liberators.[18] Word spread among Howard's men that the first French family to be liberated were popping open bottles of champagne, ninety-seven of which they had stashed secretly upon the Germans' arrival in 1940.[19] Before long, men who had carried their comrades to the aid station were sipping a little bubbly, some no doubt for the first time.[20] On the other side of Pegasus Bridge from the café, Howard was talking with a fellow officer near a pillbox. Hearing the popping corks from the opposite side of the canal, Howard crossed over to the café to investigate. He quickly sent men back to their posts and then returned to the pillbox, but not before he had had a sip of nectar himself. It was wonderful champagne and, besides, the taking of Pegasus Bridge "really was something to celebrate."[21]

A few minutes later, the skies erupted with noise and the ground shook and trembled beneath Howard's feet as Allied warships began to bombard shore defenses along a fifty-mile front. The concussive effect of the explosions felt like being punched over and over in the ears.

"Blimey, sir!" said one of Howard's men, standing close by.[22]

Howard's thoughts returned to the men on the landing craft— the first wave on the boats he had seen before midnight, the "seaborne chaps." He could see clouds of smoke rising near Sword Beach, five miles away. "I was very pleased to be where I was," he later stressed, "and not with the poor buggers coming by sea."[23]

THE LANDING CRAFT carrying some of the "seaborne chaps"— the 2nd Ranger Battalion—bucked up and down in the high seas, moving painfully slowly toward Pointe du Hoc. The craft followed a guide vessel, Motor Launch (ML) 304 of the Royal Navy, captained by Temporary Lieutenant Colin Beever. At forty years of age, he was one of the oldest men landing first-wave troops on D-Day. It was his job to lead Colonel James Rudder's force all twelve and a half miles to what looked on a map to be a small point on a craggy French coastline.

Conditions were so bad that morning that Rudder, in LCA 888, directly behind Beever, had in the darkness been able to see no more than eight feet ahead of him, following the phosphorescent glow created by ML 304's wake.[24] Rudder's and other LCAs now sat low in the water, overloaded, buffeted by the fifteen-mile-per-hour winds gusting from the west, tugged relentlessly eastward by a powerful current. Rudder had been forced to trust Beever as he stood anxiously at the bow of his landing craft—he would be the first one out—beside an armor-plated cabin where a British coxswain steered. The coxswain was under orders to act only on the command of a British naval officer, not Rudder.

When men lifted their heads and looked toward shore, they could see fires, several miles in the distance, caused by a massive naval shelling that had begun at 5:50 A.M. A black cloud of smoke and dust smothered the coastline, and an ominous red glow pulsed from just inland.[25] It seemed as if the whole of Europe was ablaze.[26]

Beever lacked experience in navigation, and as the coastline came into view, he made a costly mistake, believing that Pointe de la Percée, three miles from his objective, was in fact Pointe du Hoc.

Colonel Rudder looked ahead and did not like what he saw. In the early-morning light, the distant headland did not resemble Pointe du Hoc. Had Beever led his 250 men to the wrong place?

Rudder was not alone in his fears.

Twenty-four-year-old First Sergeant Len Lomell, a senior noncommissioned officer in D Company, stood in LCA 668 beside his friend Sergeant Jack Kuhn, the man who had helped design the ladders some men would soon use to scale the cliffs of Pointe du Hoc.[27]

"Hey, Jack, look," said Lomell. "What the hell's going on? That's not the Pointe. That's C Company's target . . ."

Kuhn stood up to get a good look.

"You're right . . . I wonder what's up."[28]

In LCA 888, just half a mile from shore, Colonel Rudder turned to a British naval officer standing behind the coxswain. *Hoc,* in Old French, meant "jib."[29] But it was no jib that loomed ahead. It was Pointe de la Percée, Rudder was convinced. Unfortunately, only the British naval officer aboard his LCA had the authority to alter course. Would he do as Rudder ordered?

Rudder politely told the officer that he thought they were badly off target.

He was ignored.

Rudder stood up.

"Goddammit, turn right!"[30]

The coxswain reacted fast, steering to the starboard.

The British naval officer signaled to other boats that they should do the same and follow Rudder's craft, which would lead the way to the correct destination. It was approaching H-Hour for the Americans, but Rudder was still at least three miles from his target. His craft plowed against a powerful current below cliff defenses manned by well-armed and forewarned Germans. There would be no surprise, no coup de main.[31] The captain of a British destroyer, the HMS *Talybont,* who stood on its deck watching Rudder's landing craft struggle slowly westward, believed the Rangers' new course was "suicidal."[32]

The Germans, sure enough, began firing at Rudder's force. All fifteen Rangers aboard Rudder's boat cowered down as shots started to ring out.[33] Five men in another craft were struck by

20-millimeter rounds and killed, their bodies ripped apart by bullets designed to bring down Allied bombers. It would take at least half an hour more to reach Pointe du Hoc. God only knew if Rudder and his men would survive the trip.

ABOVE OMAHA BEACH, at a strongpoint overlooking Easy Red sector, a young German machine gunner with the 352nd Artillery Regiment stood in a trench, peering through his commanding officer's binoculars, scanning a beach dotted with defensive obstacles—more than 3,700 of them, a higher concentration than in any other place in Normandy.

"See anything?" asked a sergeant.

"Nothing's happening. Not a thing."

The sergeant heard a distant groan from above the clouds.

"Bombers . . ."[34]

Before long, 448 B-24 bombers arrived over Omaha Beach. Unable to see through the dense cloud cover, and under orders to avoid killing American troops arriving in the first wave, the bombardiers delayed their release by vital seconds. As a result, none of their thirteen thousand bombs actually exploded on the six-mile-long beach or on any of thirteen *Widerstandsnester*—strongpoints comprising concrete bunkers and machine gun nests—but they did kill plenty of cows, as well as French civilians as far as three miles inland.[35]

Another German manning his gun at Widerstandsnest 62 (WN62) prayed as bombs rained down and the earth shook as if he were at the epicenter of an earthquake.[36] Stunned, he looked out of a slit in his strongpoint and spotted the invasion fleet.

"They've got more boats than we've got soldiers."[37]

Out at sea, on a boat ferrying soldiers of the Big Red One toward shore, Lieutenant John Spalding stood at the bow, staring up at Allied fighters soaring overhead—elegant Spitfires and rocket-carrying Typhoons with Overlord black and white stripes freshly painted on their wings to avoid friendly fire from below. (Naval gunners were notoriously trigger-happy at the sound of approaching aircraft.) Spalding's craft was soon within range of the four machine guns, two 75-millimeter artillery pieces, and two anti-tank guns at WN62. Massive volleys of rockets screeched overhead, but unfortunately, most missed their targets, falling short and landing amid the pewter-colored, swelling seas. The twenty-seven Germans manning WN62, several of them teenagers, were unharmed, and now they waited with bated breath for the order to open fire.

With Spalding in the LCA was his second in command, twenty-four-year-old Sergeant Philip Streczyk. The son of Austrian-born immigrants, Streczyk had a long face and a prominent, dimpled chin. He stood a few inches shorter than Spalding, but in the eyes of the seasick men in the craft, his stature was far greater. Although Spalding was nominally in charge of the platoon, it was to the battle-tested Streczyk that the veterans looked for clear orders and decisive leadership. Every man knew that the smart thing to do, if he wanted to survive Omaha Beach, was to trust Streczyk to lead the way.

A truck driver before the war, Streczyk knew how to get a job done. Soldiering was no different. During the Battle of El Guettar, in March 1943, amid the rocky scrub of the Tunisian desert,

Streczyk had single-handedly attacked enemy gunner positions without hesitation, destroying them. Four months later, in Sicily, with his men pinned down, he again rushed forward and cleared enemy machine gun nests. Less than a week later, he came to the rescue when officers leading his unit were killed or wounded; he "saved his company from annihilating enemy fire," according to one report, employing "brilliant tactics."[38] Now approaching the beach in his third amphibious invasion, he was the only combat veteran in E Company who had been awarded the Silver Star three times.

Every GI in the boat, cold hands gripping their cellophane-wrapped M1 rifles, knew that Streczyk would have their backs. He'd do everything he could to keep them alive. "He wasn't West Point material," one soldier said of him, "but there wasn't a braver man that ever walked the ground."[39] Nothing seemed to faze him. "Maybe he figured the Good Lord was watching over him," another man had wondered back in Africa. "He just didn't seem to care. We had an awful time keeping a helmet on him. When someone would start shooting at us, everyone would keep their heads down, taking little peeks out of the foxholes. Not Streczyk. He would be popping up like a robin."[40]

Shells fired from destroyers passed overhead, most landing well inland. It was as if the whole sky were screaming.[41] Lieutenant Spalding spotted several yellow rubber lifeboats holding soaked men, survivors from floating tanks that were supposed to have landed ahead of the infantry, clearing a path and destroying strongpoints like WN62.[42] Most of the tanks, fitted with air-filled canvas skirts—so-called bloomers—that easily kept them afloat in calm waters, had unwisely been launched more than two miles from shore. Battling fierce headwinds and heavy seas, the tanks' bloomers quickly became swamped and the heavy vehicles sank, with only a few bedraggled survivors, shivering in shock and thanking God they'd gotten out of the hatches in time.

Just two of the twenty-nine tanks put to sea off Omaha would make it to the beach to support the 1st Division's first wave, which comprised four infantry companies—some seven hundred men in twenty-four landing craft—and which was soon eight hundred yards from Omaha Beach. It was low tide, and therefore some three hundred yards of beach lay exposed, dotted with ugly defensive obstacles that would be submerged in just ninety minutes—the tide rose at an unnervingly fast rate, about a foot every ten minutes, which meant that wounded Americans, in profound shock and unable to crawl, would quickly be drowned.[43]

In an observation post near WN62, a German lieutenant waited as the first wave drew closer and closer. When the landing craft were around four hundred yards from the beach, he would give the order to open fire. He could clearly see the craft carrying E Company, approaching in two columns, lined up abreast, for the final run into Easy Red.[44] There was a strong crosswind, and the tips of sea waves were lashed into white curls.

Spalding's orders were to land to the right of a small house near the beach, lead his platoon across an area of shingle with stones the size of golf balls, then across an anti-tank ditch and a seawall before pushing inland to a village called Saint-Laurent-sur-Mer.

The young officers in E Company had been assured that by the time they arrived onshore, the air force would have laid waste to enemy defenses, clearing their way to land "without any great opposition."[45] But when Spalding looked at the beach, he saw that little, if anything, had been destroyed. "We had been led to believe German troops would be in a state of shock from aerial and naval bombardment," Spalding later recalled. "How little we knew, how great our faith! The navy promised us that we would be dumped ashore without even getting our shoes wet."[46]

There were no shell craters to offer protection, no gaps blown in the "Belgian gates"—metal obstructions designed to stop landing craft—at the waterline, nor was there any shelter a few hundred feet beyond, amid the wooden stakes with Teller mines attached, or among the steel-beamed "hedgehogs" closer to the actual beach. Nothing had been hit. Not one bomb had dropped on Easy Red, and therefore Spalding and his men were just moments from becoming ensnared in a death trap.

Coxswains aimed between the obstacles. The noise of diesel engines muffled all but shouted last orders as men checked their weapons yet again.[47] Time for a nod, maybe a quick, ironic smile at a buddy, and then they were bouncing through surf, on their way in.

In his observation post near WN62, a German lieutenant picked up a telephone and contacted a gun battery three miles inland. Machine gunners at several strongpoints overlooking Easy Red and in seventy more nests along Omaha's bluffs took aim at the first wave, in particular the crafts' ramps, ready to squeeze their triggers as soon as GIs appeared.[48]

————

ON UTAH BEACH, ten miles to the west of Omaha, the bespectacled twenty-three-year-old Lieutenant Arthur Jahnke, the commander of strongpoint 5 (WN5), looked out to sea. "Here was a truly crazy sight," he later remembered. "I wondered if I were hallucinating." Was that a tank? Floating out at sea? It was indeed. "This must be the Allies' secret weapon," thought Jahnke, who began to issue brisk orders.

With his full cheeks and thick spectacles, Jahnke may have looked like an absentminded schoolmaster, but he knew how to handle himself and those under his command when the bullets started to fly. That April he had stood proudly as he was awarded the Knight's Cross for heroism as a platoon leader on the Eastern Front, where he had been badly wounded. He had also met with Rommel himself on May 11 and was determined not to disappoint the finest German general of his generation, who had carefully inspected Jahnke's positions.[49] Rommel had been in the habit of handing out a harmonica to officers when satisfied, but along Utah the Desert Fox, as he was almost fondly known to the British, had not been impressed and had not awarded even a single concertina.[50] At WN5, he had listened impatiently as Jahnke explained how he had tried to make the best use of barbed wire.

"Let me see your hands for a minute, Lieutenant," Rommel had asked.

Jahnke removed his suede gloves, revealing scratches on his rough hands. Rommel looked pleased and nodded. "Well done, Lieutenant. The blood on an officer's hands from fortification work is worth every bit as much as that shed in battle."[51]

In the distance, Jahnke heard the drone of aircraft. The noise grew louder, becoming a constant roar. Dozens of planes were heading toward Utah, coming out of the west.

It was 6:20 A.M., and Colonel Wilson Wood was flying parallel to the Normandy coast in what was possibly the most crowded airspace in history. Two hundred and ninety-three other B-26 bombers, known as "Widowmakers" due to early models' high rates of accidents during takeoff and landing, were also converging on seven target zones on Utah, each around a hundred yards square.

Most of the planes—also nicknamed "Flying Prostitutes" because they were "fast" but had "no visible means of support"— were just two hundred feet or so below the clouds. The chance he might collide with another plane worried Colonel Wood far more than the desultory German flak that in any case he couldn't do anything about.[52] Then, at 6:24, his 250-pound instant fuse bombs were falling, whistling down toward the scraggly low dunes, and Wood was pushing his control stick to the left, banking away, back toward the whitecapped sea.[53] As he looked to his left he saw the shoreline erupting, countless explosions flashing like gargantuan Fourth of July firecrackers.

Far below, in the bow of his landing craft, Theodore Roosevelt, his face so weather-beaten it resembled tanned leather, heard a "ripple of thunder" and then saw "blazes of light, clouds of dust," and a Widowmaker from Wood's unit passing overhead, headed back to England. One of Wood's planes was hit, recalled Roosevelt, and he watched it fall to the sea, "flaming like a meteor."[54]

In all, 4,414 250-pound bombs were dropped in just a few minutes on defenders in the most accurate carpet-bombing of D-Day. Ten miles away, above Omaha, bombers had flown due south, crossing the coast in a few seconds, and it had therefore been almost impossible to hit targets along the hundred-foot bluffs. By contrast, around one in six of the bombs dropped on Utah made a direct hit on defenses. There was so much smoke and dust from debris that gun crews out at sea could no longer identify targets, and many coxswains, including Captain Schroeder's and Brigadier General Roosevelt's, lost sight of landmarks to help guide them ashore.

In his shelter, Lieutenant Jahnke crouched down, eyes shut tight. A bomb landed just a few yards away, and sand and debris buried the shelter. He was still conscious, he realized, but also in agony, wounded in the arm. He struggled, in shock, to dig himself out of the shelter.

All of Utah appeared to be aflame.

Selbst in Russland habe ich das nie gesehen.

Even in Russia I've never seen this.[55]

Yet Jahnke's agony was not over. Already hit hard, the lieutenant's unit of seventy-five men cowered, hands pressed to their ears, as yet more bombs rained down, followed by nerve-shattering naval fire. The combination destroyed all of Jahnke's heavy guns and most of the bunkers and other defenses at WN5. Almost the entire position was pulverized, with the command center receiving a direct hit.

Somehow Jahnke survived, and now he lay sprawled at the base of a bomb crater. Daring to lift his head aboveground, he groggily began to assess the extent of the destruction. There was just one anti-tank gun and a couple of machine guns left intact, nowhere near enough to stop a concerted attack. Then he looked once more out to sea and for the first time saw hundreds of ships dotting the horizon as far as the eye could see. It was low tide, yet all of his remaining guns, including the lone anti-tank weapon, which in any case was damaged, had been pre-sighted in the belief that the Allies would land at high tide. Rommel had been certain of it and given the requisite orders.

Jahnke tried his best to do his duty and ordered his shell-shocked men to shoot at the enemy. The French 47-millimeter anti-tank gun managed to fire just one round before it was destroyed. The culprit was—unbelievably, it seemed—an American tank, a white star emblazoned on its green turret, one of twenty-eight amphibious Sherman DD "Donald Duck" tanks that had reached Utah ahead of the first wave of troops and were now pounding, at close range, strongpoints with their 75-millimeter guns.[56] Fortunately, these tanks had been launched just a thousand yards from Utah rather than several miles, so only four had failed to reach the shore.

A couple of the tanks, spewing black exhaust fumes, trundled toward Jahnke and began blasting away at what remained of his positions, each cannon shot sounding like a hammer being pounded close to the head. Jahnke ordered Goliaths—small radio-controlled tanks—to be deployed, but the bombing had destroyed the cables leading to them.[57] The Shermans, with their canvas skirts raised, as if in mockery, clanked closer and closer, gears and tracks grinding.

"Looks like God deserted us," Jahnke told a man beside him. "Where's our air force?"[58]

Around 6:25 A.M., a middle-aged mess orderly emerged from his hiding place, not far from Jahnke.

"Everything's wrecked!" he cried. "Everything's wrecked."[59]
The man ran toward Jahnke. "We've got to surrender!"

Jahnke told the man he was crazy. He shouted at survivors nearby to grab shovels and dig foxholes.[60] Yet it was a vain cry for action. The few traumatized survivors could barely lift a shovel, let alone find functioning weapons amid the smoking debris of WN5. When some dared to look out to sea, they spotted landing craft in the 4th Division's first wave. What little was left of their morale evaporated.

One of the craft carried Brigadier General Theodore Roosevelt and E Company commander Captain Howard Lees. Behind both men stood Roosevelt's aide, busy puking over the side of the craft, which carried heavy equipment and a jeep.[61] The aide and other men had managed to play a few half-hearted hands of poker on its hood on the way to shore while a helmetless Roosevelt and Lees had conferred with a British coxswain steering the craft.[62]

Roosevelt looked over the side of the craft as it crashed into the waves. It was impossible to get his bearings, so thick was the haze created by the bombing. Then the beach appeared, "a long stretch of sand studded with wire and obstacles," he recalled.[63]

Meanwhile, Captain Leonard Schroeder stood at the bow of his plywood Higgins boat, at the center of a line of eight craft.[64] He was leading the first wave from the 8th Infantry Regiment toward the Uncle Red sector of the beach, in front of the once formidable WN5 strongpoint.[65] The enemy's guns made what sounded like a "raging groan"[66] as Schroeder felt the slapping of waves against his hull and smelled vomit and diesel fumes— four out of every five men on his thirty-six-foot-long craft were seasick.

The steel ramp dropped and Schroeder was off first, wading ashore, holding his .45 Colt pistol above his head. It was 6:28 A.M. "I knew my company was in the first wave, but I didn't know I was actually going to be the first ashore," recalled Schroeder. "Besides, I was too scared to think about it."[67] Then he was quickly onto the sands and sprinting, ahead of his men, across the beach toward WN5.

Theodore Roosevelt heard a crunch as his craft struck rock and sand. He, too, jumped into waist-deep water. "We splashed and floundered through some hundred yards of water while German salvos fell," he remembered. "Men dropped, some silent, some screaming." Then his feet were on the sand and he began to run, huffing and puffing, across three hundred yards of open beach toward a five-foot-high concrete seawall.

Less than a hundred yards away, Captain Schroeder saw German mortar rounds begin to explode on the beach, sending vicious geysers of sand into the air, and then he spotted Roosevelt running to the seawall while shouting and gesticulating at men from F Company, "with his hand on his cane, from which he was never separated . . . The sight of this man of fifty-six directing his troops like a conductor with his baton was something."[68] Schroeder kept moving across the gentle slope of the yellow beach, sprinting across the corrugated runnels, then dry sand strewn with driftwood and shells, heading toward the first protection, the seawall. "My mission was to breach it and then to lead my men to the small village of Sainte Marie du Mont."

Engineers blew gaps in the seawall, and from just beyond it Roosevelt watched as Captain Lees, "a great tower of a man," led

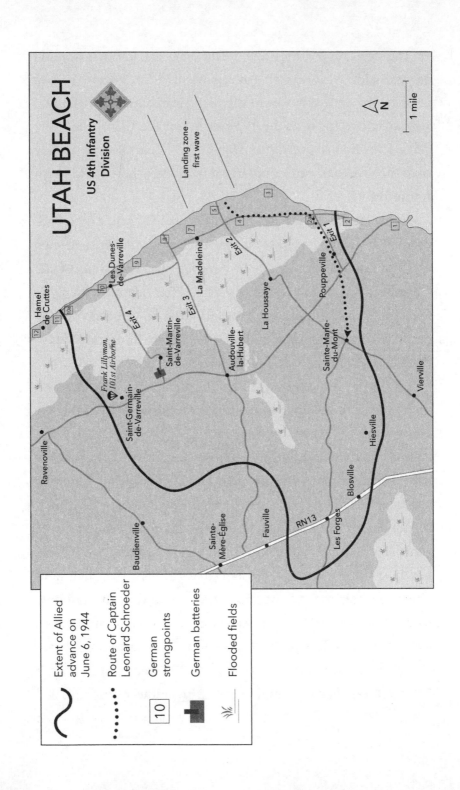

UTAH BEACH

US 4th Infantry
Division

Landing zone –
first wave

N
1 mile

Hamel
de Cruttes
Ravenoville
Baudienville
Sainte-
Mère-Église
Fauville
RN13
Les Forges
Blosville
Hiesville
Vierville
Sainte-Marie-
du-Mont
Pouppeville
La Houssaye
Audouville-
la-Hubert
La Madeleine
Saint-Martin-
de-Varreville
Saint-Germain-
de-Varreville
Les Dunes-
de-Varreville
Frank Lillyman,
101st Airborne

Exit 1
Exit 2
Exit 3
Exit 4

Extent of Allied
advance on
June 6, 1944

Route of Captain
Leonard Schroeder

German
strongpoints

German batteries

Flooded fields

his soldiers inland, moving swiftly through tall seagrass and low dunes to destroy several German strongpoints. Roosevelt tried to orient himself and quickly realized that he and the entire 8th Infantry's first wave had landed in the wrong place. He scrambled across some dunes and spotted a windmill he'd seen in reconnaissance photographs and knew that he was two thousand yards from where he should have come ashore. "I had to hot-foot it from left to right and back again," he later wrote, "setting the various commanding officers straight and changing the task." At Roosevelt's side was an aide, a lieutenant called Marcus Stevenson, "devoted and competent as always, his tommy gun ready to defend us if it became necessary." Before long, Stevenson and Roosevelt had set up a first command post and radio communication in the ruins of a building near Lieutenant Jahnke's WN5.[69]

Captain Schroeder was meanwhile leading his men to the east across dunes toward two strongpoints, WN1 and WN2, close to a small village called Pouppeville, at the very southern end of Utah Beach. Both strongpoints had to be dealt with if later waves of troops were to access a nearby causeway, leading through flooded fields. Dozens of German troops, most of them shell-shocked and terrified, emerged from dunes with their hands in the air. Some of them were Polish and Czech conscripts, no admirers of Adolf Hitler, and once they realized they would not be shot, they appeared delighted that their war was finally over.

There was the occasional heart-jolting crack of sniper fire and the odd mortar explosion, but no serious German resistance until Schroeder and his men approached the hamlet of

Pouppeville and the Germans spotted them. "Shrapnel broke my pistol in two," remembered Schroeder. "We had to carry on, to continue to advance . . . to shoot, and unfortunately, to kill . . . I killed two men. Like me, they had family, maybe children. Many years later, that came back to haunt me. But I had to look after myself."[70]

CHAPTER 7

An Angel on Each Shoulder

FIFTEEN MILES TO THE EAST of Utah, out at sea, Lieutenant John Spalding heard throttles open and then what felt like a race to shore began. "I know that the Light Brigade and Pickett's Charge flashed through my mind at that beautiful moment," recalled one of Spalding's 1st Division comrades. "It was pure excitement!"[1] The thirty-one men under Spalding's command, each with a red number 1 stitched onto a brown patch on his left sleeve, hunched down as the craft crashed violently into surf and plumes of spray flew into the air and landed on their webbed helmets.

Not one man spoke. There was no more singing, no more "whistling in the dark," no more jokes about the saucy English broads they'd left behind in England.[2] They were badly weighed down with equipment: flamethrowers, Bangalore torpedoes, heavy radios, even ladders to throw across anti-tank ditches. What would happen, Spalding worried, if they landed in deep water? Having to shout to be heard above the engines, Spalding ordered them not to jump out until he had gone first and tested the water's depth.[3] They were around two hundred yards from the beach when one of the British naval crew on his craft pulled the trigger on a machine gun mounted on the stern, and opened fire.

In a machine gun nest at WN62, the most heavily defended strongpoint on Omaha, which overlooked Easy Red sector, a twenty-one-year-old corporal watched boats in the first wave plow through the heavy seas, oddly dispersed, having been pushed off course by the strong tides and wind.

The all-important order had already been given: "Hold your fire until the enemy is coming up to the water line."[4]

There were several earthshaking explosions caused by Allied naval fire, then the corporal's immediate superior appeared, a shell splinter having hit him in the throat. "Just a little splinter, nothing serious. Everything all right here?"

"So far," replied the corporal, who then saw that the ramps of some craft were dropping. It was 6:30 A.M.: H-Hour on Omaha Beach.

The first wave had arrived.

"They're getting into the water now," someone called out.

The corporal sent a frantic message to WN62's observation post: "Landing troops disembarking."

"They must be crazy," said a German sergeant. "Are they going to swim ashore, right in front of our muzzles?"

A lieutenant finally gave the order for the men at WN62 to open fire, and within seconds a torrent of bullets were slicing toward the first wave as it landed on Easy Red, 57-millimeter rounds pinging against metal ramps, ripping through plywood hulls, zipping into the surf.

Aboard Lieutenant Spalding's landing craft, a man shouted for the ramp to be dropped, but it didn't budge. Spalding and a sergeant kicked the ramp until it slammed down.[5] Spalding was first off, dropping into heavy seas just to the left of the ramp. The noise of battle was constant as he headed for the beach. He could hear small arms fire and the distinct snarl of German MG42 machine guns, which had a far higher rate of fire than any Allied weapon. One well-aimed burst could kill his entire platoon in seconds.

The water was up to his waist and he waded toward the shore, holding his carbine above the waves, his soaked woolen trousers like lead weights, but then he came across a runnel so deep he couldn't cross it without swimming. He and men nearby inflated their life vests. "There was a strong undercurrent carrying us to the left," he remembered. "I swallowed so much salt water trying to get ashore. I came so near to drowning." Thanks to his life vest, he was able to keep his head above water.[6]

As he neared the beach, Spalding spotted his second in command, Sergeant Streczyk, and a medic. Together they were trying to carry an eighteen-foot ladder designed to cross anti-tank ditches, but they were struggling to keep ahold of it in the heavy seas.

Spalding grabbed for the ladder.

"Lieutenant, we don't need any help," shouted Streczyk.[7]

Spalding had a higher rank. He may have been in combat for only a few minutes, but he was already a changed man, no longer a callow neophyte, terrified of how he might fail. His job was to lead his men off the beach, and if he gave a goddamned order, as bullets zipped and whistled past his head, by Christ he expected it to be carried out. They were to abandon the ladder, he shouted, and they did so. Then he was able to stand once more, the water now up to his chin, surf breaking over his shoulders. "I had swallowed about half of the ocean," Spalding remembered, "and felt like I was going to choke."

A private carrying a seventy-two-pound flamethrower cried out for help, and Sergeant Streczyk told him to dump it. The private did as he was ordered, and others followed suit, abandoning equipment. Before long, Spalding's men had little left to fight with. "In addition to the flamethrowers and many personal weapons," recalled Spalding, "we lost our mortar, most of the mortar ammunition, one of our bazookas, much of the bazooka ammunition."

Spalding finally waded out of the water. He looked ahead, across three hundred yards of sand, scarred by ugly black beach defenses—mine-tipped logs driven into the sand and six-foot-high steel hedgehogs. "I was considerably shaken up. Completely soaked, my equipment, heavy when dry, seemed to weigh a ton." He saw the ruins of a house at the base of bluffs. It resembled one he had been shown in a briefing.

"Damn," said Spalding. "The navy has hit it right on the nose."

Other men moved forward and opened fire when they reached the sands. Close to Spalding, a rifleman was hit in the foot. He fell and then struggled to remove his leggings, unable to reach the lacing. Spalding helped him get the legging off and then looked up and saw some of his men crossing the hard, gray sand, bullets stitching toward them. They were soaked and too heavily burdened to sprint toward the nearest cover at the base of the bluffs. They should have gone in with as little weight as possible, like Rangers, and now looked as if they were "walking in the face of a real strong wind," Spalding remembered.[8] "It was just a slow, methodical march with absolutely no cover up to the enemy's commanding positions," recalled a fellow officer from E Company. "Men fell, left and right . . . Others staggered on to the obstacle-covered, yet completely exposed beach."[9]

It occurred to Spalding that he should contact his company commander. He crouched down with his foot-long SCR-536 radio and pulled out the antenna. "Copper One to Copper Six."

There was no answer.

"Copper One to Copper Six. This is One. Come in Copper Six."

No reply.

Spalding looked at the radio. What was wrong with it?

Its black mouthpiece had been blown off. It was useless, but Spalding's training had kicked in and he instinctively, by rote, took the antenna down, careful not to break it, and put the radio back over his shoulder, so scared he could not think straight.[10] Then he moved across some shingle, smooth gray stones slowing him, to the blasted ruins of the building that he and others would later describe in remarkably detailed after-action reports as "Roman ruins." He looked around and realized the building was different from the one in his planned landing zone, some five hundred yards to the west. As with all but one of the eight infantry companies to land in the first wave on Omaha, Spalding's unit had come ashore far from where intended.

The German fire was unrelenting, a constant stream of bullets slashing through the air above Spalding's head, pockmarking a wall a few feet from him and then killing a sergeant nearby. To his left he could see the source of the fire, WN62, and he watched as an MG42 scythed down men from F Company as they staggered across the beach. Powerless to help, he looked to his right, to the west, where E Company was supposed to have landed, and couldn't see a single GI. What had happened to the rest of E Company? Had they all been slaughtered? Down at the waterline, some landing craft had been hit and were burning, clouds of tar-black smoke spiraling into the sky. It was a truly apocalyptic scene, never to be erased from his memory. Spalding decided it was best if he didn't look back again.

A lump of shrapnel hit a private close by in the shoulder with a hard punch, the metal lodging in his upper body, knocking him down.[11] A sergeant had managed to keep ahold of a Bangalore torpedo and had placed it below curls of barbed wire, and now he exploded its charge, blowing open a gap with a sharp blast. Beyond lay thick brush and then a steep incline to the top of the bluffs. Sergeant Streczyk and a private, scouting ahead, discovered a minefield but also a path of sorts created by water that had washed through the brush.[12] The private returned and told Spalding and others to follow him. As they did so, a machine gunner directly above, near the top of the bluffs, pressed his finger on a trigger. Bullets kicked up the ground all around them, but they advanced regardless and Spalding kept his head up, scanning the bluffs.

"Lieutenant," a sergeant said. "Watch out for the damn mines."

The area was "infested' with small wooden box mines, but Spalding couldn't see any. Stepping carefully, he continued up the bluffs, through thick brush and seagrass and the gnarled stumps of windblown bushes.

"Watch out for the damn mines."

Up they climbed, and then they were through the mined area. None of his men were hurt. It seemed like a miracle. None had stepped on a mine. "The Lord was with us," recalled Spalding, "and we had an angel on each shoulder on that trip." The Lord had indeed been with them. Just a couple of hours later, several men from H Company would be lost as they crossed the very same ground.

The machine gun was still spitting bullets from above, its barrel growing hot. There was a deep boom as a sergeant fired his bazooka at the machine gun's position. But the sergeant missed and was shot in the left arm, and then a private was hit. The sergeant came up to Spalding and proudly displayed his wound—a bullet had gone through his arm just above the wrist. He'd now been in three invasions: North Africa, Sicily, and Normandy. Finally, he'd gotten the "million dollar wound" so many GIs hoped for, serious enough to be sent home but not life-threatening.

"Gee, Lieutenant, ain't it a beauty?" said the sergeant.

Men nearby looked jealous.

Spalding kept moving, following Sergeant Streczyk up the bluffs and then to within fifteen yards of the German machine gun.[13]

The gunner thrust his hands in the air to surrender. "Kamerad."

Keeping his wits about him, Spalding ordered his men to hold their fire. He needed to question the gunner, who, it turned out, was Polish. The gunner said he and his comrades had taken a vote on whether to fight and "preferred not to, but the German noncoms made them." He swore he had not tried to kill Spalding and his men.

Sergeant Streczyk, who spoke Polish fluently, glared at the gunner with withering contempt and slapped him hard over the head. "So why were you shooting at us?"

The man was clearly lying. Spalding himself had seen him hit three of his men. The gunner looked terrified, but the Americans he had indeed tried to mow down still held their fire. And then Spalding and his platoon moved into a defile near the top of the bluffs where a medic, a private from Kentucky called George Bowen, began working on several men, sprinkling sulfa powder on their bullet wounds.

All that morning, Bowen and other surviving medics from the first wave would toil without rest, jabbing dying teenagers with morphine spikes, in some cases hunting down more supplies from abandoned kit, moving back and forth along the beach and bluffs while under fire, holding men's hands as they cried for their mothers, saving lives. "No man waited more than five minutes for first aid," remembered Spalding. "[Bowen's] action did a lot to help morale." Bowen would later be awarded the Distinguished Service Cross, along with four others from Spalding's platoon.

There was no true respite for any man who had landed with

the first wave, just a minute or two to orient oneself, try to catch one's breath, and then reload. Spalding saw a sergeant carrying a Browning automatic rifle he'd picked up off the beach, firing it from the hip at a machine gun to the west, spewing bullets at such a rate that a man carrying extra ammunition could barely keep him fed with twenty-round magazines. Then a lieutenant from G Company came over, having landed in the second wave, and used the same route up the bluffs that Spalding had taken.[14] He was followed a few minutes later by Captain Joe Dawson, the lanky commander of G Company, who asked if Spalding knew where the rest of E Company was.[15] Spalding said he had no idea. He still hadn't seen any men to his right, to the west. For all he knew, he and his platoon were the only men from E Company who'd made it off the beach.

Meanwhile, a platoon sergeant set off a flare at the base of the bluffs where Spalding and his platoon had broken the trail through barbed wire and minefields. E Company's commander, Captain Edward Wozenski, pinned down on Easy Red with dozens of others from the first wave, saw the billowing yellow smoke from the flare. "I was praying for smoke," he recalled, "any kind of smoke." At last, there was cause for hope, and he decided to move his men toward the smoke. He couldn't get up the bluffs where he was—there was just too much machine gun fire from a German strongpoint. He took his trench knife and began to press the side of the blade into the backs of men lying nearby to see if they were alive. If the GI was still breathing, he rolled him over or kicked him.

"Let's go!"[16]

Back on top of the bluffs, yet another German machine

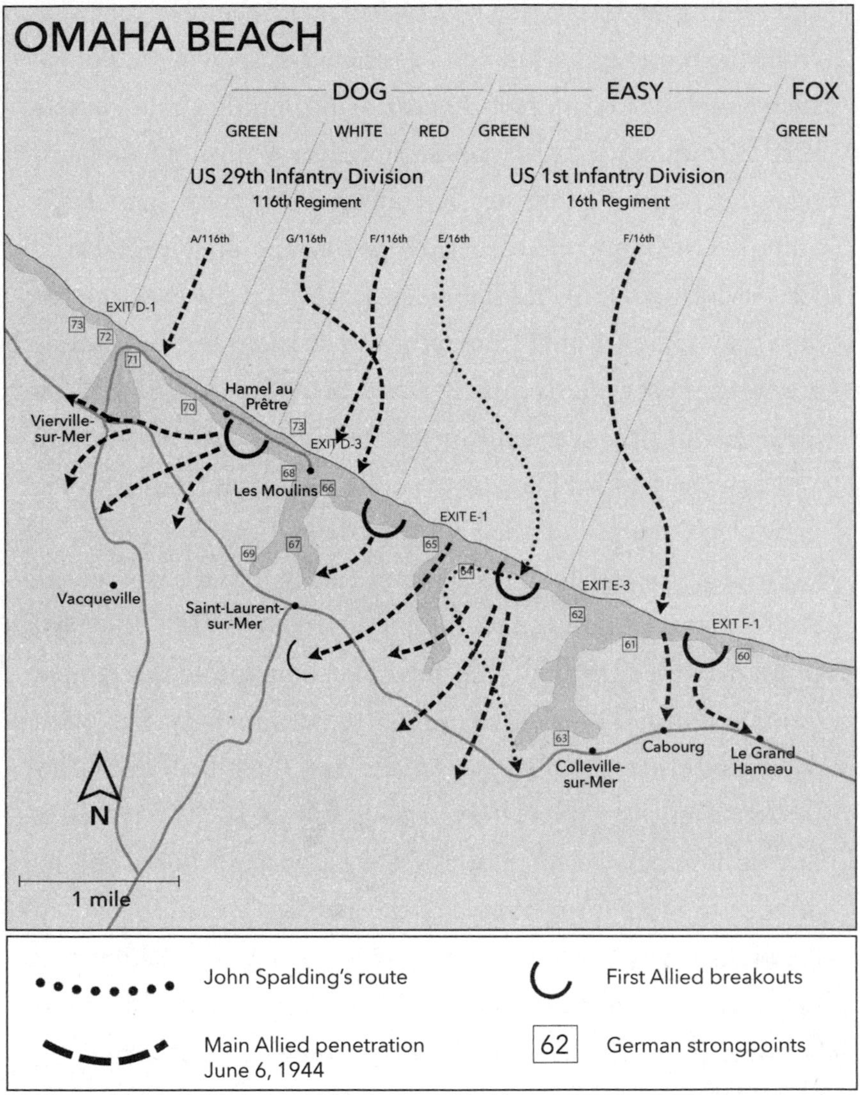
OMAHA BEACH
DOG
EASY
FOX
GREEN
WHITE
RED
GREEN
RED
GREEN
US 29th Infantry Division
116th Regiment
US 1st Infantry Division
16th Regiment
A/116th
G/116th
F/116th
E/16th
F/16th
EXIT D-1
EXIT D-3
EXIT E-1
EXIT E-3
EXIT F-1
73
72
71
70
73
68
66
69
67
65
64
62
61
60
63
Hamel au Prêtre
Vierville-sur-Mer
Les Moulins
Vacqueville
Saint-Laurent-sur-Mer
Colleville-sur-Mer
Cabourg
Le Grand Hameau
N
1 mile
John Spalding's route
First Allied breakouts
Main Allied penetration June 6, 1944
62
German strongpoints

gunner had spotted Spalding and his platoon as they moved west, toward the E-1 draw that led to the village of Saint-Laurent-sur-Mer, E Company's planned objective. There was no retreat. Those who stayed put on the bluffs or on the beach or waded back out into the bloodied waters were shot by snipers. Yet again, Spalding prepared to attack head-on. It was best to keep moving if he and his men were to see another sunrise. Hopefully, yet again, the angels wouldn't desert them.

ON UTAH BEACH, near strongpoint WN5, there was a direct hit on Lieutenant Jahnke's position, and the German officer was knocked out cold. He awoke sometime later, buried in sand. He had been hit in the back by shrapnel and felt his legs being pulled. Then he could see sunlight and began to cough up sand and dirt. There was a GI pointing his M1 rifle at his face. Close by was a machine pistol, but as he tried to grab it he was kicked in the back.

"Take it easy," said an American in a surprisingly calm voice.

Jahnke could easily have been shot, but instead the American told him to put his hands above his head. Jahnke's Knight's Cross dangled forlornly, damaged, from a shoelace around his ragged collar. And then he was being dragged toward the seawall and made to sit on it.

"Come over here!" ordered an American captain.

Jahnke was soon standing close to a Sherman tank.

"How many guns did you have?"

The German refused to answer.

The captain pulled out a silk map.

"Take a look at this. We've got it all here."

It was true. The map showed WN5 in extraordinary detail. It was labeled UTAH.

"Utah . . . that's a state . . . do you come from there?" asked Jahnke.

The captain laughed.

There was a loud explosion and Jahnke fell to the ground, hit in his stomach by a piece of German shrapnel. He was bleeding badly. An American crawled over to him and handed him some field dressing and offered him a Chesterfield cigarette. It tasted heavenly. Then the American was up on his feet and standing at attention. There was a general approaching. Jahnke lifted his hand to his bare head in a feeble salute.

Theodore Roosevelt raised his hand to return the salute but then dropped it, no doubt spotting Jahnke's gray German uniform beneath the bloodstains and dirt.

Roosevelt issued an order and before long Jahnke was being marched away with survivors from his unit and then being ordered to take off his boots and socks and wade out to a landing craft. The gold-sanded beach, where skuas could usually be seen stealing fish from black-capped sandwich terns, was now littered with the refuse of war.[17]

Roosevelt, meanwhile, walked along a narrow road that ran behind the dunes of Utah Beach, linking causeway exits. More men were landing and getting off the beach, pressing through gaps blown in the seawall, suffering minimal casualties. Roosevelt urged the latest arrivals to get the hell inland, shouting instructions when they started off in the wrong direction. "Soldiers were everywhere," he recalled. "Occasionally groups of prisoners would pass, disheveled, dirty, unshaven. There was the continuous rattle of rifles and machine guns." His only sustenance was "a cake of D-ration chocolate," but, such was his excitement, he felt no hunger, and before long he had linked up with his aide, Lieutenant Marcus Stevenson, driving Roosevelt's assigned jeep, which he had dubbed "Rough Rider." "Shells continually burst around us," he recalled, "but all I got was a slight scratch on one hand."[18] Roosevelt proudly showed his minor wound to one officer.

Roosevelt then came across General Barton, the commander of the 4th Infantry Division. "While I was mentally framing [orders]," recalled Barton, "Ted Roosevelt came up. He had landed with the first wave, had put my troops across the beach, and had a perfect picture of the entire situation." Barton had expected Roosevelt, whom he "loved," to be killed. "You can imagine then the emotion with which I greeted him when he came out to meet me."[19]

RANGER LIEUTENANT GEORGE Kerchner watched as water sloshed around his feet in his landing craft. His boots were soaked before he'd even stepped ashore. He took off his helmet. So much spray was landing in the craft that he ordered his men to start bailing with their helmets. He joined them, dipping his dark green helmet, with its red Ranger insignia stenciled on the back, into the foot-deep oily soup of salt water and vomit. Then he dumped the contents over the side of the craft as it closed on the craggy coastline of Pointe du Hoc, five miles east of Utah Beach.

Some of Kerchner's men had been assigned the role of "monkeys," because they were the best climbers; they would scale the cliffs first, pulling themselves smoothly up three-quarter-inch ropes attached to three-pronged steel grappling hooks. The hooks were to be fired from rocket launchers on each craft and also from the beach beneath the cliffs. The monkeys were lightly armed with just pistols or carbines. Kerchner and his 225 fellow Rangers about to land below the cliffs also had to be as mobile as possible. Their packs, machine guns, and mortars would arrive in later boats.[20]

Bullets stabbed the gray waters. The landing craft were now within range of German machine guns.

"Hey, boss!" shouted a Ranger. "Those jerks are trying to hit us."[21]

Kerchner could see a narrow beach, less than a hundred yards away. He gave the order to fire the rockets with grappling hooks and ropes attached. "They fired in sequence, two at a time. Out of our six ropes, five of them cleared the cliff, which was a good percentage, because some of the landing craft had a great deal of trouble. Some fired too soon and the ropes were wet and they didn't get up the cliffs."

Kerchner hoped his craft would "run right up on the beach" and he and his men could make a "dry landing."[22] It was 7 A.M., half an hour after the Rangers had been scheduled to land. The naval gunfire aimed at Pointe du Hoc had ended almost forty-five minutes before. The Germans of Werfer-Regiment 84 who had taken cover had, in all likelihood, returned by now to their positions above the cliffs.[23] The smart thing to do, if the defenders had their wits about them, would be to crawl to the grappling hooks and cut the ropes as Kerchner and his fellow Rangers scaled the cliffs.

This whole thing is a big mistake. None of us will ever get up that cliff because we are so vulnerable.

Then the ramp was down.

It was 7:09 A.M.[24]

"Everybody out," shouted a British naval officer.

Kerchner looked ahead, saw that the beach had been badly cratered by heavy bombs, and guessed that the water would be just a couple of feet deep.

"Come on, let's go!" Kerchner yelled.

Kerchner leapt into the water but quickly sank, water over his head. He had landed in a large pool. He struggled to the surface and then began to swim toward the shore. Men behind him in the landing craft jumped away from the pool, one of the many left by the massive Lancaster bombing earlier. "Instead of being the first one ashore," recalled Kerchner, "I was one of the last ashore from my boat. I wanted to find somebody to help me cuss out the Royal Navy, but everybody was busily engrossed in their own duties so I couldn't get any sympathy."[25]

A machine gun opened fire, sounding like a piece of cloth being torn close to the ear, a frantic ripping. Two Rangers fell close to Kerchner. The bullets kept coming. He was powerless, totally exposed, armed only with a Colt .45, as useless as a kid's peashooter. He grabbed an M1 rifle dropped by a Ranger who'd been shot dead. Enraged, he thought for a moment or two about hunting down the machine gunner, but he stayed focused on his mission: getting his men to the top of the cliff and then taking out the powerful German guns that could easily kill hundreds of his fellow Americans who had already landed on Utah and Omaha.[26]

Kerchner didn't have to bark orders to get the job done. His men quickly formed up and within moments were launching more grappling hooks over the bluff edges, dodging "potato masher" grenades dropped from above, then clinging to ropes as they began to climb up the cliffs.

Some of the Rangers would never forget the sight of Staff Sergeant William Stivison, scurrying up an eighty-foot ladder fitted to the base of a DUKW, which was bobbing up and down in the waves just offshore. Like a "circus performer," he was firing two heavy Lewis machine guns from atop the ladder as German tracer bullets looped toward him.[27] Ranger Jack Kuhn's top-secret consultation with a London ladder manufacturer that spring had paid off royally.

One of Kerchner's men, Sergeant Len Lomell, was close to the top of the cliffs when he saw a radioman struggling to climb any higher because of a large SCR-300 radio set on his back.

"Help me," yelled the radioman. "Help me!"

Lomell spotted another man, who was "all muscle, a born athlete, a very powerful man," and called out to him. The athlete grabbed the radioman and pulled him toward him, the radio's antenna whipping back and forth, visible above the cliffs.

"Get down!" yelled Lomell at the radioman. "You're gonna draw fire on us!"

Lomell was then over the edge of the cliff, onto grass, and rolling into a large shell crater, where he came across a captain called Gilbert Baugh, E Company's commander. "He had a .45 in his hand," recalled Lomell, "and a bullet had gone through the back of his hand into the magazine in the grip of the .45. He was in shock and bleeding badly, and there was nothing we could do other than to give him some morphine."

Baugh was one of three company commanders out of four in the battalion who were now out of action.[28]

Lomell turned to the stricken officer. "Listen. We gotta move it. We're on our way, Captain. We'll send back a medic. You just stay here. You're gonna be all right."

Lomell moved on to another shell hole, where a dozen men were cowering, out of sight of the machine gunners and snipers who were enjoying open season. Thank God for the Lancaster bombers who had cratered the entire area. From the air, the headland appeared honeycombed with holes sometimes twenty feet deep and ten yards wide, where a platoon could shelter, safe from the streams of machine gun bullets stitching the air with the *dash-dash-dash* of white-hot tracers, spitting from enemy strongpoints inland to the south and from the western edge of the battery. "We hadn't counted on craters being a protection to us," recalled Lomell. "We would have lost more men, but the craters protected us."[29]

Meanwhile, below on the beach, Lieutenant Kerchner had spotted his commanding officer, Colonel Rudder, and shouted to him that Captain Duke Slater had been lost, so he was going to assume command of D Company. Rudder, just starting up a rope ladder, couldn't have cared less and told Kerchner to get the hell up the cliffs. Scaling them was surprisingly straightforward, Kerchner recalled, a lot easier than during training in the Highlands of Scotland.

Under fire, Kerchner made it to the top of the hundred-foot

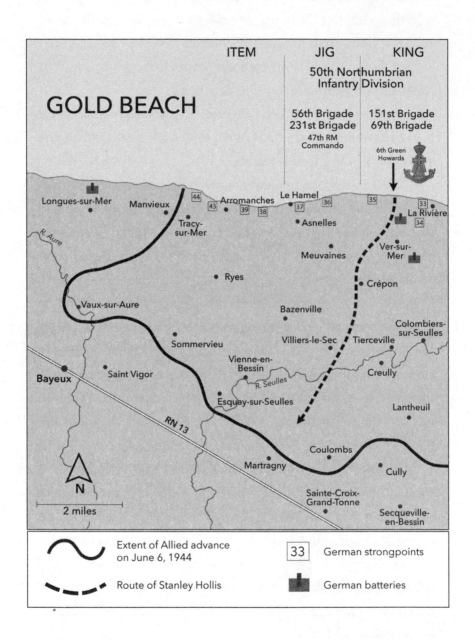

ITEM   JIG   KING

50th Northumbrian
Infantry Division

56th Brigade   151st Brigade
231st Brigade   69th Brigade
47th RM
Commando

6th Green
Howards

GOLD BEACH

Longues-sur-Mer

Manvieux

Tracy-
sur-Mer

Arromanches

Le Hamel

Asnelles

La Rivière

Ver-sur-
Mer

R. Aure

Ryes

Meuvaines

Crépon

Vaux-sur-Aure

Bazenville

Colombiers-
sur-Seulles

Sommervieu

Villiers-le-Sec

Tierceville

Vienne-en-
Bessin

R. Seulles

Creully

Bayeux

Saint Vigor

Esquay-sur-Seulles

Lantheuil

RN 13

Coulombs

Martragny

Cully

N

Sainte-Croix-
Grand-Tonne

2 miles

Secqueville-
en-Bessin

Extent of Allied advance on June 6, 1944	33	German strongpoints
Route of Stanley Hollis		German batteries

cliff and was surprised when he looked ahead. The surface of Pointe du Hoc was unlike any of the diagrams or photos he had studied so carefully. It was "just one large shell crater after another."[30]

German machine gun fire swept back and forth.

A Ranger officer and a private attacked a machine gun nest. A German saw the two seemingly demented Rangers running toward him—these were no gum-chewing, cowardly half-breeds, the kind of Americans depicted in Nazi propaganda.

"*Bitte!*" screamed the German. "*Bitte! Bitte!*"

The Ranger officer let rip with his tommy gun, killing the German. Then he turned nonchalantly to the private at his side.

"I wonder what *bitte* means?"[31]

Lieutenant Kerchner, meanwhile, kept advancing, trying to reach a crater before getting hit, moving as fast as he could in the direction of the battery of guns he'd been ordered to destroy if the American landings at Utah and Omaha were to stand a chance.[32]

TWENTY MILES TO THE EAST, the British first wave was approaching Gold Beach, the widest of the Allied landing beaches, skirted at the western end by cliffs. The wind still blew angrily, forcing many coxswains to struggle to keep on course in the steep chop. Allied bombardment had destroyed several key defenses, but on King sector, one of two areas assigned to the British 50th Infantry Division, an 88-millimeter gun—protected by thick concrete—was causing havoc. A private in the first wave would later describe the noise as "absolutely horrendous. It's not 'Bang! Bang! Bang! Bang!' It's a continual roar of sound, constantly, without stopping."[33]

As Sergeant Major Stanley Hollis stood in his landing craft as it closed on King sector of Gold Beach, he spotted what looked like a pillbox beside a railway line that ran along the beach. He lifted a heavy Lewis gun from the bottom of the craft, loaded it with ammunition, placed it on the gunwale, and opened fire on the pillbox. Then he took the Lewis gun off the gunwale. His fellow Green Howards would need it once they were ashore. "It was white-hot," he recalled, "and I got a bloody great blister across my hand, as thick as my finger!"

A self-inflicted wound and the battle hasn't even started.

The ramp came down and Hollis began wading through waist-deep water. A sergeant, weighed down with a pack and equipment, a few yards ahead of Hollis, dropped out of sight, having stepped into a shell hole under the water. A landing craft appeared, and Hollis saw its whirling propellers cut the sergeant to pieces as shells and mortars hissed through the air.

As Hollis ran across the beach, a tank exploded, its escape hatch spinning like a top across the sands, which appeared to stretch endlessly to the left and right. Ahead, there were no looming bluffs but a long, gentle slope of lush pasture. A German aircraft flew over, the black crosses on its gray fuselage clearly visible, and then Hollis reached some rolls of barbed wire skirting a minefield at the edge of the beach. An Irishman close by noticed several birds seated on the wire, oblivious to the raging battle—the crescendos of machine gun fire, the strangled cries and screams of the wounded and dying. Bullets whizzed by, but the birds stayed put.

"No bloody wonder," said the Irishman. "There's no room in the air for them!"

Hollis watched Green Howards, hunched down with mine detectors, clear a path through the minefield, laying white tape to mark a safe route, and then he and his men were stepping carefully along the trail of white tape and passing through a thick hedgerow, headed toward a gun battery at Mont Fleury, almost a mile inland, atop a rise.[34]

Other Green Howards were moving off the beach and inland. Some reached a house and stopped, preparing to throw grenades inside, when a Frenchwoman, in tears, emerged and pointed toward Gold Beach. "Is this the real thing?" she asked. "Is this the liberation?"[35]

There was the crackle of small-arms fire, like high-pitched radio static. The Irishman with Hollis was killed. It was barely five minutes after landing. Hollis pressed on, head up, running as fast as he could, sweating in his woolen uniform, knowing instinctively that it was best to be a moving target, to not stay put. He reached a crossroads, where he saw the crumpled bodies of yet more Green Howards who had been cut down by machine gun fire. He sprinted across the junction and then dropped to the ground and began to crawl uphill through a field of ripening wheat toward the Mont Fleury battery. The tall grass provided superb cover. The smell of the damp earth, of the wheat, and the occasional murmur of insects were no doubt a welcome reprieve from the din of battle and the sting in the throat from cordite and smoke.

As Hollis neared the top of the rise, the commander of D Company, Major Ronnie Lofthouse, approached him and pointed out a pillbox. The pillbox was well camouflaged, but Hollis could just make out the Germans' gun barrels. He got up and rushed the pillbox, spraying it with bullets, "hosepipe fashion," with his Sten gun. The Germans returned fire but missed Hollis, who was quickly on top of the pillbox, dropping a grenade through a slit, hearing its flat explosion, then jumping down and breaking through a rear entrance. Inside, he found two dead Germans and more than a dozen dazed and bloodied men who quickly surrendered to him, desperate to live.

It turned out some of the Germans were from a nearby command post for the Green Howards' first and most critical target off the beach, the Mont Fleury gun battery, just over the brow of the rise, a couple of hundred yards ahead.[36] As fast as possible, Hollis and D Company had to reach and then eliminate the guns aimed at Gold Beach and at the ships bringing in the second wave of Green Howards, due to land at 8:20 A.M.

Hollis couldn't spare any men to escort the prisoners into captivity, so he simply gestured in the direction of the shoreline and the Germans moved off by themselves. Not long after, Hollis paused for a few moments and looked back, out to sea. The sight in particular of twenty British battleships, cruisers, and destroyers—"Force G"—filled him with new confidence, and he turned and began to lead his men forward once more, toward the Mont Fleury battery. Thankfully, a lone flail tank, one of "Hobart's Funnies," had cleared a path off the beach through mines and then inland toward the battery. Hollis followed its trail of stamped tracks in the crushed grass. Other flail tanks and armored bulldozers, which had landed with the first wave, had been blown up or had gotten stuck in thick mud.

At some point, a piece of shrapnel had nicked Hollis's face, and now blood trickled down his cheeks. Fire came from yet another machine gun, a vicious ripping. Now a man possessed, Hollis reloaded his Sten gun, clipping in a new magazine with thirty-two rounds, and was attacking yet again, getting the job done, avenging the humiliation of Dunkirk and all the French women and children he'd seen so senselessly slaughtered in the city of Lille that dark spring of 1940.

CHAPTER 8

———————————

La Belle France

IT WAS 7:30 A.M. when a message went out by radio—"Praise the Lord"—signaling that Lieutenant George Kerchner and his fellow Rangers had scaled the cliffs at Pointe du Hoc. Now they had to cross the churned earth and twenty-yard-wide shell holes to reach the battery's guns, the nearest of which were supposed to be around a hundred yards inland. Kerchner's staff sergeant, Len Lomell, sprinted ahead of others from D Company, "charging hard and low," hearing the crack of sniper rounds overhead and the rattle of "Hitler's buzzsaw"—the MG42 machine gun—as he led others toward the casemates. "Nothing stopped us," recalled Lomell. "We waited for a moment. Just a moment. If the fire lifted, we were out of that shell hole into the next one. We ran as fast as we could over to the gun positions, to the ones we were assigned to."[1]

Lieutenant Kerchner followed behind. "The faster you moved," he remembered, "the safer you felt."[2] A few dozen yards in from the cliff's edge, he saw a German gun emplacement to his right and a gray-uniformed soldier, and he told a Ranger beside him to take out the German. The Ranger missed, firing five times without success. Not wanting to lose time, Kerchner ordered men to advance to a nearby road while he had a go at the elusive German. He couldn't get a shot on target, either, and then the German replied with a 22-millimeter anti-aircraft gun. Its bullets could easily blow foot-wide holes in a Ranger, so Kerchner quickly ducked for cover and began crawling along a deep trench. There was an explosion from a shell landing nearby, and then a sniper fired on him as he approached men from E Company. Had they seen any men from his unit, D Company? They said some of his men were farther inland, and Kerchner set off to join them.

About a hundred yards away, two Rangers came across Number 3 casemate, one of six at Pointe du Hoc. It was a charred mass of twisted steel and smashed concrete.

"Man, the navy really did a job on them," said one man.

"Yeah, but something's wrong," replied a sergeant. "There's no gun here. Looks like the Krauts had a telephone pole sticking out to make it look like a gun. Wonder what they did with the gun?"[3]

A few minutes later, the sergeant found Kerchner and told him there were no guns in the casemates.

No guns? They'd gone through months of training . . . climbed those damned cliffs . . . Kerchner shrugged off the news and pushed on along the deep trench. His primary mission was over. Now to the next: setting up a roadblock on the Grandcamp–Vierville road, which ran from Pointe du Hoc to Omaha Beach, five miles to the east. The trench snaked and he couldn't see around each turn. Would a German be waiting around the next corner?

Pointe du Hoc was a fortress with scant protection along the cliffs. The Germans had not expected an assault on the battery from the sea and so had placed minefields and strongpoints along a perimeter inland. Before long, Kerchner was closing on the perimeter and then came across some of his men. One of them was "a real fine boy" who'd been raked across his chest by machine gun fire and was dying. Other wounded lay nearby. Before Kerchner could get help to them, the Germans counterattacked, jumping from hole to hole, letting rip with Schmeisser machine pistols.

A firefight raged, feverish volleys of bullets sweeping back and forth. The Rangers managed to hold off the Germans, then Kerchner moved farther inland, coming across two men from D Company: Sergeants Len Lomell and Jack Kuhn.[4] He ordered the pair to scout ahead while he and others set up the roadblock. They crept along the road and climbed through a thick hedgerow. "We came upon this draw with camouflage all over it," recalled Lomell, "and lo and behold, I peeked over this hedgerow and there were the guns, all sitting in proper firing condition, the ammunition piled up neatly, everything at the ready."[5]

The guns had been moved from their casemates to avoid damage during bombing and were now aimed at Omaha Beach.

"There's nobody here, let's take a chance," said Lomell, who was carrying several thermite grenades; a few seconds later he was using them to destroy traversing mechanisms, cranks, and hinges.

"Hurry up, Len," cried Kuhn after several minutes. "Get out of there."

Lomell and Kuhn headed back toward Kerchner and the others from D Company, who in the meantime had set up the roadblock. "We never looked back," Lomell remembered. "We didn't waste a second." The guns had been there after all. And now they were out of action. The original, critical mission for the Rangers had been accomplished. As one of Lomell's comrades from the 2nd Ranger Battalion later put it, "Had we not been there, we felt quite sure that those guns would have been put into operation and they would have brought much death and destruction down on our men on the beaches and our ships at sea."[6]

As Lomell and Kuhn crossed a hedgerow, there was a huge explosion and both were thrown through the air. Rocks, pieces of concrete, and ramrods fell all around. Dazed, they scrambled to their feet, smothered in dirt and dust, and then sprinted "like two scared rabbits" toward the roadblock D Company had set up. Was the sudden explosion from a shell fired from the USS *Texas*, offshore? Later they learned that a patrol from E Company had detonated a nearby ammunition store.[7]

Both men rejoined the remnants of D Company, under the command of Kerchner, who was delighted to hear that they'd taken out the guns: "This was the most fantastic thing that happened in the war as far as I was concerned," Kerchner later said.[8]

Meanwhile, Colonel Rudder was standing at the edge of a casemate talking to some of his men when he heard the zing of a ricochet. He dropped to the ground, hit clean through the leg by a sniper's bullet.[9] A few minutes later, the battalion surgeon,

Captain Walter Block, was sprinkling sulfa powder on the wound and bandaging the leg. Thankfully, the bullet had missed a major blood vessel and bone, and before long Rudder was back issuing orders. "The biggest thing that saved our day was seeing Colonel Rudder controlling the operation," recalled one officer decades later. "It still makes me cringe to recall the pain he must have endured trying to operate with a wound through the leg. He was the strength of the whole operation."[10]

A shell exploded, fired short by a British cruiser, and killed an officer and blew Rudder to the ground once more, wounding him in the upper left arm and chest. "The hit turned the men completely yellow," recalled a young lieutenant. "It was as though they had been stricken with jaundice. It wasn't only their faces and hands, but the skin beneath their clothes and the clothes which were yellow from the smoke of that shell—it was probably a colored marker shell."

Despite having incurred two more wounds, Rudder continued to issue orders. Not long after the marker shell had exploded, a sergeant arrived and told Rudder that the guns were out of action.

"Ike, come over here!" Rudder ordered his communications officer, a lieutenant called Eikner. "How's our commo working out?"

"Not too good, sir!" replied Eikner. "I've tried to contact the 5th Rangers and the 29th Infantry Division but can't raise anybody."

"Well, Ike, we've got to get this message out. You ready to copy?"

Eikner was ready.

"Send, 'Located Pointe du Hoc—mission accomplished— need ammunition and reinforcements—many casualties.' Get that out, Ike."

Eikner relayed the message, but there was no reply. He kept trying. Finally, the Rangers atop Pointe du Hoc received a curt message from 1st Division commander General Huebner.

"No reinforcements available—all Rangers have landed."[11]

THIRTY-FIVE MILES TO THE EAST of Pointe du Hoc lay the seaside resort of Ouistreham, at the far eastern end of Sword Beach. Holiday villas had been razed to the ground along the seafront and ugly concrete bunkers and other defenses put in their place. Where French families had once basked in the sun, now some two thousand Germans from Infantry Regiment 736 manned more than eighty positions, which had met with Rommel's approval just the week before. These positions were the target of Number 4 Commando, to which Léon Gautier and his fellow French commandos belonged.

It was past 7 A.M. and the clouds hung low and gray as the commandos approached an area known as La Brèche, around five hundred yards west of the outskirts of Ouistreham. Some of the Frenchmen had not seen the shores of their homeland since June 1940, when, like Léon Gautier, they had answered de Gaulle's call for patriots to join him in London to fight on after France's fall. They came from many walks of life, remembered a corporal, but all had "chosen to live among commandos and to

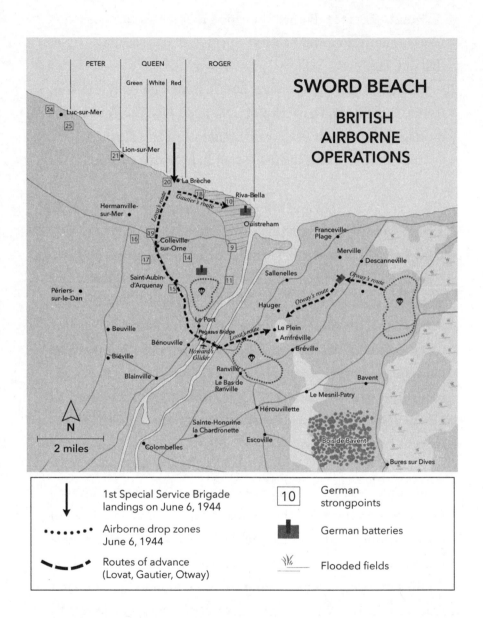

PETER   QUEEN   ROGER

Green | White | Red

SWORD BEACH

BRITISH
AIRBORNE
OPERATIONS

24 Luc-sur-Mer

25

Lion-sur-Mer
21

La Brèche
20
18   Riva-Bella
Gautier's route   10
Hermanville-
sur-Mer   Ouistreham
19
16   Franceville-
Colleville-   Plage
sur-Orne   Merville
17   14   Descanneville
Saint-Aubin-   11   Sallenelles
d'Arquenay 15
Périers-   Otway's route
sur-le-Dan   Hauger   Otway's route
Le Port
Beuville   Pegasus Bridge   Le Plein
Bénouville   Lovat's route   Amfréville
Bréville
Biéville   Howard's
Glider
Blainville   Ranville   Bavent
Le Bas de
Ranville
Le Mesnil-Patry
N   Hérouvillette

2 miles   Sainte-Honorine
la Chardronette   Bois de Bavent
Escoville
Colombelles
Bures sur Dives

↓   1st Special Service Brigade   10   German
     landings on June 6, 1944   strongpoints

•••••••   Airborne drop zones   German batteries
          June 6, 1944

- - -   Routes of advance   Flooded fields
         (Lovat, Gautier, Otway)

die if necessary and be buried with the words 'Unknown Allied Soldier' on their graves."[12]

Gautier looked across the rough seas at a landing craft, around fifty yards away, carrying some of his fellow French commandos. He could see the tall and burly figure of forty-five-year-old Commander Philippe Kieffer, mingling with his troops, giving them last words of encouragement. From farther out at sea, the battleships HMS *Warspite* and HMS *Ramillies* broke the silence with their 15-inch guns. The noise drowned out the engines on Gautier's LCI (Landing Craft Infantry) as he looked up and saw long trails of yellow smoke streaking across the sky, from the countless volleys of rockets being fired at the landing beaches. Then the boats carrying the French commandos were pushing ahead of those filled with their British comrades. Lieutenant Colonel Robert Dawson, the commander of Number 4 Commando, which included two French troops, had decided to allow de Gaulle's boys to go first.

"Messieurs les Français," Dawson had ordered, echoing a famous exhortation from the eighteenth century. "Tirez les premiers!"

Men of France—shoot first!

Gautier could hear machine gun fire. He looked ahead and from the smoke emerged the ragged coastline. France looked more beguiling than ever, despite the gunfire. Men beside him were choked with pride, some near to tears. "There was no fear," recalled Gautier. "We were just ready to do our job. When we first saw France appear out of the mist we were all emotional but very happy. One of the last things I recall was being given a tin of 'self-heating soup.' It was horrible. I threw it into the sea. I love most things English, but a Frenchman has to draw a line somewhere."[13]

Gautier adjusted his green beret one last time.[14]

On y va.

Here we go.

Just before landing, Gautier checked his grenades and the ammunition for his "precise and faithful" tommy gun. He saw that the photo in his pocket of his fiancée, Dorothy, had gotten wet. Not to worry. He'd fix it later.[15]

From his landing craft, Commander Philippe Kieffer could now see rows of beach defenses, Rommel's mined stakes, and, beyond on the beach itself, long rolls of barbed wire.[16] "We had arrived," recalled Kieffer. "A shock—a bump—we were aground. At this exact moment the sea bed seemed to rise in a rumble of thunder: mortars, the whistle of shells, staccato fire of machine guns—everything seemed concentrated towards us. Like lightning the ramps were thrown down."[17]

Léon Gautier's LCI, number 523, ground ashore and got stuck around a hundred yards from the sand. It was 7:30 A.M. and Gautier was standing beside his commanding officer, thirty-year-old Captain Alexandre Lofi. A somber-faced miner's son who had joined de Gaulle's Free French in 1940, Lofi led Troop 8 of Number 4 Commando. The English commandos had nicknamed him "Lucky Man," because he'd always come up trumps. Now Lofi would need all the *baraka*—good fortune—he could get.[18]

"Follow me everywhere," Lofi ordered Gautier. "I'm going to need you and your tommy gun."[19]

Just before he stepped off the craft, ready to wade or swim ashore, Gautier saw a shell make a direct hit on Commander Kieffer's craft, to his left, destroying its exit ramp and wounding several officers, including Kieffer.[20] Then Gautier was wading ashore, with his tommy gun above his head. Men fell close by, cut down by shrapnel from a 50-millimeter cannon firing from a concrete emplacement on the beach. Gautier knew the cannon to be a formidable weapon, capable of firing twenty shells per minute.

In the shallows, there were appalling scenes. British troops from the East Yorkshire Regiment who had preceded Gautier and his fellow Frenchmen by a few minutes were supposed to have cleared the way but were now mostly paralyzed by fear, dead, dying, or frantically trying to dig foxholes in the sand.

A commando neared a man on the ground.

"Get up, you idiot, keep going."[21]

The commando kicked the man and realized he was dead. So was a soldier beside him.

Gautier looked to his left and saw wounded men from Kieffer's craft. They were drowning amid debris, their cries muted by the water they had swallowed. He kept going, crouched low, headed toward a stretch of sand dunes. Beyond the dunes lay a holiday camp, the rallying point for Number 4 Commando's six hundred men.[22] From the left came rapid fire and more Frenchmen began to fall. A sergeant nicknamed Pepe died quietly, his stomach sliced open, guts spilling onto the sand.

Lieutenant Colonel Robert Dawson, although wounded in the leg, hobbled from one cluster of commandos to another, urging them on, bright red blood clotting in his blond hair.

"Go boys!"[23]

Gautier remembered the key order he had been given in training: "Do not stop for the wounded or dead."[24]

On Dawson's boys ran.

Gautier followed Captain Lofi, who now led Troop 8 toward some barbed wire at the edge of the beach.

Dawson's boys reached the barbed wire, which looked to one of them "like a crown of thorns covering the face of our crucified country." A sergeant called Thubé pulled out his wire cutters and snipped a gap, and his fellow commandos ran through and into a minefield at the edge of the dunes. Five minutes before, several flail tanks had worked their way through parts of the minefield before being destroyed by German fire, but thankfully they had at least cleared some mines. The others lay buried safely beneath inches of sand swept inland by a storm the previous day. The bad weather that had caused General Eisenhower to postpone the invasion had "without doubt also saved the day," recalled Gautier, for him and his fellow Number 4 commandos.[25]

Gautier followed Lofi into the relative sanctuary of the dunes, making certain to avoid moving in a straight line, to throw off German gunners. Finally, he and Lofi reached the ruins of the prewar holiday camp. They had gotten across Sword Beach and then reached their first objective on D-Day without getting hit. They were home at last.[26]

The assembly area was quickly full of commandos, giving the thumbs-up and smiling for a photographer as they sheltered in the lee of half-demolished brick walls, reloading, getting their heads straight for the attack into Ouistreham, dropping their heavy packs in piles so they would be able to move as fast as their legs could carry them. It would be close up and personal from now on, hand to hand, dagger to throat. The packs would be delivered to them later, once they'd kicked the Boche out of town, back to Berlin. "Things were unnaturally quiet," recalled one commando, "after the chaotic din of the beach, which had been almost numbing in its intensity; it seemed extraordinary that we should be able to speak in a normal tone of voice here."[27]

The commandos would now have to fight eastward for almost fifteen hundred deadly yards, past holiday villas with red-tiled roofs and neatly trimmed garden hedges, crouching as low as they could, then sprinting across road junctions and alongside high stone walls plastered with Nazi propaganda posters and painted with the name DUBONNET, a popular aperitif. They would head straight down the Rue Maréchal Joffre to a heavily defended blockhouse, the core of German resistance in Ouistreham, which had to be neutralized if operations in the Sword sector of the Allied landings were to succeed. It was a tough target indeed, surrounded by a maze of trenches and barbed wire and protected by anti-tank guns. The ugly concrete fortress had replaced a much-loved casino where some of Gautier's comrades had gambled before the war.

Gautier stayed close to Lofi as he led Troop 8 past abandoned machine gun emplacements.

"Watch out, Lieutenant," someone shouted.

There was the rip of a machine gun and a bullet holed Lofi's trousers without wounding him.

As Gautier and the rest of Troop 8 closed in on the block-house in Ouistreham, German mortars opened up and several men were hit. Gautier still stuck close to Lofi, firing his tommy gun, spraying bullets. His finger pressed the trigger, over and over, as he fired on German positions. Then there was an angry shout.

"Fire single shots. Don't waste bullets."[28]

Gautier realized he'd gone through several magazines. It was time to make each round count. A German sniper aimed at one of Gautier's comrades, Marcel Labas, and killed him as he moved along the Boulevard Maréchal Joffre. A hundred yards farther on, another shot rang out and a lieutenant called Hubert was hit in the head.

German resistance intensified, so Lofi ordered Gautier and others to take positions in the ground floors of the villas lining a road facing the blockhouse. Another group of French commandos, led by the wounded Kieffer, had made its way to the other side of the blockhouse, squeezing through a small gap in an anti-tank wall, and had also taken up positions in nearby holiday homes.

The German fire became increasingly accurate, directed by observers in a fifty-foot-high bunker some two hundred yards to the south, farther inland.

An 88-millimeter artillery piece opened up, leveling an entire house in one ground-shaking explosion.

Lofi had a feeling his position would be next.

"We've got to get out of this place right now," Lofi told Gautier and others.

He was right. Three minutes later, their position was utterly destroyed.

The French had no tanks or heavy weapons capable of destroying the 88-millimeter gun. Luckily, fifty-seven-year-old Marcel Lefevre, a World War I veteran with a neatly trimmed white mustache, braved the explosions and deadly rain of shrapnel and told a French officer that he belonged to the Resistance, wanted to fight, although he was unarmed, and added that he knew where to find and then cut communications wires leading from the main blockhouse to the 88-millimeter gun and other artillery.[29]

The wires were severed and the German fire became less accurate, but the blockhouse still had to be taken.[30] Then Commander Kieffer heard over a radio that British amphibious tanks had finally been spotted in the outskirts of Ouistreham, having cleared Sword Beach. He went in search of support and, to his men's delight, returned riding jauntily on a tank's turret, guiding it to the best position to fire on the blockhouse. Within thirty minutes, the blockhouse's guns had fallen silent.

Two French civilians approached Gautier, at first mistaking him for a British soldier because of his uniform. They were far from grateful. This was just another commando raid—a hit-and-run. What would happen once they'd gone? The Germans would be back with a vengeance. Anyone found to have helped the invaders would be shot.

"We're not leaving," said Gautier. "This time it's for good."[31]

Colonel Dawson appeared, still bleeding from a head wound and wrapped in a blanket. "Fantastic job!" said Dawson.[32] More tanks were on the way, he added.

On to the next objective. The commandos now had to link up with Major John Howard's airborne troops holding Pegasus

Bridge, six miles farther inland to the south. Gautier marched with his fellow Frenchmen back to the holiday camp where they had left their packs, marveling at the thousands of British troops now swarming across Sword Beach. Then he was heading south, walking through the village of Colleville, past gardens in full bloom.

The sun appeared from among the clouds, as if to welcome him home, and the straps on his pack bit into his shoulders as he came across bodies of British commandos who earlier had forged ahead. No one stopped to bury the dead, the contorted corpses stiffening with rigor mortis, with young faces turning a waxy yellow. Then Gautier, proudly wearing his green beret, followed his fellow commandos into the open countryside, crossing lush pasture and fields dotted with clumps of yellow cowslips and white primrose. As he headed toward Pegasus Bridge, he thanked God he was still alive. He knew he had been lucky, as the second Frenchman to put his feet on Sword Beach that morning, to survive. *Bonne chance.* Lucky indeed, unlike ten of his compatriots who had made the ultimate sacrifice.[33]

TEN MILES TO THE WEST, the first wave of Canadians from the Queen's Own Rifles were surging toward shore. Thirty-three-year-old Major Charles Dalton, a traveling tea salesman before the war, shouldered his tommy gun and issued last orders.[34] Tall and dark-haired, with a perfectly trimmed mustache and a high forehead, he was in command of the regiment's B Company, whose D-Day target was now just visible: the "Nan White" sector of Juno Beach, which had been assigned to the Canadian 3rd Division.[35]

Every now and again, Charles looked to his left and saw the landing craft of A Company, plowing against the waves toward land. Remarkably, A Company was led by his younger brother, twenty-nine-year-old Elliot, the same height but with thicker eyebrows, a wider face, and a much more carefree personality. Although more distant from his men, Charles was no less respected by them than Elliot, the more handsome of the pair, unmarried and with a reputation as something of a ladies' man. Among the entire invasion forces, they were the only brothers who were leading infantry companies that would land side by side in the first wave. They had arguably the most difficult task of all Canadian company commanders: They would assault the toughest sector of Juno, a mile-wide stretch facing the timber-and-red-brick seafront homes of the village of Bernières-sur-Mer.

The Daltons were an intensely competitive pair, whether on a tennis court in their youth or on a parade ground. "Charlie was the archetypal dashing young officer," remembered a corporal. "He really had a lot of style. He was elegant and acted the part of a fine officer. His brother was very down to earth. We would follow him to hell if we had to."[36] Neither had seen combat, even though they had been training in England since July 1941.[37] They had both wanted to command men in the first wave, even after General Bernard Montgomery visited their unit and predicted that it might suffer 80 percent casualties.

Elliot would lead his men ashore a couple of hundred yards to the east of his brother. They had tossed a coin to decide which company would go in on the right and which on the left. Their first and most important challenge was to secure key beach exits. If they failed, thousands of their countrymen, all volunteers, could be trapped and slaughtered just as they had been during the failed Dieppe raid, in August 1942—the last time a Canadian division had been sent into action in France.[38]

Earlier that morning, around 3:15 A.M., Charles had encountered Elliot on the deck of the heaving USS *Monrovia*. The brothers had stood silently at the rail, looking out into the forbidding darkness of the English Channel. Charles had reached into his mouth and pulled out an ill-fitting dental bridge, which he then threw overboard into the rough waters.

"The damn thing's killing me," he had told Elliot. "If I survive . . . I'll get a new one, maybe . . ."[39]

It had then been time to say good-bye. "I think my brother felt there should be a farewell scene," recalled Charles. "Something from *Hamlet*, maybe. Something appropriate."

Instead, the brothers had simply shaken hands.[40]

"Well, good luck," Charles had said. "I'll see you tonight."

"Fine, fair enough."

It was now five hours later, just past 8 A.M., and Bernières-sur-Mer loomed ahead.[41]

The first wave, comprising ten assault craft, was spread out over several hundred yards. Charles's A Company boats were to the right of Elliot's B Company craft, all moving hesitantly, it seemed, toward the seafront village. Which brother would be first to set foot in France and claim bragging rights?

Elliot stood at the bow of his landing craft. "I was personally convinced in my own mind that no one would ever kill me," he recalled. "My biggest fear on D-Day—I was terrified—was that I [would] not be able to lead my men properly."[42]

A shell exploded and a piece of shrapnel hit one of Elliot's men, gouging his cheek.

A crewman quickly patched the wounded man up.

"If that's the worst you get," said the crewman, "you'll be lucky."[43]

A few hundred yards to Elliot's right, Charles stared at the heavily defended beach fronting Bernières-sur-Mer. Three pill-boxes, around fifty yards apart, loomed in the distance, built into a seawall that ran along the seafront. Behind a large wood-framed house stood a small railway station. There was a park directly beside the house. It was bound to be heavily mined. On a clear day, Charles would have been able to see the 220-foot-tall steeple of a twelfth-century Romanesque church, L'Église Notre Dame, half a mile inland, but now the entire area was shrouded in smoke from bombing and naval fire.[44]

Charles thought about the last advice given by a medical officer just ten hours before: "Now look, fifty percent of you are going to be casualties. If you're hit, one of two things will happen. If you're dead, your problems will be over. If you're wounded, you're going to get better. So just lie there and keep quiet and wait for the medical people to catch up with us, but nobody else will stop to help you, because if they do the whole thing will stop."[45]

In his landing craft, younger brother Elliot moved toward the coxswain.

The coxswain was slumped down.

Elliot saw blood trailing from a bullet hole in his forehead. The man had not been steering—he'd been dead awhile.[46] Then Elliot heard his craft scraping against stones. It was 8:12 A.M. The first wave of Canadians had arrived at Juno Beach.

A sergeant major barked orders: "Move! Fast! Don't stop for anything. Go! Go! Go!"[47]

They were down the ramp, splashing through water onto hard sand, sprinting toward the seawall. "Every single one of us," recalled the sergeant major, "from Elliot Dalton, our commanding officer, who was the leader for his boat, and the other A Company boat leaders . . . was on the run and at top speed."[48]

From every direction came obscene noise as bullets and explosions ripped the air. As Elliot crossed the beach under intense fire, he looked to his right and saw a platoon being mown down by German fire from a pillbox that, he realized, had not been shown on reconnaissance maps. In all, twenty-eight men from his company quickly lay dead or badly wounded on the beach. They had, in the laconic words of an official after-action report, "caught a packet of trouble."[49] But more than a hundred others, including Elliot, were able to get to the first protection, the seawall that curved upward to a thick skirt of barbed wire.

Meanwhile, Elliot's brother Charles had arrived in a craft that ground ashore directly in front of a pillbox.[50] The ramp came down, splashing into the rough sea.

"Follow me!"[51] shouted Charles, who then stepped off the ramp into twelve feet of water, quickly disappearing as he was pulled down by the eighty-five-pound pack on his back and the

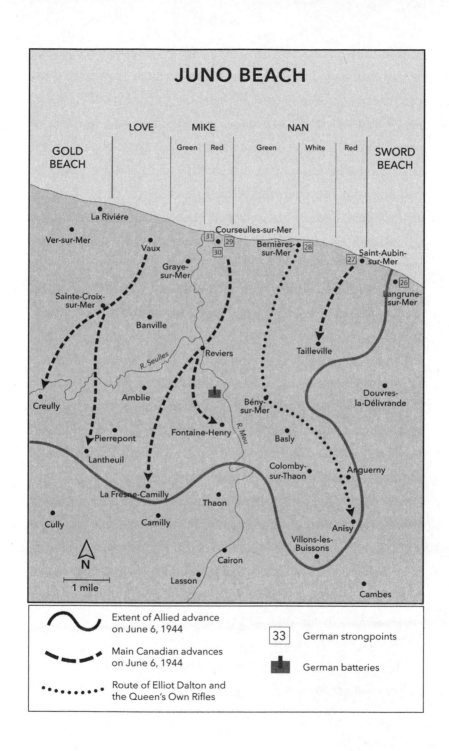

JUNO BEACH

LOVE   MIKE   NAN

GOLD
BEACH

Green | Red   Green | White | Red

SWORD
BEACH

La Riviére

Ver-sur-Mer

Vaux

Courseulles-sur-Mer

31

29

Bernières-
sur-Mer

28

Saint-Aubin-
sur-Mer

27

Graye-
sur-Mer

30

Sainte-Croix-
sur-Mer

26

Langrune-
sur-Mer

Banville

R. Seulles

Reviers

Tailleville

Douvres-
la-Délivrande

Amblie

Creully

Bény-
sur-Mer

R. Meu

Pierrepont

Fontaine-Henry

Basly

Lantheuil

La Fresne-Camilly

Thaon

Colomby-
sur-Thaon

Anguerny

Cully

Camilly

Villons-les-
Buissons

Anisy

Cairon

Lasson

Cambes

N

1 mile

Extent of Allied advance
on June 6, 1944

33   German strongpoints

Main Canadian advances
on June 6, 1944

German batteries

Route of Elliot Dalton and
the Queen's Own Rifles

ammunition strapped to him. Thankfully, he was wearing a life vest and managed to get his head above water, then waded toward the beach. A man close by was hit four times, bullets gouging his stomach and chest. It was easy to drown if wounded, or even if a man with heavy equipment on his back merely stumbled. Then Charles spotted others who had been cut down by machine gun fire from the pillbox dead center of his landing sector. Every man to his right had been killed.[52] Miraculously, he had been just out of range, by a few feet, of the machine gun's traverse.

One of his men emerged from the blood-tinged shallows and ran toward the seawall. Bullets ripped through his pack, shredding it.

"That was close."

"Yes, there goes your lunch," said a man nearby.

The next volley of bullets did not miss, and the man with the pack slumped down, dead. His fellow rifleman tried to take off his wristwatch and ID bracelet, mementos for his widow, but he had to pull back when more bullets came his way.[53]

Charles kept moving across the beach. He glanced back and was shocked to see that nobody in B Company was following him. Then he checked to the left and right: There was no sign of Elliot or his company, either. All he could see was a few soaked men, lying wounded at the water's edge, shaking with terror, being picked off by German snipers.[54]

They've gone to ground.

He felt he had failed.

They didn't follow me.

Charles reached the seawall near the pillbox and pulled out a grenade. It wasn't powerful enough to blow the door off the pillbox, so he opened fire with his Sten gun instead, but his bullets ricocheted off protective shields with a pathetic clatter. He spotted a ladder, placed it against the pillbox, climbed up, and fired into a slit. Finally, the machine guns inside fell silent. But then a German officer appeared and aimed his 9-millimeter revolver, and a bullet pierced Charles's helmet and he slid, badly wounded, stunned, down the ladder.

A medic was nearby and quickly reached Charles.[55]

"Sir, I thought you knew better than to do that," said the medic, "sticking your head over the top of that wall."[56]

"I wasn't trying to be smart," groaned Charles, "just trying to find some way to stop these people from firing . . ."[57]

The bullet had glanced off his skull, leaving a bloody furrow. As the medic wrapped his head in a bandage, Charles saw some of his men running toward him.

"Get up to the wall," he shouted as blood trickled down his face.[58]

Around three hundred yards to Charles's left, out of view, Elliot Dalton led his men over the seawall and onto a railroad track. Bullets snapped overhead and he called to his men, ordering them to follow him, and then he was up and running again, heading to a row of brick-faced houses, one of which held a machine gun nest. He kicked in a door, tossed a grenade, spattered a room with bullets, then moved on to the next room, reloading, and on to another house, a headquarters of some kind. "We'd been told it was a communications center for the whole sector of the beach," he recalled. "I'd lost track of most of my men but decided to attack it anyway, just a Bren gunner, my batman and myself. The Bren gunner starts to fire at the windows and my batman and I begin to crawl up the long garden on our bellies. Halfway there this big gold ball starts to come out of a cellar window. It was a flagpole with an enormous French flag on it. I stopped the Bren gunner firing and these fifty poor French people came out of the cellar with their hands up. They were all elderly and scared to death. There were no Germans in there at all."[59]

Elliot headed to a rendezvous point at the southwest of Bernières-sur-Mer. It was around 8:30 A.M. Hopefully, his brother would be among the survivors gathered there before they pressed inland to the regiment's next objectives.[60]

Meanwhile, Charles had been able to get to his feet and was trying to catch up with the men from his company. A medical officer spotted the bloody bandage on Charles's head and insisted on applying fresh dressings.

"You'll be back in England by tonight," said the officer.[61]

On the beach, not far away, a chaplain walked from one severely wounded man to another, giving last rites. "The noise was deafening," he remembered. "You couldn't even hear our huge tanks that had already landed and were crunching their way through the sand; some men, unable to hear them, were run over and crushed to death."[62]

Each young Canadian had the letters CANADA below QUEEN'S OWN RIFLES on his upper sleeve.

The chaplain knelt beside each dying man.

"And thus do I commend thee into the arms of our Lord of earth . . ."

Among the men led by the Dalton brothers, more than a hundred lay dead or wounded, the highest loss of any Canadian unit on D-Day.[63]

"Our Lord Jesus Christ, preserver of all mercy and reality, and the father creator . . ."

Lord Lovat saw some of his commandos aboard LCI 516 take a tot of rum. He'd forbidden officers from doing so, wanting them utterly clearheaded. But the lads needed something other than the dodgy breakfast of sardines and cocoa in their stomachs to settle their nerves. Then Lovat saw several burning craft, adrift and spewing oily clouds of smoke, sad casualties of the first wave. One badly damaged boat was returning slowly from Sword Beach, which looked, from Lovat's perspective, like a narrow strip of dark sand separating the heavy skies from the sea. "The helmsman had a bandage round his head and there were dead men on board," remembered Lovat, "but he gave us the V sign and shouted something as the unwieldy craft went by. Spouts of water splashed a pattern of falling shells."[64]

Lovat's craft picked up speed, heading for a gap among hundreds of offshore obstacles, mostly long poles with Teller mines attached. Now more buildings, their roofs holed by shellfire, and other landmarks, etched in men's minds after months of planning and training, were clearly visible. Lovat was in the right place and on time—approaching Queen Red sector, at the center of the five-mile-long Sword Beach.[65]

The officer responsible for finding a route through the defenses was a New Zealander, Lieutenant Commander Denis Glover, described by a friend as "a surprising compound of poet, craftsman, wit and devil-may-care roisterer."[66] Thirty-one-year-old Glover had ordered that Mozart be played loud on a gramophone, and now, to the rousing chords of the Austrian genius and with consummate skill "running on a timetable towards terror," he guided his hundred-foot-long LCI, carrying fifty of Lovat's commandos, through gaps in the first belt of offshore obstacles.[67] He appeared calm and collected as his passengers heard the deep rumble of enemy artillery and watched shells explode among wrecked landing craft on Sword Beach.

Within shouting distance of Glover, in LCI 519, Lord Lovat stood beside Bill Millin, who was gripping his pipes in anticipation, wearing a kilt and no underwear, his testicles exposed to the chill morning air.[68] It was 8:40 A.M. as they closed on Queen Red sector, an eight-hundred-yard-wide stretch of sand, in spots littered with the corpses of men from the East Yorkshire Regiment, who had been cut down as they bunched in panic. The tide crept in behind them.[69] Grievously wounded men screamed above the crash of the surf and the whine of artillery and the hacking of machine gun bullets. Others wore life jackets and clung desperately to beach obstacles as the still helmeted bodies of their mates bobbed against one another in the shallows.

Lieutenant Commander Rupert Curtis, in charge of Lovat's

LCI, spotted a large building at the eastern end of Queen Red sector of Sword Beach. He now knew he was in exactly the right place.[70]

"I am going in," Curtis told Lovat.

Time slowed—the "smallest detail seemed to assume microscopic clarity," Curtis recalled. Bullets and shrapnel gouged the sands ahead. The engines growled as he applied more power and then the craft entered shallow water. "At that moment," remembered Curtis, "we were hit by armor-piercing shells, which zipped through [a] gun-shield but fortunately missed both gunners."[71] Thankfully, the Germans were not using high-explosive rounds. Had they done so, Curtis later recalled, "many of us would have blown up on the beach, for we carried four thousand gallons of high-octane petrol in non-sealing tanks."[72]

The landing craft was in three or four feet of water.

Sand scraped against the bottom.

"Stand by with the ramps!"

Four sailors moved to lower the exits.

Oiled chains clattered.

"Lower away there."[73]

Bill Millin looked utterly miserable—he had been violently seasick for several hours—as he clutched his bagpipes. Lovat clambered down a ramp and leapt into the water. Millin, shorter than the six-foot Lovat, waited a second or so to see how deep the water was before he followed. A man on a ramp tumbled into the water, shot dead, and Millin decided not to hang about a moment longer, jumping into the surf. Immediately, his kilt rose to the surface and he felt the shock of cold water. But this made his seasickness vanish and, although men were dying all around him, he was aware only of finally having his feet on terra firma and of feeling immensely relieved to be off the heaving landing craft.

Millin followed the slender figure of Lovat, wading ahead of him, trailing a line of commandos snaking toward one of several tanks that had already been landed, some of them equipped with strands of metal flails for destroying mines. Amid the smoke a hundred yards ahead loomed a large three-story building, a key landmark that looked as if it had barely been touched by shelling.

Millin, remembering his orders, inhaled, pursed his lips, and blew into the tartan bag of his pipes as he, too, headed for the bullet-whipped sands.

Even amid the hue and cry of war, Lovat heard the unmistakable skirl of "Hieland Laddie" and turned toward Millin to show his approval.[74]

The cold water now numbed Millin's testicles and lifted his red-squared kilt around his waist like a ballerina's tutu.[75] He finished playing "Hieland Laddie," giving every man's heart a lift.[76]

Lovat was only a couple of yards ahead of Millin when he heard him start on another tune. "The water was knee-deep when Piper Millin struck up 'Blue Bonnets,'" he recalled, "keeping the pipes going as he played the commandos up the beach. It was not a place to hang about in, and we stood not on the order of our going. That eruption of twelve hundred men covered the sand in record time . . . As we ran up the slope, tearing the waterproof bandages off weapons, the odd man fell, but swift reactions saved casualties."[77]

Lovat suddenly noticed, amid the noise and chaos, that Millin had stopped playing his pipes.

"Would you mind giving us a tune?" asked Lovat.[78]

"Well, what tune would you like, sir?"

"How about 'The Road to the Isles'?"

"Would you want me to walk up and down, sir?"

"Yes. That would be nice. Yes, walk up and down."

It seemed a "ridiculous" idea to Millin. They were now under intense shellfire. Standing around playing the bagpipes was sheer bloody madness.

Lovat was being ridiculous, but he was not a man to be crossed.

I might as well be ridiculous as well.

The beach was "cluttered with tanks and armored vehicles," remembered one man, "and it was not exactly a health resort, for it was swept by intermittent volleys of mortar bombs, machine gun and sniper fire."[79] Already lying dead on the beach were more than two hundred men from the East Yorkshire Regiment, which had been tasked with clearing the way for the first wave of commandos.[80] Millin saw some "lying face down in the water going back and forwards with the surf. Others to my left were trying to dig in just off the beach. Yet when they heard the pipes, some of them stopped what they were doing and waved their arms, cheering."[81]

Some were not amused.

Millin felt someone's hand on his shoulder.

"Listen, boy."[82]

Millin recognized a sergeant.

"What are you fucking playing at? You mad bastard! You're

attracting all the German attention. Every German in France knows we're here now, you silly bastard."[83]

The sands trembled from yet more mortar explosions as Millin walked back and forth along the beach three times, and then caught up with Lovat. Men were running, bent down, then flinging themselves to the ground behind the nearest cover, a pillbox just beyond the beach that had been taken single-handedly by one of Lovat's best young men, a skinny lad known as "Muscles" who Lovat believed should have received the highest award for his courage that morning.

Captain Max Harper Gow scrambled behind Lovat. "We crouched beneath the eighty-pound Bergen rucksacks and, we hoped, beneath the flak the enemy were hurling at us," recalled Gow. "When we reached the sand-dunes at the top of the beach I looked up and saw Lovat standing, completely at ease, taking in the scene around him."[84]

Nearby, a Jewish commando named Peter Masters, who had escaped Nazi Austria and was serving in the British Army, was interrogating two POWs.

"Oh, you are the chap with the languages," said Lovat. "Ask them where their mortars and their howitzers are."

Masters, who was born with the name Arany but had it changed in case of capture, duly did so. There was no reply from either prisoner, and other commandos began to gather around.[85]

"Look at that arrogant German bastard," someone said. "He doesn't even talk to our man when he's asking questions."[86]

Masters realized that the prisoners were not German; they were Russian and Polish. Remembering that many Poles learnt

French at school, he switched languages. One of the prisoners began to talk.

Lovat stood a few yards away, listening carefully. He spoke far better French than Masters and quickly took over the interrogation. Then he "turned on his heel," remembered an officer, and "led Brigade HQ inland towards Pegasus Bridge and, as it happened, slap through a wired-off area, clearly marked minefields. We followed literally in his footsteps."[87] There was no time, as Lovat put it, to "play grandmother's footsteps." He and his men moved fast, blowing paths with Bangalore torpedoes through the areas surrounded by wire and marked with signs showing a skull and crossbones and the words ACHTUNG MINEN![88]

Lovat came across one of his officers lying against a pack, shot in the heart.

"He's dead, sir," cried a man near Lovat, tears running down his cheeks. "He's dead. Don't you understand? A bloody fine officer."

Medics tended to the wounded, including a redheaded man who had been shot in the legs and carried off the beach by a burly Scotsman.

"To think they could miss a big bugger like you," said the redhead, "those fucking Germans . . ."[89]

Lovat sprinted across a road and then a railway line. Smoke lifted. Open country lay beyond. He was three hundred yards inland. He had breached Hitler's famed Atlantic Wall, the series of concrete bunkers, pillboxes, coastal batteries, and other defenses stretching all the way from Norway to Spain. After the uproar and numbing clatter of the beach, the open fields seemed an oasis of silence. Men felt the difference intensely, as if going from hot water to ice cold.

An officer nearby looked at his watch.

"That round lasted eleven minutes."

Lovat paused as an aid post was set up, and then several wounded men arrived. He was called to a radio. One of his finest officers, Lieutenant Colonel Derek Mills-Roberts, leading Number 6 Commando, had good news.

"Sunray calling Sunshine. First task accomplished. Report minor casualties. Now on start line regrouping for second bound. Moving left up fairway on Plan A for Apple. Still on time. Do you read me? Over."[90]

Lovat read him loud and clear.

There was less pleasing news, too. Lovat now learned that Colonel Dawson, leading Léon Gautier's Number 4 Commando, had been wounded in the leg and head.[91] Commander Kieffer had also been hit badly in his left thigh by a mortar fragment but was struggling on.[92]

Lovat checked the time. He knew that Major John Howard's men had successfully seized the Orne bridges, which were intact. The challenge now was to reach Howard, some six miles away, as soon as possible.[93] If he didn't make it, Howard and his men would be done for.

IT WAS AROUND 9 A.M. when the remnants of Lieutenant Colonel Terence Otway's unit, having left the rendezvous at the calvary cross, moved into the outskirts of a village called Le Plein, on the northern end of a ridge that overlooked the Orne River.

Otway was following behind several scouts when one of them spotted two French prostitutes sauntering down the road toward them. "I should imagine they'd been up to the German barracks and were on their way home," recalled one of Otway's men. "They'd got painted legs, short skirts. Frightened me more than the Germans!"

A corporal told the women to run to safety.

"Arse off, get out of the way."

The women moved off, laughing. A vast army of new clients, armed with condoms, had just arrived.

The scouts carried on.

Two Germans riding bicycles appeared around a corner.

The scouts stared in disbelief.

"Well shoot the bastards then!" someone cried.

A man opened fire, killing one German and hitting the other in the shoulder.

"Hier, Doktor," cried the wounded German, "hier, Doktor."[94]

Otway advanced once more, moving farther into Le Plein.

A Frenchman wearing a distinctive blue suit walked over to Otway and greeted him.

"A very good morning."

The Frenchman asked if Otway would like to stop by his home for a coffee when the fighting was over. Before Otway could respond, Germans nearby opened fire. The Frenchman stood with "not a care in the world," smoking a pipe, looking down at Otway as he took cover in a ditch.[95]

The firefight ended and Otway sent a patrol ahead to probe the German defenses in Le Plein, but the patrol was forced to retreat and its leader was killed—clearly the Germans held the village in force. With the remnants of his battalion, Otway decided to head instead to the elegant Château d'Amfreville, less than a mile away, where he planned to set up a temporary base and wait to be relieved by Lord Lovat and his men of the 1st Special Service Brigade.[96]

How long would Lovat's commandos take to reach him? An hour or several? Otway knew he would be in serious trouble if the Germans managed to deploy an armored force anytime soon. Yet such a counterattack was inevitable. Whoever controlled a ridge east of the Orne would decide the opening chapter of the Battle of Normandy in the British sector. At all costs, the Germans must be prevented from setting up artillery and moving panzers into the woods running along the high ground. If they did so, they would be able to destroy the entire eastern flank of the Allied invasion.

As OTWAY and his men made their way toward Amfreville, the leader of the Third Reich was finally awoken at the Berghof, Adolf Hitler's home in the Bavarian Alps. Despite the flood of news from the Normandy front throughout the night, none of his flunkies had dared wake the Führer, knowing he would be furious if he slept less than five hours; he had gone to bed at 4 A.M. with his mistress, Eva Braun, as was often his habit. But finally General der Artillerie Alfred Jodl decided enough was enough. Hitler had to be informed of the invasion.

Before long, the Führer was standing in his dressing gown, being briefed about the invasion. He appeared to be delighted, relieved that the waiting for the inevitable Allied assault was finally over.

"The news couldn't be better," Hitler exclaimed. "As long as they were in Britain we couldn't get at them. Now we have them where we can get at them!"

Hitler did not believe, however, that the landings in Normandy were anything but a diversion. "This is not the real invasion yet," he insisted.[97] The major assault was still to come, at the Pas-de-Calais, where the English Channel was at its narrowest and where there were key ports, such as Calais and Boulogne.

Luckily for the Allies, the general entrusted with repelling the invasion in Normandy, Field Marshal Erwin Rommel, was now nowhere near the landing beaches but instead hundreds of miles away, dressed in a red-striped dressing gown, at his home in Herrlingen, having decided to visit his wife to celebrate her fiftieth birthday. Not long after Hitler learned of the invasion, Rommel, too, was informed.

"How stupid of me."

If only he had stayed in Normandy. He would not have hesitated, as others had, to deploy all the forces that could be mustered. The one division that could have quickly inflicted serious damage, easily mopping up Otway's meager force and stopping Lord Lovat in his tracks, was the 21st Panzer Division, based around Caen. It had finally been released, but far too late. It would be midafternoon before the division moved in strength against British forces north of Caen, losing seventy out of 124 tanks but nonetheless preventing the seizure of the city, a vital Allied objective on D-Day.[98]

Dressed in a dark leather coat, Rommel was soon racing back to Normandy in a black Horch.

"Do you know," he told an aide, "if I was commander of the Allied forces right now, I could finish off the war in fourteen days."[99]

CHAPTER 9

All the Blue Bonnets

Lieutenant John Spalding hunched down amid the brush at the top of a bluff above the Easy Red sector of Omaha Beach. He was the first officer to lead men off Omaha, an extraordinary achievement, without doubt one of the most heroic and notable of D-Day, given how deadly the sands below had proved for so many of his fellow Americans. In the distance, tiny figures from later waves of troops struggled ashore, wading in ragged lines through the bullet-whipped surf. Abandoned equipment, corpses, and weapons cluttered the waterline. Some men clustered around burning tanks and landing craft as others clung in terror to beach obstacles.

Spalding got back to business, leading his men once more along the top of the 120-foot-high bluffs toward the E-1 draw, a few hundred yards away, the vital exit at the western end of Easy Red sector. Not for first time, Sergeant Streczyk volunteered to scout ahead. Spalding wasn't about to stop him. Streczyk had more than lived up to his formidable reputation. He'd stepped forward first, inspiring others to fight and follow ever since they'd gotten across the beach. "We crossed through two mine-fields," recalled Spalding. "One had a path through it, which looked like it had been made for a long time. When we got through it we saw the Achtung Minen sign. No one was lost."[1]

It was around 9:50 A.M. Out at sea, the chaos and carnage on the beach was clear to any man with binoculars. Rear Admiral Carleton F. Bryant, commander of the Omaha bombardment force, sent an urgent message to the captains of his destroyers: "Get on them, men, get on them. We must knock out those guns. They are raising hell with the men on the beach, and we can't have any more of that. We must stop it."[2] Twelve destroyers duly responded, some scraping the seabed as the ships edged closer to the shore in search of targets of opportunity.

All along Omaha Beach, men were trapped below the bluffs, being methodically picked off by German snipers and machine gunners, their bodies jolting with the impact of bullets and shrapnel. It was all so one-sided. The enemy couldn't be seen, and few men returned fire, not knowing what to shoot at or not wanting to expose themselves. In any case, many men's rifles were jammed by sand and salt water. The wounded, if they could find the strength, scrambled to stay ahead of the flood tide, only to be shot by snipers. Young Americans, too badly hit to crawl, held out their arms to their traumatized comrades, just feet away but out of the field of fire, and screamed and begged them to reach over and pull them to safety.

Parts of the beach, those nearest to the heavily defended ex-its, resembled a slaughterhouse. There were simply too many wounded for medics to cope with. And still, mercilessly, the Germans kept up the massacre, carrying out Rommel's orders that the invaders be defeated, at all costs, on the beach, before they could press inland. "These goddam Boche just won't stop fighting," complained General Huebner, commander of the Big Red One.[3] Another message was brutally succinct: "We are being butchered like a bunch of hogs."[4]

Aboard the USS *Augusta*, a gravely worried General Omar Bradley was seated at a plotting table, wearing spectacles and a helmet, asking aides what the hell was happening on the beach and wondering what he should do next.[5] The operation had largely been his plan, and now it appeared to be a bloody disaster. His failure, above all, to destroy defenses had cost so many hundreds of men their lives. He had almost no information from officers on the beach—so many radios had been lost and so many men carrying them killed. But from observers aboard boats closer to shore, he understood that there had been "an irreversible catastrophe." The situation seemed hopeless. Should he order an evacuation?[6]

Should more waves of men be needlessly sacrificed? If Omaha remained in German hands, there would be a thirty-mile gap between British and American forces that Rommel, a master of swift counterattack, would ruthlessly exploit. The success of the entire invasion now appeared to be at stake. Omaha had to be secured, but to do so, hundreds of ever more desperate junior officers would need to follow Lieutenant Spalding's example and get their units off the damned beach.

The first two waves from the 1st Division had suffered great casualties, but at least they had enjoyed an element of surprise when landing. Subsequent waves had walked into the sights of hot-barreled machine guns. "It was very tragic," recalled E Company commander Edward Wozenski, pinned down on Easy Red. "It was real sad to see the number of bodies that were in the water. Wave action will normally distribute logs or bodies or anything else head to toe along any given length of beach. But there were so many bodies that I saw a number of areas where they were two and three deep, just rolling in the waves."[7]

Frontal assaults on the heavily defended draws would not work. At the E-1 draw and other exits, they had led only to slaughter and defeat. The least fatal routes off Omaha were via the bluffs farthest from German strongpoints. But to get up the bluffs would require extraordinary courage and leadership: officers like Spalding who could make petrified men stand up and follow them into the line of fire.

So many young Americans were now jumbled in traumatized clusters, for the most part leaderless. Where Lieutenant Spalding was supposed to have landed, near the E-1 draw, men lay like a "human carpet" on a pebbly rise, not daring to lift their heads above the large stones.[8] One German machine gunner, hidden in a nest overlooking the draw, would later claim to have fired twelve thousand rounds. "The number of dead was appalling," recalled a medic with the 16th Infantry Regiment who had landed near the draw in the third wave. "The water was pink, and there were many bodies floating face down as well as body parts."[9] It seemed that men were literally drowning in their own blood.[10]

"Medic! Medic!"[11]

A corporal from the 16th Infantry Regiment was among those pinned down near the entrance to the E-1 draw. He heard a scorching *whoosh*—a sergeant had blown a gap in thick wire, opening a way for him and others to get away from the beach.

The corporal yelled with relief.

An officer nearby screamed at the corporal, but he could barely hear him, so loud was the noise of the battle.

The officer yelled again.

"Go back to Colonel Taylor."

Taylor commanded the 1st Division's 16th Infantry Regiment.

"Where's the command post?"

"It's supposed to be on our left!" the officer barked. "Find the colonel . . . Now!"

The corporal sprinted across the beach, searching for Colonel Taylor. "Scurrying like a mad rabbit, I jumped over all the corpses," he remembered. "I stumbled once on somebody's leg and fell onto a dead dogface. Getting up, I careened into the surf, but the bodies blocked me. Swerving from the water to the sand and back again, I ran until I thought my heart would burst."

The corporal spotted Taylor, crouched behind a seawall with another officer. He dropped down beside Taylor.

There was a way through.

The corporal stared in disbelief as Taylor calmly got to his feet and stood straight up.

He was crazy, surely?

Other men saw Taylor standing upright, seemingly oblivious to enemy fire.

"There are two kinds of men out here!" Taylor shouted. "The dead! And those who are about to die! So let's get the hell off this beach and at least die inland!"[12]

Taylor paced the immediate area, cursing, exhorting, kicking, ordering men to get off their backsides and get off the goddamn beach, transforming a "bewildered mob," as one report put it, "into a coordinated fighting force."[13]

"It's better to be shot to death than drown like rats on the beach!"[14]

Men did as they were ordered, some pushing in single file up the narrow, winding path that Spalding's unit had used, and which Sergeant Streczyk had first scouted, scanning the scuffed ground warily for any sign of mines. Still more men followed, and before long, according to an official after-action report, "the entire [force landed on Easy Red] was attempting to clear inland by [Spalding's] route despite the fact that it was being swept by machine gun, artillery, mortar, and anti-tank fire."[15] No junior officer or platoon had done more to change the outcome of the battle on Omaha than Spalding and his men. Against the longest odds, in the worst imaginable circumstances, their courage and initiative had made a critical difference when it mattered most.

As soldiers escaped the charnel house of Omaha via the route that he and his platoon had first opened, Spalding was peering into a half-built pillbox above the E-1 draw.[16] Inside were radios and what Spalding remembered as "excellent sleeping facilities." Spalding moved on to another pillbox, close by. One of his men approached a ventilator, grenade in hand.

"Hold on a minute," said Sergeant Streczyk, who fired three

times down the concrete steps that led into the pillbox and then cried out in both Polish and German for the men inside to get out. Four men emerged, carrying two wounded comrades with them. Again the rip and snarl of an MG42. This time the bullets came zipping from the right, farther west.[17] Two of Spalding's men scouted ahead, determined to take out the machine gun. Then the earth shook and the sky erupted with noise. Express trains seemed to be barreling overhead. Destroyers had moved closer to shore, and their fire was now being directed from the beach by forward observers. The results were devastating as 5-inch shells from one destroyer, the USS *Doyle*,[18] a thousand yards off Omaha, exploded in the nearby E-1 draw and amid its defenses.[19]

Around 10 A.M., the naval fire abated. Spalding and his men began mopping up the last German positions at WN65, overlooking the eastern slopes of the E-1 draw. "We had a short fight with thirteen men," he recalled. "They threw three grenades at us, but they didn't hit anyone. We found one dead man . . . but don't know if we killed him. If we did, he was the only German we killed. [Then] I did a fool thing. After losing my carbine in the water I had picked up a German rifle, but found I didn't know how to use it too well. When I started to check on the trenches I traded the German rifle to a soldier for a carbine and failed to check it. In a minute I ran into a Kraut and pulled the trigger, but the safety was on. I reached for the safety catch and hit the clip release, so my clip hit the ground. I ran about 50 yards in nothing flat . . . That business of not checking guns is certainly not habit forming."[20]

Meanwhile, one of Spalding's men, nicknamed "Dig," was

clearing out a pillbox with a flamethrower, sending jets of scorching gasoline inside. After thirty seconds, the flamethrower's tank was empty and some Germans, their uniforms on fire, scurried out with their hands in the air.

Again the sky seemed to be torn asunder as naval fire hit what was left of German defenses around the E-1 draw. Spalding and his men took cover as shells screeched overhead. The concussive effect of the shells was powerful enough to uproot trees and could leave men stripped of their uniforms, totally naked. Before long, Spalding and his men were "getting pretty jittery," in Spalding's words, so he ordered one of his men to let off a yellow smoke grenade, the last he had, so the *Doyle* would direct its fire away from them.[21]

It was around 10:45 A.M. when the burly Captain Wozenski, Spalding's company commander, approached him from the east, having followed in his footsteps up the bluffs.[22] Spalding was delighted to see Wozenski, who told him he should head next to the nearest village, Colleville-sur-Mer. It had been a tough morning for the company. Three of Spalding's fellow platoon leaders had been killed on the beach.[23] The landing had been a bloodbath, but now, finally, hundreds of men from the regiment were attacking inland.

All along the six-mile-long crescent of Omaha, young leaders like Spalding also had men on the move, seizing strongpoints and exits from the rear and flanks, pulling victory from the jaws of defeat.[24] "The battle belonged that morning," General Bradley would write, "to the thin, wet line of khaki that dragged itself ashore on the Channel coast of France."[25]

———

ON UTAH BEACH, where less than two hundred men had fallen—ten times fewer than on Omaha—every exit from the beach had been secured by midmorning and thousands of Americans from the Ivy Division were landing in successive waves, weaving with ease between the few landing craft and vehicles that had been hit, greasy smoke hanging over them. Senior officers were both surprised and relieved that the operation had been so successful. The lack of steep bluffs and the intense and accurate bombing of beach defenses had made all the difference.

By 10:30 A.M., Captain Leonard Schroeder, leading F Company, had moved off Utah Beach and seized a group of farm buildings labeled LA GRANDE DUNE on his map, seven hundred yards from where he had landed, encountering occasional sniper fire. Farther inland, a group of Germans surrendered to Schroeder and his men. "They were armed to the hilt," recalled Schroeder, "so I pulled out my trench knife and proceeded to cut all their web equipment from their bodies. One German soldier hit the panic button and ran toward the beach. I suppose half of the company put bullets into him, thinking he was trying to get away."[26]

Meanwhile, one of Schroeder's fellow officers, twenty-six-year-old Lieutenant Colonel George Mabry, led the battalion's advance. As he neared a bridge rigged with demolition charges, gunfire rang out, and Mabry spotted around a dozen German paratroopers running toward him. He and his men opened fire, hitting several of the enemy soldiers as they neared the bridge. As it turned out, the Germans had been fleeing the 501st Parachute Infantry Regiment of the 101st Airborne, and now, realizing they were trapped between two American forces, they quickly surrendered. Mabry pulled out an orange flag—to avoid incidents of friendly fire, the army had provided the flags to be waved if a unit's identity was in doubt. Mabry lifted the orange flag, attached to a stick, over his head. An orange flag appeared in response. Then a 101st Airborne paratrooper jumped into his path, pointing his M1 rifle at Mabry.[27]

Realizing they were on the same side, the pair shook hands. The paratrooper told Mabry that General Maxwell Taylor, the commander of the 101st Airborne, was not far away. A few minutes later, forty-two-year-old Taylor, the first Allied general officer to land in France on D-Day, crawled out of a hedgerow. Mabry saluted and shook hands with Taylor, a tall, ramrod-straight West Point graduate fluent in several languages.[28] It was a momentous encounter, "an historic moment," according to Taylor, "the long-planned junction of the air and seaborne assaults on Hitler's fortress Europe."[29]

Captain Leonard Schroeder and F Company pushed on, through minefields and orchards, alert for the assassin's stab of a sniper and for booby traps at gates. German resistance stiffened more the further they probed. There was the sudden stutter of a machine gun and Schroeder was hit in the arm by two bullets. He was so excited, so focused, that he felt no pain, even as blood soaked the sleeve of his uniform. He carried on leading his men forward, through yet another minefield, toward the village of Sainte-Marie-du-Mont, five miles inland from Utah, finally arriving just two minutes before schedule. Schroeder had done his job. He had reached all of his D-Day objectives on time. He had led the first men to break out from Utah Beach. But he had also lost a great deal of blood and now he collapsed. A medic came to his aid. It was a million-dollar wound. He'd survive, but his war was damn sure over. And he'd be very lucky to keep the arm. It was a mangled mess.

Schroeder lost consciousness. He came to several hours later in a tent, surrounded by doctors.

"We're going to have to amputate your arm."

Schroeder blacked out again.

He awoke once more many hours later, this time in a British medical clinic. "The guy in the stretcher next to me had a bullet in his head," he remembered, "and another guy had the skin covering his entire back torn off. He died the next day. For me, the war was over but I had five more operations before the surgeons succeeded in saving my arm. I wanted to go back to the front to join my true family. It was forbidden."

One morning, a nurse brought Schroeder some newspapers.

He refused to read them.

The nurse insisted. "Read them. Look. You're a hero!"[30]

It was true. Back home, in the American press, Schroeder had been tagged as "the first GI to invade Europe." According to his hometown paper, *The Baltimore Sun*: "When his boot touched French soil, it was a great moment in history."[31]

AS THE PARATROOPERS and foot soldiers converged behind Utah Beach, Lord Lovat and his commandos crept into the village of Saint-Aubin-d'Arquenay, two-thirds of which lay in smoking ruins, the result of Allied bombardment.[32] Shards of broken glass frosted the sidewalks, also strewn with smashed tiles and pieces of masonry. Telephone wire lay in twisting coils on the ground between snapped poles. Lovat was now less than two miles from Pegasus Bridge, where Major John Howard awaited reinforcement. He had a sense of foreboding—he hated street fighting, which suited German snipers, their cheeks bruised from the recoil of their Mausers, over the fast-moving, lightly armed commandos. At a road junction in the village, some distraught Frenchmen and women pointed at a building that had been destroyed. Family members lay badly injured in the ruins, desperate for medical aid. Lovat turned and gestured toward medics who were some way behind him. A sniper's bullet hit a wall close to Lovat's head with a startling crack. Stone chips flew through the air.

"He's over there," shouted one of Lovat's men as he sprinted across the street, determined to kill the sniper who had fired on Lovat. A grenade through a window. A flat explosion. A door kicked in. Tommy gun bullets spraying a room. Dead and done.

Germans were spotted, around thirty, crossing nearby fields, sun in their eyes, unaware of Lovat and his men.

Lovat pulled off his eighty-pound Bergen rucksack. It felt good to be free of the weight. He knelt down behind it, aiming his short-barreled US Army carbine.

The Germans kept coming, oblivious. Some of Lovat's men set up a Vickers K machine gun on the roof of a shed.

Whispered orders.

"Pick the officers and NCOs and let them come right in."

A blond-haired German officer spun as he fell, dust flying off his back as bullets thumped into his chest. Others who had bunched up lay in a grotesque heap, riddled by the vengeful commando fire.

Lovat pressed on, hearing the sound of intense fighting in the distance, the dull hammer blows of artillery and the steady *tonk* of mortars firing. He knew it was the Germans counterattacking. "The Airborne sounded in trouble," Lovat recalled, "and it was our job to bail them out."[33]

At Pegasus Bridge, Major John Howard had just one thought.

How long could he and his men hold out?

He had been given very clear orders.

Hold until relieved.

Howard looked at his watch.

Come on lads . . . Where are the bloody commandos?

Howard's nerves were raw. The wait was excruciating, perhaps the hardest part of the whole D-Day operation.

Hold until relieved.

Hold until relieved . . .

But how long for?[34]

It was approaching 1 P.M. when Howard heard an odd sound amid the crackle of machine gun fire and distant explosions.

Several hundred yards away, out of Howard's view, Bill Millin walked at the front of a group of commandos, playing his pipes.

Lord Lovat sauntered behind Millin as they passed a row of poplar trees.

Millin spotted a sniper in one of the trees, off to his right.

The sniper opened fire and Millin saw a flash. Lovat dropped to his knee, and Millin stopped playing the pipes. Then several commandos ran past, firing at the sniper, who shimmied down the tree and sprinted into a cornfield. "I could see his head bobbing up and down," recalled Millin. "Lovat was shooting, his rifle was blazing away, and then we stopped and Lovat sent some commandos into the field to drag the body out and we dumped him at the side of the road."

Lovat ordered his men to keep on toward Pegasus Bridge.

"Well, start playing your pipes again, piper."[35]

The sound of pipes could now clearly be heard on Pegasus Bridge. Some of Howard's men thought they were dreaming—it had been a very long morning.

Not far from the bridge, a paratrooper turned to a man next to him.

"I can hear bagpipes."

"Don't be stupid," replied the man. "We're in the middle of France, you can't hear bagpipes."

Then they spotted Millin playing his pipes.

"Do the Germans play the bagpipes?" asked another man.

"I don't think so," someone said.[36]

John Howard was astonished at the sight of Millin marching along the towpath beside the Caen Canal. With the wail of the pipes, modernity in that moment fell away. The skirl was answered by another ancient noise, evoking battles from distant ages. "A bugle sounded in reply from the 7th Para," recalled the major, "and the skirl of the bagpipes became louder. We could see Lovat striding ahead of his men, clad in his trademark Aran wool jumper with Millin beside him blowing away for all he was worth."[37]

Some men broke into tears as the pipes grew louder.[38]

Millin stopped outside the Café Gondrée, just a few yards from the bridge. His arrival with his fellow commandos had not gone unnoticed by the enemy. German snipers opened fire from wheat fields to the southwest. "Even where I was standing," Millin remembered, "I could hear the shrapnel or the bullets, whatever, hitting off the metal side of the bridge. The wounded were being carried up from along the canal banks and into the café. It was a real hot spot."[39]

Lovat approached John Howard.

They shook hands.

"About bloody time!" said Howard.[40]

Lovat apologized for being a few minutes late.

"John," he added, "today we are making history."[41]

Howard advised Lovat to keep on going.

Lovat turned to Millin.

"Right, we'll cross over."

Millin put his pipes on his shoulder, ready to play.

"No, don't play," ordered Lovat. "Wait until you get over."[42]

Millin ran across with a group of commandos while Lovat walked calmly, unflustered by the intense *crack, crack, crack* of sniper fire. Howard watched Lovat cross and would never forget his "courage and panache," for which he would always have "an immense respect."[43]

On the other side of Pegasus Bridge, Lovat caught up with Millin. "Right," said Lovat, "play now and keep playing all the way along this road, about two hundred yards, until you come to the Ranville Bridge and keep playing right across that. No matter what, just keep playing."[44]

Millin did as he was told.

The fields nearby were a grim spectacle. Lovat saw dead horses lying with their legs in the air, "while others dragged around, tripping on spilled insides, bellowing their agony."[45]

They arrived at the narrow, metal-sided Ranville bridge, which spanned the Orne River.

Millin spotted two British airborne troops in a slit trench on the other side of the bridge.

"Get back!" called one of the troops.

The bridge was under sniper fire.

Millin then saw that Lovat was walking ahead, yet again as calm as could be, as if he were strolling along a lane on his 200,000-acre estate in Scotland.

"Carry on, carry on," ordered Lovat.[46]

Again Millin obeyed, this time playing "Blue Bonnets over the Border," with its stirring words, so familiar to every proud Scotsman:

> *March! March! Ettrick and Teviot-dale,*
> *Why my lads dinna ye march forward in order?*
> *March! March! Eskdale and Liddesdale!*
> *All the blue bonnets are over the border . . .*

Snipers quickly opened up on Lovat's commandos, several falling as they hurried across the Ranville bridge. "You didn't hear the shot," remembered one man, "you just saw them crumple. These chaps with great big packs, loaded up, had marched inland and were jolly tired. They were so tired. I think they felt

Lord Lovat after returning from the Dieppe raid, August 1942. He would lead a force of British commandos with legendary panache and courage on D-Day. COURTESY OF THE IMPERIAL WAR MUSEUM

Brothers Elliot and Charles Dalton. They would both lead Canadian infantry companies in the first wave on D-Day.
COURTESY OF THE QUEEN'S OWN RIFLES OF CANADA REGIMENTAL MUSEUM AND ARCHIVES

Lieutenant John Spalding, section leader, E Company, 16th Infantry Regiment, 1st Division. The first officer in the first wave to lead men off the Easy Red sector of Omaha Beach on D-Day.

COURTESY OF THE COLONEL ROBERT R. McCORMICK RESEARCH CENTER

Lieutenant Colonel Terence Otway, the British officer who was given arguably D-Day's most perilous mission—to seize the Merville Battery.

COURTESY OF THE MUSÉE DE LA BATTERIE DE MERVILLE

Sergeant Major Stanley Hollis, the only Allied combatant to receive Britain's highest award for valor, the Victoria Cross, for his actions on D-Day.

COURTESY OF THE GREEN HOWARDS MUSEUM

Captain Leonard Schroeder, F Company commander, 2nd Battalion, 8th Infantry Regiment, 4th Infantry Division, reportedly the first American to wade ashore on D-Day.

Captain Frank Lillyman, 502nd Parachute Infantry Regiment, 101st Airborne Division, with customary cigar during a practice jump. As commander of the first American pathfinders to jump into Normandy, he would be celebrated as the first American to land in France on D-Day.

US invasion troops at a final prayer service before embarkation for D-Day.
COURTESY OF THE NATIONAL ARCHIVES, US

American bombers from the 9th Air Force attack Pointe du Hoc before D-Day.
COURTESY OF THE NATIONAL ARCHIVES, US

General Eisenhower talks with 101st Airborne paratroopers on the evening of June 5, 1944. Corporal Bill Hayes is shown directly behind Eisenhower's thumb.

The first Americans to fight in Normandy—the pathfinders of Stick 1, Team A, 502nd Parachute Infantry Regiment, dropped by Plane 1 at 12:15 A.M. on June 6, 1944.

American paratroopers bound
for Normandy, June 6, 1944.
COURTESY OF THE NATIONAL ARCHIVES, US

American paratroopers about to jump into
Normandy, June 6, 1944.
COURTESY OF THE NATIONAL ARCHIVES, US

Soldiers from the US 1st Infantry Division wade ashore onto Omaha Beach, June 6, 1944.
COURTESY OF THE NATIONAL ARCHIVES, US

The path taken by Lieutenant John Spalding and his platoon as they broke out from the Easy Red sector of Omaha Beach.

COURTESY OF THE NATIONAL ARCHIVES, US

Troops from the US 4th Infantry Division cross the seawall on Utah Beach, June 6, 1944.

COURTESY OF THE NATIONAL ARCHIVES, US

Devastating naval fire on D-Day.

Troops approaching Omaha Beach on D-Day.

Rangers take a rest from
combat at Pointe du Hoc.

COURTESY OF THE NATIONAL ARCHIVES, US

British commandos land on Sword Beach,
June 6, 1944. Piper Bill Millin and his
pipes are shown in the foreground. Lord
Lovat, commander of the 1st Special
Service Brigade, is shown wading ashore
just to the right of his men, directly
ahead of Millin.

COURTESY OF THE IMPERIAL WAR MUSEUM

British casualties from the initial assault on D-Day are helped ashore on Sword Beach.

TRINITY MIRROR / MIRRORPIX / ALAMY STOCK PHOTO

Dead soldiers from the 16th Infantry Regiment, 1st Division, on Omaha
Beach, June 6, 1944.   COURTESY OF THE NATIONAL ARCHIVES, US

Wounded troops from 1st Division receive cigarettes and rations, Omaha
Beach, June 6, 1944.   COURTESY OF THE NATIONAL ARCHIVES, US

The top brass watching operations from the bridge of the USS *Augusta*. Lieutenant General Omar Bradley, commander of the US First Army, is second from left. COURTESY OF THE NATIONAL ARCHIVES, US

American casualties being transferred from a landing craft to a larger ship.
COURTESY OF THE NATIONAL ARCHIVES, US

Captain Frank Lillyman, center, backed by other paratroopers from the 101st Airborne, Normandy, June 1944.
COURTESY OF MICHEL DE TREZ

Rangers demonstrate how they climbed the cliffs of Pointe du Hoc.

Rangers after being relieved at Pointe du Hoc, June 8, 1944.

Rangers meet with a relief force on June 8, 1944. Sergeant Jack Kuhn of D Company is shown far left. COURTESY OF THE NATIONAL ARCHIVES, US

Lieutenant Colonel James Rudder congratulates D Company commander, Lieutenant George Kerchner, after both men had received the Distinguished Service Cross for their actions on D-Day.

COURTESY OF THE NATIONAL ARCHIVES, US

General Bernard Montgomery pins the British Military Medal on the uniform of Sergeant Philip Streczyk of the US 1st Infantry Division for extraordinary gallantry on Omaha Beach, Normandy, France, on D-Day. Award presented July 7, 1944.

COURTESY OF THE NATIONAL ARCHIVES, US

General Eisenhower on July 2, 1944, in Normandy after decorating twenty-two
men from the 16th Infantry Regiment for their bravery on D-Day.

Major Charles Dalton receiving the
Distinguished Service Order from
General Montgomery.

A 1946 photo of Pegasus Bridge with, on left, Georges Gondrée, owner of Café Gondrée; and Major John Howard, center, commander on D-Day of D Company, Oxford and Buckinghamshire Light Infantry.

COURTESY OF THE PRESS ASSOCIATION

The calvary where Lieutenant Colonel Terence Otway and his men gathered after attacking the Merville Battery.

PHOTOGRAPH BY JOHN SNOWDON

The view from a strongpoint of the section of Juno Beach where Major Charles Dalton landed with B Company, Queen's Own Rifles, in the first wave.

PHOTOGRAPH BY JOHN SNOWDON

The view from atop Pointe du Hoc.
FROM THE AUTHOR'S COLLECTION

French commando Léon Gautier, photographed in May 2017 wearing his green beret at his home in Ouistreham, less than a mile from where he came ashore on D-Day.
PHOTOGRAPH BY JOHN SNOWDON

'If we're going to be sniped then we're going to be sniped' sort of thing."

Still piping, Millin crossed the Ranville bridge as the sniper fire pinged around him. "The two airborne chaps in the slit trench thought we were crazy . . . But I got over, stopped playing the pipes and I shook hands with the two chaps. Then from across the road appears this tall airborne officer—red beret on. He came marching across, his arms outstretched towards Lovat. 'Very pleased to see you, old boy.' Lovat said, 'And we are very pleased to see you, old boy. Sorry, we are two and a half minutes late!'"[47] The critical linkup between seaborne forces and para-troopers had now been achieved on both flanks of the fifty-mile-long Allied front.

Beyond the Ranville bridge, two senior officers were waiting for Lovat in the shelter of tall trees on a rise.[48] Lovat learned that he had arrived just in time. Elements of the 21st Panzer Division were finally attacking in strength from the south. Lovat's com-mandos would be needed to fend off the counterattack and to aid Lieutenant Colonel Terence Otway, whose force had been reduced to just two hundred men and had now taken up posi-tions in Amfreville, two miles north on the high ground run-ning to the east of the Orne.

The real test of Lovat and of his men's mettle was imminent. Time now for hard pounding. "So far, so good," he recalled. "We retained the initiative and events had clicked into place. The sea crossing, dry landing, rapid break through and intact bridges were bonus marks. Shock tactics had proved a complete success. [But] how would we get on after losing the element of surprise?

It is one thing to go on the warpath; quite another to stay put and take what's coming to you . . . We'd had a flying start: could we prove our staying power and face the music?"[49]

BY 2:30 THAT AFTERNOON, the Green Howards' Sergeant Major Stanley Hollis found himself in command of 16 Platoon—its previous leader, a young lieutenant, had been killed just thirty minutes before. "We advanced inland through fields of ripening corn and small green pastures surrounded by banks and hedges—the dreaded Bocage," recalled Hollis's commanding officer, Lieutenant Colonel Robin Hastings, who accompanied Hollis and D Company's commander, Major Ronnie Lofthouse,[50] and who was before long giving orders to clear the enemy from buildings near the village of Crépon, 2.5 miles inland from Gold Beach.

Hollis and his platoon approached an old farmhouse and passed through a gate. The front entrance to the farmhouse was locked, so Hollis broke the door in.[51] "I went up the stairs into the various bedrooms," he remembered, "and I burst into one of the bedrooms and there was a small boy about 10 or 11 years old, and I just saw him disappear round the corner . . . I was covered in blood and he must have been terrified. I'm convinced he thought I was going to kill him."[52] There was no sign of Germans, so Hollis decided to reconnoiter behind the farmhouse. As he looked around a corner, a bullet blew a chunk from the wall, splintering the stone inches from his head. He saw a hedge in the distance. Two dogs stood in a gap in the hedge, wagging their tails. Hollis knew their German owners must be close by.

Hollis turned to some of his men.

"Just open up with Bren guns and shoot the hedge up."[53]

The men sprinted into the open near a rhubarb patch. A stream of bullets greeted them. All were killed, "stone dead," in a few moments.

Hollis pulled back and reported to his company commander, Lofthouse.

"Get a PIAT gun," said Lofthouse, "and crawl forward through that rhubarb patch."

Hollis located a PIAT, powerful enough to destroy a field gun, and selected two men to accompany him. They slithered through the rhubarb patch toward the Germans, Hollis leading the way. Once in position, obscured by a rhubarb plant, he poked his PIAT through the leaves and fired, but he missed the German position, hitting the roof of a nearby house instead. Pieces of stone and masonry flew through the air.

A German machine gun snarled and Hollis's two companions were wounded, hopelessly pinned down in the rhubarb patch, bullets whipping above their heads. Having spotted the source of the enemy fire, Hollis reacted instantly and sprinted across open ground, spraying rounds at a hedgerow, within a few seconds silencing the German machine gun. Then he and the two men scrambled back toward the rest of D Company. "Stan Hollis was a remarkably resolute fighter," recalled one of Hollis's senior officers. "He was one of those people who through the force of his own personality could change the course of a battle."[54]

Later that afternoon, D Company regrouped and mopped up the last German resistance in Crépon and then pushed on, heading for the unit's final D-Day objective, a main road leading from Caen to Bayeux. For risking his own life to save two others, as well as for exemplary and extraordinary courage throughout D-Day, Sergeant Major Stanley Hollis would receive the Victoria Cross, the highest award in the British Army for valor.[55] Incredibly, he was the only British warrior to be so recognized for his courage on June 6, 1944.

WHILE STANLEY HOLLIS was saving the lives of his fellow Green Howards, Lord Lovat and his commandos prepared to attack the village of Le Plein, two miles north of Pegasus Bridge. The village ran along high ground with a main street of creamy yellow limestone buildings a half mile long and was occupied by a large force of Germans who'd been ordered to hold their vital positions overlooking the Orne River valley.[56]

Piper Millin watched as the commandos under Lovat's command checked their Bren and Sten guns and then began to advance along a lane, shoulders hunched like boxers ready to parry and jab. Lovat was standing at a crossroads, urging his men on, when the Germans launched a well-aimed mortar strike, groups of bombs landing and spraying chunks of shrapnel in erratic patterns, bracketing commando positions, slicing and slashing at feet and legs. Clearly, Lovat and his men were under close observation. Two valuable officers were wounded. Enemy fire intensified, the violence of explosions steadily mounting. "The fire fight was thickening," recalled Lovat, "but men were being killed; the Germans had started to react fiercely. We had run into trouble. The enemy had to be dislodged without delay."[57]

Millin moved closer to Le Plein, coming across a quarry

where badly wounded commandos had been placed. He was deeply saddened to see so many men in agony—they were also petrified by the German mortars landing near the quarry. He returned to the crossroads, where he found Lovat still issuing orders for the attack on Le Plein.

Mortar fire grew more intense, dozens of explosions ripping up open ground. Millin took cover in a ditch, where he looked back at Lovat.

"Goodness, thirty-two years of age," thought Millin. "Right enough he's old . . . But what a responsibility, aged thirty-two, and all these people have been killed and seriously injured."[58]

On the road leading into Le Plein, one of Lovat's young commandos, an eighteen-year-old private, saw a sergeant get hit. A phosphorus grenade in the sergeant's pocket exploded and he began to burn fiercely. A fellow officer appeared and shot the sergeant to death—he had to be put out of his misery.

The battle for Le Plein raged on. Several men near the private were felled by anti-tank fire from a Russian-made gun. A man a few feet away had his stomach gouged by shrapnel and died in the private's arms. Yet another commando had gotten it in the "arse," and someone else had lost a foot.

The young private was carrying a first-aid kit and realized that he alone could help the wounded. His unit's medical officer was busy back on Sword Beach.

"Is my wedding tackle all right?" asked one wounded man. "Is my wedding tackle all right?"

"For Christ's sake," replied the private. "You've got it through the arse. You haven't got it through anything else."

The private applied a field dressing to the man's backside.[59]

"Hold it. Get your hand on it. Hold it and really push in."

The mortars were still firing with a furious whooshing sound. Then came the crash of explosions and the hiss of countless shards of shrapnel slashing through the air.

It was safest to keep moving or get underground.

One man approached, covered in blood. He was barely able to stand and was dragging a tommy gun along the road.

"Well," thought the private, "he ain't going to go far."

The private moved toward the man.

Someone called out.

"Let him go . . ."

It was a waste of time for the private to try to help the man. Another commando was dragged over to the private, who ripped open the man's brown canvas jacket. He was a hopeless case, too, his chest "just one mass of jelly."[60]

The private pulled out some morphine vials. He could ease the pain, at least. The man with the chest wound could not speak. Blood seeped from his nostrils and mouth. Then he died, yet another one of Lovat's finest killed in his prime.

Meanwhile, Lovat had spotted a group of cows around four hundred yards from where he had taken up position, just outside Le Plein. He was convinced that a German, perhaps a sniper, was hidden close to the cattle. Time for a little hunting. "Two animals were taking an interest—as cows do, sniffing and throwing their heads—at a thorn bush," recalled Lovat. "It was good light, but the carbine did not get the distance. The first round from a borrowed rifle, however, scored a bull's eye, winging a prone civilian who jumped up, nicked through the fleshy part of his shoulder."

A sergeant was sent to bring in the "shifty-looking yokel in plain clothes." While doing so, he paced off the distance of Lovat's superb shot. The yokel was clearly a spy: He had a pair of binoculars and a wad of cash and spoke in a strange accent. Lovat handed him a spade and made him dig a trench, and he looked relieved not to have been shot.

The afternoon dragged on as Lovat waited for Number 4 Commando to arrive to reinforce his men as they fought their way through Le Plein. German shells landed sporadically, keeping every man on his toes, nerves taut. All of Lovat's lads, their Fairbairn-Sykes fighting knives close to hand, many wearing their green berets rather than helmets, were before long in the fight, bayonets fixed, their blood up, hunting Germans from yard to yard and house to house in Le Plein.

There was no reserve. They had no backup.

Would help reach them before the formidable tanks of the 21st Panzer Division?[61] Who would arrive first: the tanks or their fellow commandos?[62]

By midafternoon, Lieutenant John Spalding and his platoon were several hundred yards inland from Omaha, having received orders to head across cow pastures to the village of Colleville. Roses were in bloom, their scent mixing in some places with the sickly-sweet stench of animal corpses—countless cows had been killed by bombardment and shelling, and in the fields some were still standing, stiff with rigor mortis. On the outskirts of the village, near a stone church where snipers had earlier lurked, Spalding and his unit joined others from the 1st

Division, and in all some forty-five men set up positions, using drainage ditches near an orchard so they did not have to waste energy digging in.

It was around 3 P.M. when the Germans tried to kill Spalding yet again. One man nearby had his gun shot out of his hand, the stock shattering as he was hit in the thigh by a shell fragment. A medic quickly gave first aid, and others joked that the wounded man was "too big to be missed." The next casualty was no laughing matter. The sergeant who had kicked down the ramp on Spalding's craft that morning was hit in the throat and face and killed.[63]

If this was not sobering enough, at around 4 P.M. a navy artillery shell landed just a couple of hundred yards away. Then another exploded and another, sending shock waves along the ground, knocking men off their feet. Spalding and his men were under friendly fire, a common experience for men on D-Day on both sides. Spotters out at sea could finally identify landmarks, including the church, and now began to level it, not realizing Americans were in the vicinity.

One of Spalding's fellow officers, Captain Joe Dawson, G Company commander, hunkered down as yet more shells flew over, landing in and all around the village of Colleville, shredding apple orchards, leaving only splintered stumps, reducing buildings to mounds of stone, and killing or wounding seven of Dawson's men. He had already lost all thirty-three soldiers who had lined up behind him in his landing craft at H-Hour, obliterated by a direct hit from artillery. The shelling had "leveled the town," he recalled, "and in doing so we suffered the worst casualties we had the whole of the day—not from the enemy, but from our own Navy. I was angered by it, angered beyond all measure, because I thought it was totally disgraceful . . . I was frantically throwing up smoke bombs to alert them to the fact that we were in the town, but it was too late."[64]

Spalding watched as orange and yellow flames stabbed toward the low gray skies.[65] All they could do was curl up in the rotting leaves and dirt of the ditch and make themselves as small as possible, hands over their ringing ears or their genitals, and curse and curse or pray the next shell would not have their name on it. Finally, after what must have felt like an eternity, around 5 P.M., the naval fire stopped.[66] Spalding looked back toward the beach and to his shock saw several squads of Germans heading his way, and then a GI out in the open, a runner from G Company. The Germans opened fire on the runner and he fell to the ground. Spalding watched as they then pumped at least another hundred rounds of machine gun bullets into the young American.[67]

Spalding and his men were before long in a ferocious firefight and starting to run low on ammunition. Spalding counted his rounds—he had just six left. In all, he and his men had fewer than a hundred bullets between them. In a lull in the fighting, Spalding and two other lieutenants discussed the situation with Sergeant Streczyk, the most experienced combat veteran among them. What should they do? There were mumblings about surrender. Neither Spalding nor Streczyk was having any of that. "We decided to fight our way back to the battalion," recalled Spalding. "We sent word for men to come to us in the ditch where we were; we were several hundred yards south and west of Colleville."

Reinforcements did not arrive, so early that evening Spalding and others crawled in single file along a ditch, hoping they had not been spotted. They came to a road, sprinted across it, thankfully without hearing the crack of a sniper's round, and then made their way, combat jackets covered in mud and grass stains, along another ditch. "We passed a German machine gun with two dead Germans and one live German," remembered Spalding. "Without saying a word we exchanged the German's life for our own safety. I was sure that I saw a twinkle in the German's eye as I crawled past him."[68]

Finally, no doubt to their great relief, Spalding's platoon came across men from C Company who had been sent to help them. Before long, they had found extra ammunition and set up new positions, guarding a road into Colleville, half a mile from where they had been surrounded earlier. After the friendly fire incident, they knew it was suicide to not dig in or find cover belowground.[69] Thankfully, Spalding and his platoon were now reinforced by men from C Company and several squads operating heavy machine guns. The extra firepower was reassuring indeed.[70]

Spalding later recalled being "tired, hungry and scared" as he settled down to await an inevitable German counterattack.[71] In a medical report, he would state that he had "adjusted well to his first combat experiences." He had felt "normal fear" but had been able to control it. He should have been killed or wounded. Indeed, he had been exceptionally lucky to survive, given that "Germans [were] sitting there waiting for us." In his view, "no man" in the first wave on Omaha "had a right to come out alive."[72]

For several hours that morning, the outcome on Omaha had

been uncertain. Victory had depended on Spalding and others of his ilk, young men who had risked their lives over and over as they led terrified Americans off the beach—these were the exceptional warriors who had ultimately won the day on Omaha. According to an after-action report, Spalding's company had in fact tipped the scales in favor of the invaders: "It is an obvious fact that Company E, as much as, if not more than any other unit, seemingly by strength of will and courage alone, saved the entire beach-head from being thrown back in the sea. It was an experience few men underwent and lived, and for a month afterwards, those who did, remained almost in a daze."[73]

Later that afternoon, the commander of E Company, Captain Wozenski, did a head count and was stunned when he saw how few soldiers had survived the twelve hours since landing in the first wave. Of the men in E Company who had stormed the beach with him, only sixty remained to fight. "Sixty of us left!" he shouted. "Where are my men? . . . What did they promise us?"[74] E Company had in fact suffered more than any other 1st Division unit, with forty men killed, forty missing, and thirty-seven wounded.[75]

They had been told it would be a cakewalk. The air force was supposed to have bombed the entire beach, but nothing had been touched. It had been as flat as a pancake, with not a single crater to offer the promised protection. Indeed, not one bomb "was dropped on Omaha Beach by our airplanes," recalled a naval commander.[76]

Wozenski and E Company, like so many others in the Big Red One, had deserved far better. They had done their duty in North Africa and Sicily, only to be sent like so many cattle to the slaughter. It had been a damn waste of good soldiers, warriors who should by rights have long since been sent home. So many had been cut down before even firing a shot.[77]

As survivors huddled in foxholes, shaking from nervous exhaustion, startled by the slightest sound, some of their comrades—from the 35,000 men landed that day on Omaha—still lay in agony among minefields along the bluffs, still waiting for a medic to reach them before they bled to death.

In all, the United States had landed some 55,000 men on D-Day. By far the greatest losses had been suffered on Omaha, where more than nine hundred were killed.[78] For their heroism on Omaha Beach, 153 men would receive the Distinguished Service Cross, America's second-highest award for bravery. Remarkably, among the thirty-two men in Lieutenant John Spalding's platoon, three other than Spalding and Streczyk would get the medal.[79] No fewer than ten men from the platoon earned the Silver Star. Seven men had been wounded that June 6. Miraculously, only two had been killed.

Some of the medals received for extraordinary courage on Omaha should have been Medals of Honor—without doubt in both Spalding's and Streczyk's cases—but army officials far from the maw and horror of the front lines worried that "too many men" would get the highest award for bravery and its significance would somehow be diminished.[80] In the end, scandalously, just three soldiers would receive the Medal of Honor for their actions on Omaha Beach, two of them belonging to the Big Red One.[81] Of the three, only one would survive the war.[82]

CHAPTER 10

Tallyho!

IT WAS A glorious evening. Around 7 P.M., at Pegasus Bridge, a soldier was seated at a table outside the liberated Café Gondrée, waiting to be treated for his wounds. "Georges Gondrée," he remembered, "brought me a glass of champagne, which was very welcome indeed after that sort of day . . . There was a tremendous flight of aircraft, hundreds of British aircraft. They came in and they did a glider drop and a supply drop between the bridges and the coast on our side of the canal. It was a marvelous sight, it really was . . . It only seemed a few minutes afterwards that all these chaps in jeeps, towing anti-tank guns and god knows what, were coming down the road."[1]

Army vehicles began to cross Pegasus Bridge.

"You're a bit late, mate!" called out one of Major John Howard's men.

"Hey!" shouted another. "Where've you been? The war's over."[2]

One of Howard's men looked on in awe at the reinforcements, fresh-faced, their uniforms undusted.

"My God," he thought. "We've done it!"[3]

BACK IN ENGLAND, thirty-two Horsa gliders had been lifted by towplanes into the evening sky from an airfield southwest of London, part of an operation called Keokuk that was to provide heavy weapons, ammunition, and medical supplies to the 101st Airborne. The Screaming Eagles, numbering three regiments, dropped near Utah Beach more than eighteen hours earlier, were now in urgent need of resupply. It was the job of Captain Frank Lillyman and his pathfinders to mark the landing zone for the Keokuk gliders.

Near a village called Hiesville, as the shadows began to lengthen, Lillyman searched for a field that had been cleared of defensive obstacles and was large enough to fit the gliders. As he and his men positioned the Eureka sets and smoke pots that would guide the Horsa pilots,[4] German troops infiltrated neighboring fields. Lillyman stood at the center of the T that marked the landing zone, unaware that dozens of Germans were lurking, heavily camouflaged, in surrounding hedgerows. It was just before 9 P.M. when the Horsa glider pilots separated from their towplanes, crossed Utah Beach, and spotted the T of Lillyman's drop zone.

The Germans opened fire as the gliders swooped in to land. Some pilots panicked and crashed into trees. Lillyman ran toward a smashed glider to help men get out but then felt a scorching pain as a bullet hit his arm. Someone shouted his name, and he looked at his sleeve and saw blood flowing from his arm, then collapsed as a piece of mortar shrapnel sliced his face.[5] A medic treated Lillyman and he was taken to an aid station. His wounds were not life-threatening, but for Captain Frank Lillyman, the first American to land in France on June 6, 1944, D-Day was finally over.

Three miles due east of Hiesville, beyond flooded fields where dozens of Screaming Eagles had drowned, the oldest American to fight on D-Day was meanwhile still going strong, despite his weak heart and arthritis. On the outskirts of the village of Sainte-Marie-du-Mont, a dusty Brigadier General Theodore Roosevelt came across the gruff thirty-nine-year-old Colonel Robert Sink, commander of the 506th Parachute Infantry Regiment of the 101st Airborne. Sink's men had suffered the highest losses of the three regiments from the Screaming Eagles on D-Day: Some 230 men had been killed in action or had died later from their wounds. In all, the division had lost almost nine hundred men killed and around 2,300 wounded. More than 660 were missing in action or captured.[6]

Roosevelt and Sink saluted each other and shook hands.

Roosevelt took off his helmet. "The removal of my helmet is symbolic," he said. "I would like to take my hat off to every member of the 101st Airborne."[7]

AT POINTE DU HOC, as the light started to fade, D Company commander Lieutenant George Kerchner nervously manned a roadblock three-quarters of a mile inland from the sheer cliffs of the Pointe. He was badly outnumbered: At least five hundred

Germans were busy preparing to infiltrate and take back lost ground. "They had the advantage of knowing the terrain," remembered Kerchner, "and of having underground rooms and passageways."[8]

He had no idea that reinforcements, although not many, were in fact fighting toward him. A bedraggled group of two dozen Rangers from A Company of the 5th Ranger Battalion were indeed slowly moving through mined pastures and booby-trapped orchards from Omaha Beach toward Kerchner. "The hours had passed so fast that what some call 'the longest day' was to me the shortest," he recalled. "For a while, we weren't even sure that the Americans had not pulled everyone out, gone back to England, and left us alone. We only knew of a group of Rangers at the command post with Col. Rudder, where they were also treating the wounded, and that a naval shore fire control party and a couple of guys from the 29th Division Recon were on hand."

Thankfully, the small band of Rangers from A Company were led by the highly capable Lieutenant Charles "Ace" Parker, who would be remembered by one of his men for his "cool head."[9] Nothing seemed to faze the twenty-five-year-old, who had learnt during the Depression in Minnesota that "pride" and a sense of "responsibility" were what really allowed men to carry on, to function, to not give up.[10] For Parker, recalled one Ranger, "life was just a bowl of cherries . . . An officer always used to carry a pistol but Ace always carried an M-1 and would cradle it in his arms like he was going out hunting deer or something. He reminded me of Davy Crockett."[11]

Parker and his men now crept along a narrow lane, parallel to the coast, feeling ever more isolated and vulnerable. In reconnaissance photographs, the hedgerows had seemed to be like those in England, where his unit had trained—a few feet tall, mere thin strips—not high, thick walls that blocked the light and made it impossible to see where the enemy lurked. It was like fighting through a maze, a claustrophobic nightmare.

Germans shouted and then hurled "potato masher" grenades. A German machine gun opened up and Parker and his men were quickly pinned down, taking cover behind a wall. It appeared that Ace Parker's luck had finally run out, but then a Ranger leapt over the wall and sprinted toward the machine gun, bullets ripping through his pack, one hitting him in the jaw. The Ranger threw himself to the ground, finding cover beneath a hedgerow, checked his wound, and, to his relief, discovered that a German slug had gone clean through his face. Then he spotted two Germans nearby, shot both dead with a German machine pistol he'd picked up, and finally scrambled back to the wall, where he found Parker.

"Look at what I got," he told Parker, pointing to his badly wounded jaw.

The soldier was far from done. Consumed by vengeance, not caring if he lived or died, he walked into the open and then along the road, as if inviting the enemy to finish him off. He'd gone well and truly "kill crazy," in Parker's words.

"I'm going to get that son-of-a-bitch," the soldier declared.

The German machine gun snarled once more and the soldier ducked out of the line of fire. A while later, Parker heard the metallic purr of a machine pistol, and then the soldier who'd gone "kill crazy" returned with two German prisoners, toting an extra Schmeisser MP40 submachine pistol and ammunition.

"Look what I got!"[12]

Around 9 P.M., Parker and his men moved once more toward Pointe du Hoc. A scout led the way, skirting a high hedgerow, followed by a backup man, knowing that a German could be hiding on the other side of the wall of earth and knotted roots, just feet away, finger ready to squeeze the trigger of a machine pistol.

It seemed to Parker that perhaps he and his group were the sole survivors from the thousand men of 5th Ranger Battalion, which had landed on the Dog White sector of Omaha Beach more than twelve hours before.

Are we all that's left?

As Parker tramped on, he heard a voice in some bushes.

"What's the password?"

He had come across Lieutenant George Kerchner and his men, positioned on the other side of a road. He had never heard "such a nice sound" as the voice of the American asking for a password.

"Tallyho!" replied Parker.[13]

Parker's platoon of two dozen exhausted men from the 5th Ranger Battalion emerged from thick hedgerows and muddy ditches and joined forces with Kerchner. "We were so happy to see them," recalled Kerchner. "[They were] the first men from Omaha Beach. Now we realized the invasion was here to stay."[14]

Rudder, at his command post, was told that Parker and his band of stalwarts had arrived.

A message arrived for Parker from Rudder.

"Where the hell is the rest of the 5th Battalion?"[15]

Where indeed were the other men from the 5th Ranger Battalion who had landed that morning on Omaha?

"I don't know," replied Parker. "I thought they were here. They must be right behind me."[16]

They were not. As the minutes passed and night began to fall, it became clear that Parker and his men were the only 5th Rangers to have in fact carried out their pre-invasion plan. They were most welcome, but until the rest of the 5th Battalion arrived, the 2nd Battalion at Pointe du Hoc would remain in mortal danger, outnumbered by a fiercely determined, well-armed enemy under orders to take back Pointe du Hoc at all costs. "Our main worry was our reduced ammunition supply and lack of food," recalled Parker, who huddled in a foxhole a hundred yards west along a thick hedgerow from Kerchner. "Survival was the only thing on our minds."[17]

At six minutes past ten, the sun finally set.[18] Yet still the light lingered, as if D-Day refused to end. It wasn't long before the Germans started to infiltrate the fields nearby, sliding on their bellies alongside familiar hedgerows, closing on Kerchner's foxhole. Then three Germans were up and running across open ground toward Kerchner, but they were quickly cut down. Just fifteen minutes later, dozens more were spotted, heavily camouflaged, preparing to attack from behind a wall fifty yards away. Kerchner sensibly ordered his men to pull back, in good order, three hundred yards, and join up with the ragged remnants of E and F Companies and form a new line of defense.

After taking up his new position, Kerchner started to feel strangely buoyant. He actually felt confident, he later noted in his diary, that the war was "maybe almost over."[19] He and his battered unit would surely be relieved by the 5th Battalion, which was in Vierville-sur-Mer, just a few miles away. Then he and the rest of the 2nd Battalion, elite troops who'd pulled off the impossible at Pointe du Hoc, would be sent back to England for rest and recuperation. Surely?

DARKNESS HAD DESCENDED. Seven miles inland from Juno Beach, one of Major Elliot Dalton's men from the Queen's Own Rifles began to process the momentous day. The losses. The pain. The great achievement. "We were the only regiment to capture and hold the assigned D-Day objective," he recalled. "Half of our original company—those I had joined up with in June 1940—had been killed or wounded."

In all, the 3rd Canadian Division, an all-volunteer force, had landed more than 21,000 men on Juno, of whom 304 had been killed and almost six hundred wounded.[20] The Queen's Own Rifles had suffered disproportionately, and for some survivors from the first wave the losses were soul-crushing. "The tears came," recalled one of Elliot Dalton's sergeants. "I went behind a wall. So many had been lost. I found myself questioning— idiotically—why war was conducted this way. Four years of training and living together, a common purpose, friends who became brothers—then more than half of us gone. Why didn't they just round up any collection of men in uniform and throw them into this killing machine? Why these, when anyone— somebody else, but not these—could have paid this price in human life? In grief there is not always good sense. It was one of those times. Gradually, though, in asking helplessly what we could do, we would find an answer—we could carry on and do our best, that's what."[21]

At some point, a medical officer found Elliot Dalton at his command post and informed him that his brother Charles had been killed. Decades later, Elliot would still remember the moment vividly: "How did I react? I know it sounds sort of cold-blooded, but all I thought was 'Tough luck.' Tough on his wife and his young daughter. I didn't feel much more. There had been so many killed that day. Men in my own company. Now somebody else had been killed. You're numb. As I say, it sounds awful."[22]

CLOUDS HID THE MOON. On the outskirts of Le Plein, Lord Lovat had set up his 1st Special Service Brigade's headquarters in an abandoned German command post, complete with trenches and sandbagged entrances. The commandos now manned the left flank of the Allied bridgehead, the key villages running along the heights to the east of the Orne River. Lovat's lads had taken "a lot of stick." Several senior officers had been wounded, a mere fraction of the 10,500 Allied casualties on D-Day, but a significant blow to the commandos.[23]

Lovat's trusty piper, Bill Millin, decided to seek shelter near the brigade headquarters. He was soon walking with another commando toward a trench, looking forward to finally getting some rest. "Everything was still and the firing had ceased," he remembered. "Everything was nice and quiet and there was the smell of the corn and the flowers and we're just walking along. Suddenly, 'Swoosh!' and two mortars exploded in the cornfield and of course shrapnel came thudding into the wall of the farmhouse. I got right down and scrambled away back the way we

had come and then another 'Swoosh!' and another two explosions. Well, I was in the trench by this time. The other chap was
a big beefy man and I heard him running, his big thudding feet
running along."

The man dropped into the trench, almost crushing Millin.

"For Christ's sake," cried Millin, "you're a hefty character!"

Millin fell asleep, and awoke about an hour later to find the
hefty character lying motionless in the bottom of the trench.
"There wasn't no snoring nor sound of breathing in the darkness, so I felt the back of his head and his back and of course
there's all blood. Obviously he'd been hit with several pieces of
shrapnel in the back and one in the back of the head and he'd
been dead all the time."[24]

SERGEANT MAJOR STANLEY HOLLIS ended his D-Day seven miles
inland from Gold Beach, with the survivors of the 6th Battalion
of the Green Howards, just below a hill close to the Caen–Bayeux
road.[25] He had added another dozen dead Germans to his wartime tally that day, bringing his total to more than a hundred.
The British operation at Gold Beach had largely been a success,
although by nightfall troops were almost four miles short of their
assigned objectives, which included the town of Bayeux.[26]

Around 350 men had been killed in operations at Gold,
where twenty thousand had come ashore. Hollis had lost 180 of
his fellow Green Howards, most of them killed on the beach.[27]
Yet Hollis and those from the first wave had, according to their
after-action report for June 6, "suffered surprisingly low casualties." Tanks had cleared paths through minefields skirting the

beach.[28] Men like Hollis had then pushed men forward quickly, thereby saving lives. No man, in fact, had fought harder than the redheaded sergeant major. No other warrior had better exemplified the aggression and initiative needed to get the job done.

Hollis's commanding officer, Lieutenant Colonel Robin Hastings, who would make the written recommendation that Hollis receive the Victoria Cross, was intensely proud of what his men had achieved on D-Day. Yet already he had begun to mourn. Two of his company commanders had been lost, as well as several highly experienced NCOs. "We lay down with a feeling of relief at having achieved a landing without excessive cost," he remembered. "Little did we know what we had to look forward to."[29]

TWENTY MILES TO THE EAST, at the farthest edge of the Allied bridgehead, Léon Gautier dug in with his fellow French commandos on high ground on the outskirts of a village called Hauger, having been told to prepare a defensive perimeter.[30] He had spent the long afternoon marching nine miles, often under fire, a heavy pack on his back, from Ouistreham to the Orne River and then up to high ground at Hauger.[31] There was time for a quick brew-up, using the standard-issue "Tommy" Primus stove, and to swallow a few rations and then pull a Player's Clipper cigarette from the metal tin each man carried containing fifty "fags."

It was quiet, "menacingly" so, as one commando remembered.[32]

"We are here to stay," an officer said, "so if we can keep quiet till we're properly ready, we'll be able to sort them out if they do attack."[33]

Gautier's unit, Number 4 Commando, set up a headquarters on the grounds of an elegant château, under new orders: "to stay, hold on, and fight, and not yield an inch."[34] No one was to fire on the enemy unless under direct attack. Gautier and his fellow commandos were to lie "doggo" in their trenches, hewn with miners' pickaxes, hidden from the Germans.[35]

Gautier had come through D-Day without a single scratch. His fellow French commandos had suffered twenty-one killed and ninety-three wounded, a casualty rate of more than 50 percent. "In the end [D-Day] was much less hard than I had feared," he recalled. "I had expected a lot tougher. It could have been worse. It was thanks to our discipline. In the British Army you had to be disciplined—which was something the French were not very good at."[36]

AT POINTE DU HOC, around 11:30 P.M., Lieutenant George Kerchner heard the piercing shriek of whistles and then Germans shouting orders. A flare soared above, bathing the shell-holed landscape in an eerie glow. Then grenades were exploding nearby. The seemingly endless day of intense combat was not yet over. So began the most terrifying moments of Kerchner's life. "The Germans had planned a well-coordinated night attack," he recalled. "It seemed there were hundreds and hundreds of Germans running toward us. From their firing, we began to see their outlines; it was not real dark. We started firing, and although they did not break our lines, we suffered casualties."

The Germans pulled back and an infuriated Kerchner tried to round up his men to give chase. Offense was the best means of defense, and besides, he was through with sitting back and waiting to be killed by a tossed grenade or a sharp blade slashed across his throat. "I could only find ten men, and before we could organize, Jerry hit us again on our left flank, using 75mms, mortars, machine guns, and grenades." The Germans quickly captured Kerchner's command post and killed several of his men. "After this attack, F and E Companies withdrew without my knowledge to Pointe du Hoc, leaving us completely surrounded and cut off."

Yet Kerchner was still keen to counterattack. He was "quite rattled" when, he recalled, he jumped into a foxhole and told the sergeant in it to join him and go after the Germans.

"Now, George," said the sergeant. "What do you expect to accomplish by this? First, you don't know how many there are. Second, you don't know where they are. Let's talk it over."

Kerchner did so and calmed down enough to see the folly of attacking the Germans with so few men, all of whom were cold and hungry and dog-tired after almost twenty-four hours of high tension and combat.[37]

The last few men from D Company, as with the other Americans surrounded at Pointe du Hoc, had only one option: to hold their positions until help arrived.

IT WAS NEAR midnight. Major Charles Dalton of the Queen's Own Rifles was laid on a stretcher on the beach fronting the village of Bernières-sur-Mer, where he had landed. Out of 125 men in his company, he had lost eighty-three.[38] Those from the

Queen's Own Rifles who had survived the landings in the most heavily defended sector of Juno Beach had performed magnificently, pushing farther than any other Allied troops, eight miles inland, achieving all that could reasonably be expected of green troops.

The knowledge that his men, the spearhead of Canadian forces on D-Day, had succeeded in breaking through one of the toughest sectors of German defenses was of scant comfort to Charles Dalton as he lay in agony with other wounded below the bullet-scarred seawall at Bernières-sur-Mer. At high tide, there were just a few yards between the lapping waters and his feet. The beach as far as he could see was a smoking junkyard of burnt-out and abandoned vehicles. The bodies of so many of his men lay stiff under coarse blankets. Had his brother Elliot survived? How could he go home alone, without his brother, and explain to their parents that he had survived and Elliot had not?

Walking wounded passed by Dalton. Back in Canada, at his modest home on Castlefield Avenue in Toronto, his wife and young daughter would have learnt of the invasion by now and why he had been absent in their lives, overseas for so long.[39] Five long years of training for just a few minutes of fighting. He could feel the wet, scratchy sand inside his bloodstained uniform. Finally, it was midnight. D-Day was over. At some point, a soldier placed a cigarette between Charles Dalton's lips. Another gave him some rum, thinking maybe it would help, but neither the nicotine nor the alcohol could even begin to kill the pain.[40]

PART THREE

The Killing Fields

The heavy shells exploded like doors slamming at the end of long, echoing corridors, and the machine-guns faintly rattled like dried peas shaken in a bag.

—DOUGLAS GRANT,
41st Royal Marine Commando

CHAPTER 11

The Bocage

THE SUN ROSE on June 7 above the beaches of Normandy. Skies were clear. The wind had dropped, and the sea, dotted with thousands of gray vessels, had calmed. For fifty miles, the Norman coastline was scattered with countless landing craft and abandoned tanks, many still smoking. More than 160,000 Allied troops had crossed the Channel on D-Day, of whom more than four thousand had been killed. Survivors lay huddled in foxholes and ditches, ears ringing, hungry and cold, steeling themselves to once again get up and move into the line of fire. Berlin was still a long way away.

Villages just inland from the five invasion beaches lay in smoldering ruins, masonry and pieces of honeyed stone strewn across streets where villagers formed shocked groups and mourned their dead neighbors, not sure whether their liberators were about to be kicked back into the sea. More than two thousand French civilians lay dead, killed mostly by Allied bombing, in the skeletons of churches and collapsed cottages and beachside villas. Countless farm animals had been slaughtered, and their already rotting carcasses dotted the shell-blasted fields. Near the Orne River, the pastures were strewn with hundreds of crashed gliders with ripped canvas wings and crushed cockpits, the shards of their smashed Perspex windows glinting in the early-morning sun.

On Omaha Beach, German soldiers, now prisoners of war, carried dead Americans in wheelbarrows to a temporary graveyard below steep bluffs, where hundreds of blankets covered the fallen. Omar Bradley's troops, some 35,000 men, held a "sliver of corpse-littered beach five miles long and about one and a half miles deep," as he put it.[1] There was still enormous chaos and confusion among the 24,000 airborne troops, some dropped as many as fifty miles from their intended zones. None of the key towns inland—Carentan, Caen, and Bayeux—had been seized, although each had been a D-Day objective. It would be several increasingly bloody weeks before they were finally in Allied hands. The Germans, caught wrong-footed on D-Day, were stirring in their tens of thousands. Panzer divisions were clanking toward the front. Erwin Rommel was back in Normandy at his headquarters, furiously orchestrating massive counterattacks.

At Pointe du Hoc that morning, amid the deep craters and "the ripped-open dirt," Lieutenant George Kerchner and his fellow Rangers prepared once more for the worst.[2] There had been frenetic German attacks at 1 A.M., and then again at 3 A.M. from a different direction. He had no communication with Colonel Rudder and he was running low on ammunition.

At his command post in a concrete bunker just above the cliffs, Rudder was just as desperate. He commanded only ninety men, from an original force of 225, and was hemmed in on three sides; the only direction from which the Germans could not infiltrate was by way of the cliffs behind him. He knew that the Germans were masters of the counterattack and able to time their strikes seemingly at the point of maximum fatigue and exposure of the Americans, who in most cases had not slept properly for two days. They were surely as good as done for. It certainly seemed that way to a *Stars and Stripes* reporter holed up in Rudder's cramped command post: "I gave up hope of getting off Pointe du Hoc alive. No reinforcements in sight, plenty of Germans in front of us, nothing behind us but sheer cliffs and [the] Channel . . . We were up a creek not only for food and water but also ammunition."[3]

Forty miles away, Major John Howard had meanwhile moved, under mortar fire, with his men from D Company to the village of Escoville, three miles south of Pegasus Bridge. Veterans of the 21st Panzer Division, wearing camouflage smocks uncannily similar to those of British paratroopers, were waiting in force. Howard set up his headquarters in a farm building and then, around 11 A.M., joined his forward platoon. Before long, they were in the crosshairs of several snipers. Just like Howard's sharpshooters, the Germans were trained to drill officers first. Shots rang out. Howard moved along a wall, holding his binoculars, wanting to get a glimpse of the action.

"Watch out, John," warned an officer. "Those snipers are deadly."

Howard foolishly stepped beyond the wall. A sniper spotted him and pulled the trigger on his Mauser. A split second later Howard collapsed, blood flowing from his head.

It looked as if Howard had been shot dead, but then he was heard groaning in agony.

"He's alive!" shouted one of his men. "For God's sake get him."

Howard was pulled to cover and then helped back to his command post, where a medic looked at his wound. "I'd had an amazing escape," recalled Howard. "The sniper's fatal accuracy had pierced my helmet from front to back, the bullet actually grazing the top of my head . . . I could legitimately claim to have had my hair parted for me by a German bullet."[4]

The battle for Escoville intensified that afternoon.[5] Cut off, attacked from the east and the south, every one of Howard's platoons suffered heavy losses. Finally, after managing to withdraw with the remnants of D Company to the village of Hérouvillette, a mile to the north, Howard made a tally: he had lost fifty-eight men that day, killed, missing, or wounded.[6] It was, as he described it, "the saddest reckoning of my life." He sank into a terrible depression, "an agony of remorse and bewilderment."[7] The startling success at Pegasus Bridge had been so quickly supplanted by tragedy and despair: "I never got over the devastating shock of what happened to D Company in Escoville on 7 June 1944."[8]

Back at Pointe du Hoc, there was finally good news. Around 3 P.M., two landing craft arrived on the beach below the cliffs. They carried ammunition, fresh water, and food, along with twenty-four men, one of whom informed Rudder that relief

from the 5th Ranger Battalion, which had been ordered the previous evening to stay and hold Vierville-sur-Mer, was on its
way.[9] Rudder's men gorged on Spam, bread, and jam and reloaded their weapons. The landing craft then left with fifty-two
badly wounded men aboard.

At five o'clock that afternoon, Rudder made contact with the
relief force.

"Try and fight thru to us."

The reply was far from heartening. The relief force had been
halted by a massive crater on the road from Vierville-sur-Mer to
Pointe du Hoc. Minefields flanked the road. The force had then
come under heavy artillery fire. There was also a truly alarming
report: Other Americans in the area had been defeated in a
fierce German counterattack. This was not true, but the senior
officers in the relief force did not yet know this and were under-
standably confused and deeply concerned—for all they knew,
they were the last remaining American unit in the area, facing
concerted German attacks. And so they halted, just fifteen hundred yards from Rudder, and waited for more information. Several hours later, they finally learned that the "invasion was
definitely a success" and that earlier reports had been mistaken.[10]
But they were ordered not to advance toward the Pointe until
the following morning.[11]

Rudder and his men had to spend a second night, cut off,
under continual German attack. Their only support was the
navy. Through the night of June 7–8, the battleship *Texas,* an-
chored offshore, poured accurate fire into the fields surrounding
D Company's George Kerchner and his two dozen men, all that

remained of the more than 150 he had commanded on June 6. Shells landed just fifty yards from a ditch where they were taking cover, gouging craters, sometimes five feet deep and twenty feet wide, in the heaving ground.

Kerchner later jotted down his memories of these harrowing hours: "I was plenty scared and worried about my men and didn't get any sleep until about 0630—I was awakened at 0730 by a rustling in the brush about twenty yards down the ditch. However, I was relieved to find it was two 'E' company men who were left when their outfit pulled out. They were doubly welcome as one had matches which I used to light some Jerry cigars I had gotten earlier . . . We could see a number of Jerries around and heard lots more as they fought off our own troops. I didn't know if all my men were alive, dead, or captured. The brush in the hedgerow was too thick to crawl through and Jerry had machine guns at all four corners of our field. About all I could do was pray, worry and alternately clean my pistol and M1. Most of the time I sat with my pistol in one hand and a grenade in the other."[12]

Kerchner had a prayer book in his pocket. He cowered in the ditch and prayed to God for salvation—to stay alive, to be spared. He turned the pages as shells exploded and eventually read the prayer book from cover to cover. There was no relief from other Rangers under Rudder's command; Rudder had by now assumed that D Company had been killed or captured. Finally, early on the morning of June 8, the *Texas* stopped firing. The Germans appeared to have lost their stamina and did not launch any further counterattacks. A badly shaken Kerchner crawled out of his ditch and moved along a nearby hedgerow, trying to find some of his men. Just a dozen had survived.

Kerchner came across a man who had a bad shoulder wound but was so delighted to see Kerchner that he "almost kissed" him.

There was the clank and clatter of tank tracks.

In a foxhole not far from Kerchner, Sergeant Len Lomell listened as the sound grew louder.

We're about to be overrun by Germans.[13]

Someone spotted soldiers marching behind a Sherman tank. Americans.

A few yards behind several scouts strode Colonel Charles Canham, the grizzled commander of the 116th Infantry Regiment. He had landed the morning of June 6 on Omaha and managed not only to survive but to then organize his battered regiment and finally lead it toward Pointe du Hoc. Forty-three-year-old Canham, a bespectacled West Point graduate with a neatly trimmed mustache, had been shot in the wrist on Omaha and now toted a pistol in his good hand.

It was around 11 A.M. when Kerchner ordered some men to cover him and then ran toward Canham's relief force. "I was so weak and stiff I fell two or three times," he recalled, "but it was a wonderful sight to see American troops on the road. They didn't know if Pointe du Hoc was still held by our own men."

"Where are the Germans?"[14] asked Canham, ever eager to fight.

Canham and the tank pressed on, past Kerchner's position, toward Rudder's command post. Other tanks followed, but several were disabled by mines. Then tragic confusion played out.

Some of Rudder's men had been forced to scavenge whatever weapons they could find in the previous two days of fierce fighting around the Pointe and were firing German machine guns. The relief force, recognizing the high rate of fire coming from the guns, opened up on the Rangers' positions.[15] Two men were in fact killed by Canham's relief force.[16]

One of Rudder's men snapped, jumped up onto a Sherman, banged on its turret, and then put a gun to the tank commander's head to bring the fratricide to an end. Meanwhile, at his command post, Rudder hurriedly helped some of his men hold up an American flag to show Canham's trigger-happy force that they were not Germans.

Rudder then received a message from the *Texas*, where observers had heard the tanks firing.

"Are you being fired upon?"

"Yes."

"Do you want me to fire on them?"

"No."

"Are you being hit by friendly fire?"

"Yes."[17]

Not long after, the firing stopped.

At around 4 P.M., Kerchner and his fellow survivors from the assault on Pointe du Hoc set up camp in a muddy apple orchard, where they finally were able to lie down on bedrolls, eat C rations, drink fresh water, and start to come to terms with the enormity of the trauma they had survived and the loss of so many close friends.[18] On either side of a road leading from the orchard lay dead Americans. "The gold and silver insignia of rank on the officers' collars," recalled one of Rudder's men, "caught the sun and sent it back along the road in little pin-points of dancing light."[19]

Of the 225 Rangers who had landed on D-Day, fewer than seventy-five were still able to fight on.[20] In all, 152 men from the 2nd Ranger Battalion, which would be awarded the Presidential Unit Citation, had been wounded, seventy-seven of them fatally—a casualty rate of some 67 percent.[21]

Lieutenant Kerchner and Colonel Rudder, wounded twice at Pointe du Hoc, would both receive the Distinguished Service Cross for their heroism at those cliffs, as would Sergeant Len Lomell and eleven other Rangers.[22] "Rudder talked to you softly but firmly like a big brother," remembered Lomell, who would become a successful lawyer after the war. "He inspired you to do your best. He was a man you would die for."

At an awards ceremony seven miles inland from Pointe du Hoc, two weeks after D-Day, Rudder's courage and persever-ance were cited by a senior general as Rudder stood before the survivors of his 2nd Battalion. With tears rolling down his cheeks, Rudder turned to his men. "This does not belong to me," he cried out, referring to the medal, whose cost had been so great. "It belongs to you."

"You keep it for us!" shouted one of his men.[23]

BY THE TIME THE RANGERS at Pointe du Hoc were relieved on June 8, the acclaimed war correspondent Ernie Pyle, approach-ing a nervous breakdown after covering the war in Europe since 1942, was surveying the grim aftermath on Omaha Beach. In the western sector, Colonel Canham's 116th Infantry Regiment had been decimated, suffering more than a thousand casualties, with 247 men killed.[24] Some of their bloated corpses were now washing in with the tide.

Pyle walked amid a haunting flotsam and jetsam: broken and discarded weapons, pocket Bibles, moldy oranges, tennis rackets, hastily written last letters. "There were toothbrushes and razors," observed Pyle, "and snapshots of families back home staring up at you from the sand. There were pocketbooks, metal mirrors, extra trousers, and bloody, abandoned shoes. There were broken-handled shovels, and portable radios smashed almost beyond recognition, and mine detectors twisted and ruined."[25]

Pyle tried his best to convey the price of D-Day to his millions of readers in the United States, but words, he knew, could never adequately convey the extent of the devastation, human and material: "The wreckage was vast and startling. The awful waste and destruction of war, even aside from the loss of human life, has always been one of its outstanding features to those who are in it. Anything and everything is expendable."[26]

That same afternoon, Major Charles Dalton of the Queen's Own Rifles found himself on a hospital ship in the middle of the English Channel. The sun shone on calm seas. Was his younger brother Elliot alive, still in action? He felt proud that he had led the first men to secure Juno Beach, the deadliest stretch of sand on D-Day after Omaha.

Belowdecks, stretchers had been stacked three high, full of wounded Canadians. Cigarettes were hard to come by, so everyone shared. Dalton would light a smoke and take two puffs and then pass it to the man above him, who also took just a couple of drags. If nobody cheated, the cigarette would go all the way up to the top rack and back down and Dalton would then get to fill his lungs once more. Several decades later, he would remember how not one man took more than his fair share: "Most people would say, 'Here I am, and I don't even know if I'm going to be alive by morning, so I'm going to take a really good drag on it,' but nobody did. And that's what people missed when they got home."[27]

FROM SWORD AND GOLD, just two days after D-Day, long lines of British infantry snaked inland beneath bright blue skies to reinforce the front line, "plodding steadily up dusty French roads," recalled a British officer, "single file; heads bent against the heavy weight of all the kit piled on their backs; armed to the teeth . . . sweat running down their cheeks and their enamel drinking mugs dangling at their hips; never looking back and hardly ever looking to the side . . . while the jeeps and the lorries and the tanks went crowding by, smothering them in great billows and clouds of dust."[28]

Every single Tommy was needed in what had rapidly developed into a bitter slugging match on the eastern flank of the Allied bridgehead. Even a cursory look at a situation map had made it clear to Rommel that the Allies had to be prevented from seizing Caen, the hub of several critical roads that led across open ground to the Seine and Paris, 120 miles away. If Caen could be held, the Allied breakout from Normandy could be stalled. As many tanks as possible were rolling under cover of darkness—daylight movement was suicidal, due to the Allies' complete mastery of the skies—toward the heavily bombed city and the high ground to the city's east above the Orne River.

The Allies had enjoyed the element of surprise on D-Day. But now the stunned German defenders were being reinforced by tens of thousands of soldiers led by field officers who were fiercely determined to not only hold their ground but also strike swiftly at the many weak points in the Allied front lines while continually pummeling the invaders with artillery and mortar fire. It was essential to inflict maximum terror and violence, especially in critical sectors such as the high ground to the east of the Orne, where, by June 8, Lord Lovat and his brigade of two thousand commandos were only just managing to hold on. Indeed, Lovat's lads were close to the breaking point, rattled and worn down by the continual shelling and surprise counterattacks by elements of the 21st Panzer Division. Red-eyed, quick to anger, slow to laughter, they were utterly oblivious to anything but the basics of survival, blind to the beauty of the Normandy countryside bathed in golden sunlight and to the clusters of blooming cabbage roses dangling from the windows of houses that had escaped shelling.

There was no dawn chorus of birdsong on June 9. The nightingales and larks had fled. The ripening corn could be heard swaying in the breeze as men tried to kick up as little dust as possible moving from one covered hole to the next. The crack of a twig underfoot could draw a sniper's bullet. The silence between eruptions of violence was full of desperation and fear. "We felt that we must whisper," recalled one commando, "and each noise in the distance clinked sharply like a chink of light suddenly breaking into a dark room."[29]

Men no longer laughed when Bill Millin abandoned his pipes and dove for cover upon the resumption of still more mortar shelling. "With the crashes of sounds one's brains seemed to be blown out as well," recalled Lovat. "Words came slowly from afar, and although the mind raced in mental overdrive it became increasingly hard to concentrate."

Prolonged and accurate artillery fire was even more terrifying than the seemingly endless mortar "stonks," shredding men's nerves, driving some insane. "The fury of artillery is a cold, mechanical fury," remembered one particularly articulate soldier, "but its intent is personal. When you are under its fire you are the sole target. All of that shrieking, whining venom is directed at you and no one else. You hunch in your hole in the ground, reduce yourself into as small a thing as you can become, and harden your muscles in a pitiful attempt at defying the jagged, burning teeth of the shrapnel. Involuntarily you curl up into the fetal position except that your hands go down to protect your genitalia. This instinct to defend the place of generation against the forces of annihilation is universal."[30]

On June 10, the Germans launched attack after attack on the British positions near a village called Bréville, on the high ground overlooking the Orne. It was the fiercest combat Lovat had yet encountered. The day's final assault left a "hushed silence" and many fatalities. Commander Philippe Kieffer, as "brave as a lion," in Lovat's words, had been badly wounded. Léon Gautier's commanding officer, Robert Dawson, who had headed Number 4 Commando, was also evacuated. "The survivors, as always, rose magnificently to the dark hour," recalled Lovat. "Burial parties performed their appointed duties: 'The Band of Brothers'

were very close that day. The quick and the dead . . . There was a
tenderness under the apple trees as powder-grimed officers and
men brought in the dead; a tenderness for lost comrades, who
had fought together so often and so well, that went beyond rever-
ence and compassion."

Many dear friends went into the earth that sunlit evening.
One young man had been killed by a German bullet that had cut
the ribbon of a decoration for bravery sewn onto his chest. Lovat
finally left the apple orchard on tiptoe, "not to disturb our comrades' sleep."[31] Later that evening, he held a meeting with other
depressed and jittery officers. The news was grim: Almost three
hundred men from the brigade had been lost. The Germans
were counterattacking every few hours, sensing victory. It was
but a matter of time, Lovat knew, before his and so many of his
men's turn would inevitably come to "bite the dust."[32]

FINDING NO SUCCESS in attacks on Caen from the north, an increasingly under-pressure General Montgomery decided to en-
circle the German defenders from the 21st Panzer Division and
then finish them off. Meanwhile, farther west, the Americans
encountered stiff resistance as they tried to push inland toward
the city of Saint-Lô—like Caen, an important road hub. Fighting raged all along the Allied front line, from the heights above
the Orne River to Carentan, at the neck of the Cotentin Peninsula, sixty miles to the west. "There can be no question of fighting a rearguard action," Hitler ordered his generals, "nor of
retiring to a new line of resistance. Every man shall fight and fall
where he stands."[33]

At the center of the Allied line, the Canadians fought one costly engagement after another as the battle for Caen intensified, with both sides "blasting at each other day and night," remembered a Canadian corporal, pounding away like demented "hockey players."[34] In an afternoon attack on June 11 near the village of Le Mesnil-Patry, the Queen's Own Rifles came under fire from 88-millimeter guns, the most feared German artillery pieces of the war, which were well dug in just eight hundred yards away. Major Elliot Dalton was leading A Company, following behind Sherman tanks, when the high-explosive, armor-piercing shells landed all around.

As the advance unit, A Company were easy pickings. The first men were killed, turned to hamburger by thousands of shards of flying white-hot metal before they even heard the sound of the high-velocity shells, which traveled almost three thousand feet per second. The Germans were able to fire up to twenty rounds per minute from each gun, and as they did so, more and more of Elliot Dalton's men frantically tried to escape tanks that were hit or about to be. "Hatches came up," recalled a sergeant major in Elliot's company, "and tank men struggled to get out—mostly with uniforms on fire—and the drivers with our riflemen tried to put out the flames both in the machines and on the men." It was impossible for Elliot to keep control of his company as tank drivers panicked. "The drivers couldn't see the ground directly ahead or under them, so a soldier on the ground had almost as much fear from his own raging tanks—twisting, speeding up, retreating, flames everywhere—as from enemy fire."[35]

A mortar exploded near Elliot Dalton.[36] "It blew off part of

my uniform and one shoe," he recalled. "But the worst part was
the indignity. I fell face down in a cow flap and I had this . . . this
stuff all over me. Two girls looked over a wall and started laughing. I was so mad I wanted to shoot them. I even took out my
revolver. I was only half-conscious, you see."[37] In less than fifteen minutes, two companies from the Queen's Own Rifles had
been decimated, almost a hundred men killed or wounded.[38]
Nineteen tanks were destroyed.

Elliot Dalton's men found him bleeding badly and quickly
applied a tourniquet to his leg. Before long, he was on his way to
a crowded aid station, then back to England, to a hospital at
Cliveden, the lavish estate of Lady Astor, on the banks of the
Thames in Buckinghamshire. "I got there on the 14th June," remembered Elliot. "I was on a stretcher at the door and a nurse
comes up to me. She wants to know why I'm not in my bed. I tell
her I've just arrived. She tells me to stop joking and wheels me
off to a ward. We stop by a bed. Someone is sleeping in it with a
sheet over his head. The nurse tells this fellow it's someone else's
bed. What's he doing in it? Who is he? The fellow says he's Dalton of the Queen's Own."

The nurse was having none of that.

"Dalton of the Queen's Own is over there on a stretcher."[39]

The man in the bed sat up. He was indeed a Dalton: Major
Charles Dalton.

Elliot and Charles looked at each other in amazement. "That
was the first time I knew my brother wasn't dead," recalled Elliot.[40]

Two days after Elliot was admitted to the hospital, Queen
Elizabeth toured the wards, spending three hours chatting with

the wounded. She wore a long gray coat, one starstruck reporter noted, "an upturned hat with a blue bow in front, and the diamond maple leaf pin given to her by the women of Canada."[41] When she talked with Charles, who was photographed in his uniform with his head bound in bandages, she learned that he had been part of her guard of honor when she visited Toronto before the war.

Both brothers would make speedy recoveries but would do so in different hospitals. According to one report: "The brothers were celebrated throughout the Canadian military for their shenanigans as well as their bravery. After disrupting the hospital with wheelchair races and escapes to the local pub, they were finally sent to separate hospitals."[42] The Daltons would eventually return to action with their regiment and survive the war. Charles would leave the army in 1945, and Elliot seven years later. Asked if they were no longer competitive, fifty years after the war, Elliot smiled. "Well, no, not exactly," he explained. "Charlie and I still play tennis a couple of times a week."[43] Each brother still hated to lose to the other.

ON THE SAME afternoon that Elliot Dalton was wounded, June 11, Sergeant Major Stanley Hollis's Green Howards prepared to attack a village called Cristot, just two miles to the west of where the Queen's Own Rifles had been stopped in their tracks and badly mauled. There was confusion and delay, but finally, around 5 P.M., they received the order to advance. Hollis was leading 16 Platoon of D Company of the 6th Green Howards as rain poured down and men moved out.

"A lousy day for anything," thought Hollis, "anything, particularly war."[44]

Just a straightforward, simple job. That was what Hollis and his men had been told. Capture a small hill south of Cristot. But the planning had seemed rushed to Hollis. It had all the makings of a botch job. Little did he know he was about to encounter, for the first time, the full force of the 12th SS Panzer Division, which had already routed the Canadians earlier that day before receiving Rommel's orders to seize and hold Cristot. Of all the German armored divisions rushed to Normandy, the 12th SS, otherwise known as the Hitler Youth Division, fought most fanatically and, arguably, inflicted the greatest carnage, earning a truly fearsome reputation.[45] The Green Howards were no match.

As C and B Companies from Hollis's battalion started to cross the wheat fields,[46] the 12th SS opened fire from a farm around a hundred yards away. C Company's commander was killed, the second leader of the unit to lose his life since D-Day, and B Company was hit even harder, with its most senior officers killed and wounded. Battalion commander Lieutenant Colonel Robin Hastings learnt that both companies had been halted by intense fire and decided to bring A Company into the fight, but it, too, came under withering fire, so he ordered his only reserve, D Company, into action.

Hollis found himself beside Hastings, leading 16 Platoon to the left of a tank along a sunken and shaded lane, skirted by trees and high banks, near the village of Cristot. They had not gone far along the lane when they heard the familiar rattle of a Spandau, an MG42 machine gun. "The first thing Hollis did was grab me and shove me behind the tank," recalled Hastings. Rain still poured down, turning the churned ground, stamped with tank tracks, into a muddy mire. The tank ground to a halt. Hollis couldn't work out why. "Maybe [the tank driver] could see over a hedge and see another tank knocked out in the field," he recalled. "I think he knew what he was in for and that's why he stopped."[47]

Hollis gathered his platoon on the edge of a nearby orchard, making sure they carried as many rounds and grenades as possible, and then led them forward on his hands and knees until he could see Germans firing from behind a tree. Hollis was flat on his stomach and spotted two more Germans, in gray uniforms, firing quick bursts down a lane and then ducking back into cover. He watched closely. Every few seconds they would appear, fire at the Green Howards, and then drop out of view.

Well, we'll have to see what we can do about that.

Hollis grabbed for a grenade in a pouch that held his Bren gun's extra ammunition but instead found a shaving brush and a pair of socks. He'd checked so thoroughly that every man in his unit had packed extra ammunition, but he'd forgotten to do so himself. He turned to the man behind him. "For Christ's sake give me a grenade!"

The next time the Germans jumped up, Hollis was ready. He threw a grenade as if he were lobbing a cricket ball—he'd never got the hang of doing it the regulation army way. The Germans saw the grenade arcing through the air and ducked down as Hollis sprinted toward them. "I ran right behind [the grenade] . . . I hadn't pulled the bloody pin out! Of course the Germans didn't know that and they kept down, waiting for it to go off. By the time they realized it wasn't going to go off, I was on top of them and shot both of them."[48]

A company commander approached Colonel Robin Hastings, saluted, and asked if he could go in search of men who had come under German fire and had not reported back.

Hastings had lost too many officers already that evening. "No, certainly not," he replied. "You can go as far as that hedge—no further."

The company commander found a gap in the hedge, but almost as soon as he peered through it, he was killed, shot through the head.

Hastings decided he should explain his position to superiors at brigade level. Then he heard what sounded like a fierce tank engagement to his rear. He realized that elements of the 12th SS Panzer Division had counterattacked, leaving his battalion in danger of being cut off and then surrounded.

"We are on the edge of our objective and under intermittent fire," reported Hastings to a superior over a radio. "We have had severe losses of officers. We are not in touch with any friendly troops on either side. What are the orders? What am I to do?"

"Do what you think best."

"I suggest we withdraw . . ."[49]

Hastings went to his decimated companies, one by one, and gave the order to pull back. He then stood in the sunken lane, not far from where Stanley Hollis had earlier killed the German machine gunners, and watched as his weary men withdrew. "They carried their wounded and marched past me bloody but fairly unbowed," he remembered. "I noticed amongst the prisoners some in the Panzer Lehr uniform who must have arrived since the morning; these were the toughest of all German SS soldiers. After the last man had passed through, I walked back down the lane of death, leaving a great part of my battalion dead among the Normandy hayfields."[50]

It had been a disastrous day. Hastings would later learn that nine tanks had raced ahead of his battalion through orchards, only to be ambushed. Just two of the tanks had made it back to British lines, and many of Hastings's men, separated from armored support, had then been massacred by heavy fire from the 12th SS as they crossed several fields. The final butcher's bill for the fateful evening's fighting was depressing indeed: 250 casualties, with twenty-four officers lost.

Hastings had been dubious, like Hollis, about the operation from the start, believing it was "not on."

"I think there's a lot of work for you to do, padre," Hastings told his unit's priest, who attended to so many dying and grievously wounded that he quickly took up smoking, so affected was he by the carnage.[51]

THE FOLLOWING DAY, June 12, the battle for control of the all-important heights on the eastern bank of the Orne continued from the cold dawn until the late dusk, with both sides suffering ever greater casualties. As darkness fell, Lord Lovat called a meeting at a command post he had set up in some farm buildings near the village of Bréville, at the southern perimeter of the British positions. Suddenly, shells exploded all around with devastating effect, setting roofs ablaze. Several men were killed and others collapsed, badly wounded by flying white-hot shards of shrapnel. Lovat's close friend, thirty-five-year-old Lieutenant Colonel Derek Mills-Roberts, entered a stable and came across a badly wounded Lovat: "He was a frightful mess; a large shell fragment had cut deeply into his back and side."

Lovat was in agony but extraordinarily calm.

"Take over the brigade," he told Mills-Roberts, "and whatever happens—not a foot back."[52]

Lovat repeated his order again and again.

Not a foot back . . . Not a foot back . . .

A captain watched as Lovat called for a priest and was then evacuated: "Those who saw Lovat could not believe he could possibly survive."[53]

Lovat's final orders were obeyed. The heights to the east of the Orne were held, but his men paid a terrible price in doing so, eventually spending eighty-three days in combat without being rested. "Of the 146 officers and 2,452 other ranks who had taken part," recalled Mills-Roberts, "77 officers and 890 other ranks had become battle casualties, killed, wounded or missing."[54]

Such was the toll on just one British unit that had landed on D-Day and then refused to give up ground.

THAT SAME SUNNY, mild evening of June 12, Lieutenant Colonel Terence Otway, still leading the 9th Battalion of the Parachute Regiment, was inspecting his men's positions close to Bréville when a shell landed nearby, killing a young lieutenant, wounding a sergeant badly, and blowing Otway several yards across a road. He was shaken but visibly unhurt. The following morning,

Otway and his men were finally relieved by a unit from Major John Howard's 2nd Battalion of the Oxford and Buckingham-shire Light Infantry, some of whom were deeply shocked by the evidence all around them of intensely violent combat.

Men stood in small groups, utterly dazed, with bewildered eyes. In every hedgerow, remembered one man, body parts and mangled corpses rotted in the June sun. A lifeless Scot held fanned-out playing cards, not far from a corporal with his fin-ger on the trigger of a Thompson submachine gun, one eye still open, killed as he was taking aim at a German who was also dead but still gripping his dagger.

One eyewitness saw a paratrooper who had been "run through the middle of his body by a German rifle and bayonet which had pinned him to a tree. At the same time, he had reached over . . . and plunged his dagger into the middle of his opponent's back. The two had died at some time during the night but in daylight could be seen propping each other up."[55]

Otway and his men had fought to the end of their endurance and were barely able to stand as they left Bréville, with its sickly odor of burnt wood and smoldering flesh, carpeted with broken twigs, branches, and singed leaves.

On June 17, Otway and the few survivors from his battalion who had seized the Merville Battery were pulled off the line and sent for rest in a quarry near the village of Amfreville.[56] As soon as Otway arrived, he went to meet with a fellow officer in a building. As he entered, he looked back at his men. They were laid out on grass nearby, in a deep sleep after just a few seconds, having collapsed to the ground in exhaustion.[57]

Otway himself had not emerged unscathed. The blast that

had thrown him across a road had increasingly severe after-effects. At first he had pains in his neck and headaches, but then he lost his vision for a while. As the battle for the heights east of the Orne continued, he was diagnosed with a serious concussion and was sent back across the English Channel to a hospital in Wales. To his great and everlasting frustration, he was told he was unfit to serve in combat again.

CHAPTER 12

A Dirty Bush War

THE FIGHTING GREW ever more intense in Normandy later that June as the summer heat settled over the dusty, shell-scarred pastures and began to bake the ruins of hundreds of villages. Eisenhower's driver and confidante, Kay Summersby, recalled that her boss, ensconced in his spartan trailer on the grounds of Southwick House, near Portsmouth, was "very much depressed" by the news filtering back from the front: "Most of the time we simply sat in the trailer in the woods waiting. We stayed late every night waiting for just one more report to come through. I would call up the mess and have them send sandwiches over for supper, and I would boil water on the little spirit stove for Ike's powdered coffee. He would sit there and smoke and worry. Every time the telephone would ring he would grab it."[1]

One of Eisenhower's men, Captain Frank Lillyman, wasn't prepared to wait for good news on the wrong side of the English Channel. Already feted in the American press as officially the

first American to land in France on D-Day, Lillyman went absent without leave from a hospital in England after just a few
days of treatment for his wounds, determined to rejoin his men
in Normandy. He wrangled his way onto a supply ship on June
14 and reported for duty back in France.

The 101st Airborne's commanding general, Maxwell Taylor,
having just encountered savage German resistance at Carentan,
was far from pleased to see his wayward, now famous pathfinder, and according to one report he "waved the papers for a
promotion under Lillyman's nose and then ripped them up."[2]
Press footage of the 101st Airborne in Normandy showed an
ever cocky Lillyman, surrounded by his fellow Screaming Eagles, tommy gun in hand, nonchalantly answering questions. A
few weeks later, Lillyman paid the price for going AWOL and
was ordered to change units, moving to the 3rd Battalion of the
502nd Parachute Infantry Regiment. His days as a swashbuck-
ling pathfinder were over.

Meanwhile, back in England, General Eisenhower grew increasingly frustrated with Montgomery's lack of progress and
his excuses for not seizing Caen, the key British and Canadian
objective on D-Day. "Naturally I and all my senior commanders
and staff," recalled Eisenhower, "were greatly concerned about
this static situation near Caen. Every possible means of breaking
the deadlock was considered and I repeatedly urged Montgomery to speed up and intensify his efforts to the limit. He threw in
attack after attack, gallantly conducted and heavily supported
by artillery and air, but German resistance was not crushed."[3]

The Germans who carried the greatest burden in maintain-
ing the deadlock were the beleaguered panzer crews, living

short and brutal lives that more resembled those of men aboard hunted U-boats. Trapped by day in their dug-in and heavily camouflaged Mark IVs and Tigers, low on fuel and ammunition, hidden in the lee of honeysuckle-draped walls and hedgerows, covered in clods of lush pasture and leaves, Rommel's amphetamine-fueled youths watched and waited for their prey to stir. No longer crack offensive units, masters of blitzkrieg, the panzers were now used mostly as armored anti-tank artillery, islands of static defense. Turrets reeked of fuel and of feces filling empty shell casings and of anxious boys' sweat. Gingerly, tankers climbed from their turrets only at night and filled their lungs with fresh air.

There were a million Allied soldiers in Normandy by late June, but still the front barely moved. British generals had long been haunted by the bloodletting and stalemate of the Great War in France, when mazes of trenches had swallowed the best of their generation. Now it seemed as if the ghosts of the Great War had been resurrected. There had clearly been a monumental oversight in planning—not one of the legions of intelligence officers who had pored over reconnaissance photos had spotted the high, ancient banks of hedgerows known as the bocage. It made swift movement impossible and provided the perfect defensive landscape for the Germans.[4] An entire infantry company, filled with confused and untrained replacements, could be engaged all day to seize just one field, one small patch of the infernal tapestry stretching from Caen to Cherbourg, the port at the tip of the Cotentin Peninsula whose liberation would cost the Americans 22,000 casualties after an agonizing slog.

The Allies had made another costly error in planning: They

had vastly underestimated the will of the German soldier to fight so long and so hard in Normandy. Germany's survival depended on the outcome of the battle. Even the foreign conscripts from Russia and Poland killed with determination, until the moment they decided it was safe to surrender and emerged from their bullet-scarred pillboxes. "Why did I fight for the Germans?" said one Polish prisoner of war, interviewed by journalist Alan Moorehead in a POW cage on the Cotentin Peninsula. "Like to see my back? It's got scars across it from the neck down to the arse. They hit me there with a sword. Either you obeyed orders or you got no food. Certainly I went on firing. There was a German standing behind me with a revolver. It wasn't enough just to shoot. You had to shoot straight. If you didn't you got a bullet through your back. Don't believe me? Ask the others. Like the Germans? I'd like to tear their guts out."[5]

On June 27, as Americans entered the shattered outskirts of Cherbourg, Sergeant Major Stanley Hollis and the Green Howards were still fighting near Caen, almost three-quarters of which would become a blanket of rubble, burying some of the three thousand civilians killed in Allied bombings beneath a shroud of blasted masonry and creamy yellow limestone.[6] That day, beside a flower-speckled field, where the bloated corpses of cattle rotted, their feet jutting skyward, Hollis's battalion lost its irreplaceable leader: Colonel Robin Hastings, who had led the first wave ashore on D-Day, was badly wounded in the leg by mortar fire.[7] Medics rushed to help Hastings, and his unflappable demeanor fell away. "Don't hurt me," cried Hastings as men carried him to a jeep. His nerve had finally gone.

As he was being taken to an aid station, Hastings came across a senior officer whom he detested, the kind of "bloody old fool" who had sent so many men over the top and to their deaths in World War I and was now doing the same a generation later. "What are you doing back here?" the officer asked Hastings. "I think you're perfectly fit."[8] A medic, perhaps taking umbrage at the insult, showed the officer a large pool of Hastings's blood in the ambulance.

Hollis and his fellow Green Howards, most of them scared young replacements, fought on under new but less capable and loving leadership, in what the men trying to kill them now called a "schmutziger Buschkrieg"—"dirty bush war."[9] And it was foul indeed, forcing men on both sides to casually cross moral lines, to become glib and debased, to do what once had been unthinkable—especially if it meant staying alive. Hollis would later tell his daughter of an incident that would haunt his fitful sleep for decades. "He had to kill a young German soldier who was wounded," she explained, "one of the Hitler Youth, not much older than his own son, Brian. The boy, in SS combat uniform and helmet and carrying an automatic weapon was aged about 14 or 15 when captured in the deadly Bocage. The Green Howards pulled this boy into their foxhole, fed him, gave him water, dressed his wounds and shared what little they had. They were looking after him because he was so young. When they thought [they were] safe from the fighting, they relaxed. But that was when the boy grabbed one of their guns and shot one of Stan's men dead. In a flash, [Hollis] grabbed his gun and shot him and killed him and that was what his nightmares were about. They were awful and plagued him for years afterwards."[10]

It was these most demented worshippers of Hitler, these

"German problem children," pallid and dusty-haired, who most disturbed their captors and journalists such as Alan Moorehead.[11] The more he saw of them, the more he gave up hope for the German people. They embodied the utter nihilism and amorality of Nazism. They were the ones who had gotten drunk fastest and raped without conscience, who had most shamed the nation of Beethoven and Goethe, who had been in kindergarten when Hitler promised them a Jew-free thousand-year Reich.

CHERBOURG FELL ON JUNE 30, three weeks behind schedule. Brigadier General Theodore Roosevelt was installed as the proud military governor of the port, which had been so badly destroyed by the Germans that it could not be used until the middle of August. On July 10, General Montgomery and General Bradley met to discuss plans to finally seize Caen and then to break out of Normandy. Operation Goodwood would commence on July 18 and become the largest tank battle ever waged by the British. Operation Cobra was scheduled to begin a week later, preceded by three thousand aircraft carpet-bombing a narrow section of the front, thereby punching a hole in the German lines.

The day after the Allies' senior generals met, twenty-four-year-old Quentin Roosevelt II, who had landed with the Big Red One on Omaha Beach on D-Day, visited his father in Cherbourg. They sat together until 10 P.M., recalled Quentin, chatting about "home, the family, my plans, the war . . . having a swell time." General Roosevelt confessed that he was "very tired" after two years of war. In fact, he had had several minor heart attacks. Quentin insisted his father take it easy, "stay low." After he bade him good night, Quentin paid a visit to his father's doctor, and then to the general's aide, pressuring the man to promise to "hold" his father down if he got sick again. Just a couple of hours later, around 2 A.M. on July 12, Quentin arrived back to his unit and learned that his father had suffered yet another heart attack.

"The lion is dead," Quentin wrote to his mother.[12] D-Day's oldest general, the eldest son of one of America's greatest presidents, was buried on Bastille Day, July 14, 1944, in Sainte-Mère-Église. Among the honorary pallbearers at what Quentin described as a "warrior's funeral" was General George Patton, who would write in his diary that Roosevelt was the bravest man he ever knew. The funeral was like "the magnificent climax of a great play," Quentin wrote. After his body was moved, at the request of his widow, Theodore Roosevelt Jr. would be buried near Colleville-sur-Mer beside his brother, a pilot who was killed during World War I.[13]

Four days after Roosevelt was placed in the ground, Operation Goodwood began with an attack of three armored divisions. The British lost five hundred tanks, more than a third of their total in Normandy, but Goodwood managed to strain the Germans severely, drawing in vital reserves of men and matériel. Six hundred German tanks were engaged against the Canadians and British, four times the number deployed against the Americans farther west.

On July 25, all of Caen was finally liberated, although not

much of it was left standing.[14] "Where three and four story houses had been, there were now merely craters in the ground," recalled one journalist. "New hills and valleys wherever you looked. The very earth was reduced to its original dust." Bulldozers were needed to open routes through rubble piled twenty feet deep. "It was like an archeological excavation into a lost world."[15]

As the traumatized citizens of Caen searched for loved ones in the ruins, in some cases turning their backs angrily on their British liberators, the Americans launched Operation Cobra. The aim was to finally escape the infernal hedgerow country that had stalled the American advance with its dense barriers, up to fifteen feet high, of blackthorn, hazel, and brambles. Near Saint-Lô, which, like Caen, was a critical crossroads, six hundred bombers pulverized a three-hundred-yard-wide strip of ground, punching a hole in the German line, held by the once elite Panzer Lehr Division.

The gap was expanded by a further eighteen hundred Eighth Air Force bombers, some of whom tragically dropped their loads on their own forces, wounding almost five hundred Americans and killing 111, including General Lesley McNair, the highest-ranking US officer to lose his life in Europe in World War II. "A bomb landed squarely on McNair in a slit trench," recalled General Omar Bradley, "and threw his body sixty feet and mangled it beyond recognition except for the three stars on his collar."[16] The fratricide "cast a gloom" over Eisenhower, as he remembered, and indeed over Bradley, but Cobra proved a stunning success, allowing the Americans to finally push into open country and regain mobility.[17]

On August 1, General George Patton's Third Army was acti-
vated and would sweep through Normandy into Brittany, ex-
ploiting open ground, and then threaten to envelop German
forces west of the Seine.[18] In response to the looming threat of
defeat in France, Hitler ordered a massive counterattack, the
Mortain offensive, to "annihilate" the Americans in the US VII
Corps in the area of Mortain.[19] On the night of August 6, just
hours before the main German offensive began, SS troops struck
hard at the Big Red One, in particular at Lieutenant John Spalding's 16th Infantry Regiment. His and other platoons appeared
to be surrounded. The SS attacked several times throughout the
night, but the men who had fought their way off Bloody Omaha
yet again refused to buckle.

It had now been exactly two months since Spalding first
heard the *zip-zip* of bullets over his head on D-Day, and the
haunting wail of Nebelwerfer rockets, which sounded like the
"high-pitched scream of despairing women" and, remembered
one officer, made it "difficult to retain any self-control under
their horrible and obscene noise."[20] During the subsequent slog
through the hellish bocage, he had "figured that if [the Ger-
mans] didn't get him then they wouldn't get him at all." He was
blessed, surely immortal. A later medical report noted that he
had "developed a feeling of personal invulnerability which was
reinforced as he saw so many of the others become casualties.
Frequently he felt that if he weren't an officer he would stay put
and not move forward, but he pushed himself on because of his
responsibility to his men and declared that if they were going to
get him they would regardless of where he was."[21]

The following morning, August 7, patrols detected in a nearby

village a large and well-armed German force, part of the 9th SS
Panzer Division, which appeared to be preparing for a knockout
blow on the 16th Infantry Regiment.[22] Spalding braced himself
for the onslaught. There had indeed been an angel on each of his
shoulders, as he put it, on D-Day. He had survived the odds on
Omaha, but now, in the mined mud of hedgerow country, the
waiting for the young fanatics of the SS to die for their Führer
finally pushed him to the breaking point. He was, after all, merely
human, and his nerves felt ever more raw and jagged. Near the
village of Mayenne, with his regiment widely dispersed, he heard
that SS paratroopers had been seen nearby. He would later tell a
doctor that the tension of waiting for them to attack had become
unbearable. "Patient started to worry," a subsequent medical report noted, "apprehensive that he would make poor decisions
which would be costly to his men."[23]

As it turned out, the purported SS avengers never turned up.
The Mortain offensive had been supported by just three hundred tanks, and by noon on August 7, as the morning mist burnt
off, they became fatally exposed to Allied aircraft. Before long,
Hitler's supermen were retreating, anxiously scanning the skies
for "Jabos," RAF Typhoons that swooped low and massacred every living thing in their gunsights, including countless horses,
their large eyes bulging in death with such pain that one pilot
felt as if his "heart would burst."[24] On August 8, realizing that
the German lines throughout Normandy were about to collapse,
Bradley declared, "This is an opportunity that comes to a commander not more than once in a century. We're about to destroy
an entire hostile army and go all the way from here to the German border."[25] Spalding and his regiment played their part,

capturing and destroying elements of the 9th and 10th SS Panzer Divisions as Hitler's generals desperately tried to pull troops from what became known as the Falaise pocket.[26] Just 460 men from the 9th SS Panzer would escape.[27] A typical SS armored division at full strength had twenty thousand men.

The numbers were numbing. At least eighty thousand German troops were caught in the Allied encirclement at Falaise, of whom more than ten thousand were mercilessly annihilated. A favorite tactic of the Typhoon pilots, remembered one RAF wing commander proudly, "was to seal off the front and rear of a column by accurately dropping a few bombs. This imprisoned the desperate enemy on a narrow stretch of dusty lane, and since the transports were sometimes jammed together four abreast, it made the subsequent rocket and cannon attack a comparatively easy business against the stationary targets."[28]

It was jolly good sport, although a tad too easy, like shooting fish, packed together like squirming sardines, in a barrel. Back and forth the vengeful RAF pilots flew, strafing, bombing, slaughtering the swarms of ragged men until their twelve Browning machine guns were smoking hot and their ammunition spent and it was time to gun the Rolls-Royce engine and soar away to get yet more rockets.[29] "After each run," remembered one pilot, "which resulted in a large vacant path of chopped up soldiers, the space would almost immediately be filled with other escapees."[30] Ambulances carrying grievously wounded men were turned to pitiful pieces of carbon. Another pilot recalled seeing pieces of uniform "plastered to shattered tanks and trunks . . . human remains hung in grotesque shapes on the blackened hedgerows."[31]

———

AMONG THE ALLIED units mopping up final German resistance were Sergeant Major Stanley Hollis and his fellow Green Howards, embittered foes of Hitler's finest killers since 1940. Toward the end of the battle of the Falaise pocket, as Hollis waited with other men at his company's command post, he heard the familiar whine of an incoming mortar. It exploded and a man on a radio was "killed stone dead where he sat," recalled Hollis, who was seated less than a yard away. Hollis himself was gravely wounded by dozens of mortar fragments. As one account had it: "His temple had been hit and his skull fractured, and his nose and the front of his face were badly damaged. He was also deaf in his left ear from the blast and his leg was wounded. His comrades were amazed and relieved to find him alive after what had been virtually a direct hit. This incident only served to add to Stan's already considerable legend among the troops. If the Germans couldn't kill him now, then surely nothing would."

Doctors attached a silver plate over Hollis's skull fracture and sent him back to England to recover. After five serious wounds and four years of combat, his time in the front lines was finally over. His tally of dead Germans stood at 102. Hollis would still be recuperating in a hospital in Leeds, in his native Yorkshire, several months later when he was told that he would receive the Victoria Cross. No Yorkshireman ever deserved it more. According to Lieutenant Colonel Robin Hastings, the commanding officer of the 6th Green Howards on D-Day, Hollis "was absolutely personally dedicated to winning the war—one of the few men I ever met who felt like that."[32]

In the Falaise pocket, two panzer divisions and eight infantry divisions were captured "almost in their entirety," recalled Eisenhower, who visited the battlefield two days after the pocket was sealed on August 21 and was met by "scenes that could be described only by Dante. It was literally possible to walk for hundreds of yards at a time, stepping on nothing but dead and decaying flesh."[33] Only with the first frost would the dark clouds of flies covering the area begin to lift. The stench of death, which aircrews could smell far above, took just as long to dissipate.

There remained one final, glorious chapter in the Battle of Normandy, which had seen the defeat of one of the greatest armies in the history of war.[34] On August 25, Paris was finally set free after more than fifteen hundred days and nights of increasing terror and starvation under the Nazi jackboot. The marvelously warm and sunny weather made "the day the war should have ended," in the words of American writer Irwin Shaw, all the more memorable.[35] Elements of the 4th "Ivy" Division, which had landed with Captain Leonard Schroeder on Utah Beach, fought to the very heart of the delirious city, seeing action just yards from Notre Dame cathedral. To many jaded reporters, who had recorded the Allies' agonies for several years, the sight of GIs embracing genuinely ecstatic Frenchwomen was never to be forgotten, the most joyous memory of the entire war. "Any GI who doesn't get laid tonight is a sissy," quipped Ernie Pyle.[36]

Five days later, Hitler's last troops retreated across the Seine, trudging east to defend their homeland. Since D-Day, as many as half a million of their compatriots had been killed, wounded, or captured or were missing.[37] So many others had also made the ultimate sacrifice during the Battle of Normandy, since the Allied first wave hit the beaches in the early hours of June 6. More than 15,000 French men, women, and children had been killed, mostly by Allied bombing. The Allies had suffered more than 200,000 casualties on the ground, with almost 40,000 dead and 20,000 missing.[38] Of 20,000 American fatalities, 9,385 would eventually lie in just one graveyard, near the village of Colleville-sur-Mer, overlooking Omaha Beach.[39] In a chapel at the center of the cemetery, the following words would be inscribed: "Think not only upon their passing. Remember the glory of their spirit."

CHAPTER 13

Defeating Hitler

SOME OF THOSE who had landed in the first wave were still alive and on the front lines as the long, bloody summer turned to fall. On September 1, less than a week after the liberation of Paris, Lieutenant George Kerchner of the 2nd Ranger Battalion, who had led men up the cliffs at Pointe du Hoc, was wounded in the shoulder by artillery fire while taking a German position, labeled "Hill 63" on maps, close to the village of Ty Baol, near the port of Brest, in Brittany.[1] In his diary, Kerchner noted, "Attack. Rough! Got hit. Million dollar wound. On way back."[2]

Four days after Kerchner's war ended, Major John Howard arrived back in England with what was left of D Company from the Oxford and Buckinghamshire Light Infantry. One hundred and eighty men, packed into flimsy wooden gliders, had accompanied Howard to France on the night of June 5; now, three months later, on September 5, his boat docked in Southampton with just forty soldiers. The regimental band heralded their arrival, and Howard's men enjoyed a shower and a hot meal before returning to the very barracks they had occupied during training for D-Day. Howard gazed at the empty beds where his men had once slept. So many had been killed or wounded in ninety-one days of war.

Howard felt terribly alone. "I was the only original officer left with D Company," he recalled, "for none of my friends or junior officers returned from Normandy with me. I had lost all of my sergeants and most of the corporals. I had seen my closest friend [Den Brotheridge] killed in the first minutes of action in battle. I found myself home, unscathed but for a couple of scars, and I couldn't wait to see my family again. I can remember trying to pray—to thank God for bringing me back alive—but, instead, I put my head in my hands and wept."[3]

Howard was at his home in Oxford, reunited with his wife, Joy, and their two young children, a fortnight later on the morning of September 17. He looked up and saw "planes milling about" in the clear sky, towing Horsa gliders, one of which was flown by Jim Wallwork, the pilot who had landed Howard so close to Pegasus Bridge on D-Day. Howard now knew some large-scale operation was in the offing and that Wallwork, as a highly experienced glider pilot, would be involved. "I silently wished old Jim good luck," Howard recalled.[4] Indeed, Wallwork would be in the thick of the action once again, this time as part of Operation Market Garden, the Allied airborne assault intended to shorten the war by dropping a large force across the lower Rhine in Holland. Beyond the Rhine lay the road to final victory and Berlin.

After landing his glider, Wallwork became involved in

desperate fighting, wielding a rifle near the Arnhem bridge, the famous "Bridge Too Far." Due to faulty intelligence and bad planning, Market Garden ended in major defeat for the British, with the 1st Airborne suffering a crushing blow, losing more than eight thousand men. It never went into combat again.[5] "We held one end of the bridge and the Germans held the other—and they wouldn't give up," remembered Wallwork. "Not too sporting of them."[6] Wallwork's unit, the Glider Pilot Regiment, had suffered greatly: More than 17 percent of Wallwork's comrades were killed.[7]

The British airborne forces had been humiliated, but Captain Frank Lillyman's Screaming Eagles enjoyed considerable success during Market Garden. More than 90 percent of Lillyman's fellow fifteen hundred paratroopers gathered in assembly areas less than ninety minutes after landing, a significant improvement compared with their drop on Normandy.[8] At a canal crossing in Best, north of the city of Eindhoven, one of Lillyman's fellow paratroopers, Private Joe Mann, died protecting his brothers-in-arms when he threw himself on a grenade. Mann was posthumously awarded the Medal of Honor, one of just two men from the division, incredibly, to receive the medal in World War II.[9]

Throughout his time in combat, Lillyman had carried a small 16-millimeter movie camera. He had used it on D-Day, recording color images of his fellow Screaming Eagles at an assembly point, and again filmed some of his men in Holland as they escorted more than a thousand German prisoners away from the Best battleground.[10] Lillyman then moved north with the rest of the 101st Airborne to an area southwest of Arnhem that would come to be known as "the Island," where the division would be deployed as regular infantry, fighting off concerted German attacks without yielding a yard of ground.[11]

Meanwhile, Lieutenant John Spalding, serving still with E Company of the 16th Infantry Regiment, had led his platoon through Belgium in just five days and entered Nazi Germany. For thirty-eight days, according to an after-action report, his company would fight in rain and fog, under "terrific shelling," beating off "almost continuous strong counterattacks" by Germans determined to hold Aachen, the first German city threatened by the Americans.[12]

On September 27, Spalding's luck finally ran out. In yet another shelling, the concussive effect of explosions twice knocked him to the ground and he was hit by shrapnel.[13] He managed somehow to crawl to an aid station and was sent back to England, wounded in his right thigh, one of five thousand US casualties in the battle for the ancient seat of Charlemagne's Holy Roman Empire, regarded as the First Reich by Hitler and his followers. The struggle for Aachen was deeply unnerving to the American high command, who had not expected such ferocious resistance. How many more GIs would have to die before the rest of Germany was defeated?

AS FALL TURNED TO WINTER, the Allies became bogged down in the Hürtgen Forest, east of Aachen, in a bitter attrition that would consume eleven American divisions and become the longest single battle ever fought by the US Army. Spalding's regiment from the 1st Division endured some of the fiercest combat, as did the 2nd Ranger Battalion, which had fought so heroically at Pointe du Hoc, only to be decimated by artillery fire while seizing just one hillside in the Hürtgen. The Americans suffered an extraordinary 71,000 non-battle casualties—trench foot, frostbite, and trauma—so hellish were the conditions in the dark forests, dubbed "the meat grinder" by the fortunate survivors.

One day that dreariest of Novembers, Spalding's fearless comrade from the first wave, Sergeant Phil Streczyk, finally reached his limit. Wounded in the neck in the Hürtgen, he had refused medical treatment, because it would mean leaving his men; combat had become a sacrament, bonding him to those he commanded as if in holy alliance. But the mortar screams, the vicious wails of Nebelwerfer rockets, and the time-on-target shelling from 88-millimeter guns were too much for even the man whose commanding officer on D-Day had described him as the bravest he had ever met. As shell fragments sliced through the air and tree bursts blasted jagged wooden shards in every direction, he began to shake from head to toe, and then lost his mind. It took several men from E Company to control him before he could be pulled off the line, by which time he had earned four Silver Stars and six Bronze Stars, having fought from North Africa via Sicily to northwest Europe, logging more than 440 days of frontline combat.[14]

Fighting in the Hürtgen ended on December 16 when Hitler launched his last great offensive in the west, called the Battle of the Bulge because of the sixty-mile-deep penetration of thinly held Allied lines in the Ardennes. The surprise attack involved thirty German divisions, including the reorganized 12th SS Panzer Division, which had been almost completely destroyed in Normandy. The battle would become the largest ever fought by the US Army, with almost twenty thousand US fatalities.

On December 18, with the Allied high command stunned and panicked, Captain Frank Lillyman and the rest of the 101st Airborne were ordered to board trucks and travel, in bitter winter conditions, to the Belgian city of Bastogne to set up a defensive ring. Bastogne was before long surrounded by German troops who outnumbered the besieged Americans three to one. As supplies ran desperately low for the ill-equipped defenders, it was decided that when the skies cleared, a forty-plane resupply mission should be carried out. Two planes of pathfinders would lead the operation, dropping men near Bastogne so they could set up smoke signals and Eureka sets for the main body of C-47 transports bringing in ammunition and medical supplies.

The lead pathfinder plane left England bound for a snow-covered Bastogne at 6:45 A.M. on December 23.[15] At the controls was Lieutenant Colonel Joel Crouch, seated beside Vito Pedone, the very same pair who had dropped Captain Lillyman into Normandy on D-Day. Again they were leading the way in a vital mission, this time to help save Lillyman and his fellow Screaming Eagles.

Shortly after takeoff, twenty-five-year-old Sergeant Jake McNiece, a veteran pathfinder, put his head into the cockpit and introduced himself to Crouch and Pedone.

McNiece looked worried.

"You don't have much confidence in this, do you?" asked Crouch.

"Change that to little or no confidence," replied McNiece. "I don't think you can hit Bastogne."[16]

"Let's synchronize our watches," said Crouch.

They did so.

"At eight-fifteen on the dot I'll pull us down out of this soup and you'll see the ground," said Crouch calmly. "We'll be right over Lille, France."

At exactly that time, Crouch pulled out of the clouds, and there, sure enough, was the city of Lille spread out below.

McNiece was impressed.

"The next place we'll hit is Brussels," said Crouch.

Crouch gave an exact time.

Again, on the dot, Crouch arrived over Brussels. Again, McNiece poked his head into the cockpit.

"Well," said McNiece, "this gives me a little more hope."

"In about fifteen minutes," said Crouch, "I'm going to give you a green light. You get out of here. If you do your job, I'll do mine."[17]

"I gotcha."[18]

It was just after 9 A.M. when Crouch approached Bastogne. He had hoped for a fighter escort from the Ninth Air Force, but the promised protection had not shown up, so he found himself flying alone in an unarmed plane, just above the heavily forested Ardennes. Crouch peered through his windscreen, looking for a cemetery he'd been told to use as a landmark to guide his way.

There it was—dead ahead.

Crouch looked at Pedone, who switched on the green jump light.

"Stand up and hook up!"[19] cried McNiece.

Men were about to jump when anti-aircraft fire filled the sky, the explosions like dry peas shaken in a tin can. Tracers fizzed past the plane's windows and shrapnel hit the fuselage with a hollow popping sound. One piece punctured the plane's thin skin and passed right between two paratroopers. Crouch could see the German guns ahead of him. He dived fast, throwing his passengers off balance, buzzing an artillery emplacement, and then quickly regained height. "The suddenness of this maneuver," recalled one pathfinder, "caught us by surprise and most of us sank to our knees due to the 'G' force exerted."[20]

Crouch pushed forward on his control stick.

"As soon as I level off," he told Pedone, "give them the green light."[21]

Sixty seconds later, the green light flashed once more and the pathfinders scrambled out of the C-47's door and into the frigid air, dropping into the graveyard and then letting off orange smoke grenades.[22] One pathfinder turned a switch on the radar set strapped to him. Crouch spotted blips on the cathode ray screen of the radar set in his cockpit. He sent a radio message— the supply operation was a go—and then was heading for home. He spotted German tanks below and gave their position over the radio in the hope that dive bombers could destroy them.

Later that day, guided by the pathfinders Crouch had delivered, forty C-47s dropped vital supplies out of the blue skies. The cloud cover had finally lifted, allowing a clear view of the battlefield and heralding round-the-clock bombing sorties by the Allies for the first time during the Battle of the Bulge. Hundreds of brightly colored parachutes drifted down above Bastogne as paratroopers, some of them down to their last few rounds of ammunition, raced to bring in the bundles that proved an invaluable lifeline. In less than five hours that day, 114 tons of supplies were dropped to the Americans holding Bastogne.[23]

The day after Christmas, elements of George Patton's 3rd Army reached Bastogne and the German siege ended. Elsewhere in the Ardennes, the Allies fought to push the Germans back in temperatures that plummeted to twenty below zero. The relief of Bastogne was headline news around the world, and the Screaming Eagles' heroics lifted spirits back home, where the grinding war in Europe and the Pacific, as well as escalating casualties, had some politicians wondering about the public's stomach for finishing off both Nazi Germany and Imperial Japan.

On January 16, 1945, the Screaming Eagles were once more on the attack, pushing the Germans back toward the fatherland. Eight miles northeast of Bastogne, Captain Frank Lillyman ordered his unit from the 502nd Parachute Infantry Regiment to take the town of Bourcy. One paratrooper remembered Lillyman telling him to operate a machine gun in a tank and being grateful when another man climbed up into the screeching and squealing Sherman instead. In an encounter with a German Tiger or Panther tank, the Sherman stood little chance unless fitted with a high-powered British 76.2-millimeter gun. Standard rounds from a regular M4 Sherman "bounced off the [German tanks] like ping-pong balls," recalled one of Lillyman's comrades.[24] If you were unlucky enough to find yourself in a Sherman when hit, you had just a few seconds to get out. If the tank burnt, as most did with startling ease, you had a 50 percent chance of surviving.[25]

The Allies had forced the Germans back to their starting line in the Battle of the Bulge by January 22. The last great battle on the Western Front was over. Hitler's final gamble had failed, at the cost of 100,000 German soldiers. The defeat of Nazi Germany was now inevitable as the remnants of Hitler's once glorious armies were squeezed between the western Allies and the vengeful Red Army, which was sweeping inexorably from the east toward Berlin, raping and pillaging as it did so with Bolshevik abandon.

Victory felt as distant as ever to those serving in the Allied front lines. Indeed, there was no respite from the bitter winter, the coldest in living memory, for the grunts pushing deeper and deeper into the Third Reich, trudging through snowdrifts, seeing the stiff corpses of dead comrades piled up in gruesome stacks. It was so cold that half the weapons in some units ceased to function, unable to fire bullets. In one day alone, Lieutenant John Spalding's E Company in the 1st Division lost twenty-two men from frostbite.[26] One man was carried from a foxhole, frozen in a sitting position. On February 24, near the Roer River, Spalding himself, having only recently returned to his unit, was admitted to a rear aid station with an "upper respiratory tract infection," according to a medical report.

Spalding was also suffering from depression and severe anxiety, also known as combat fatigue.[27] The body and mind could take only so much. There were no "iron men" on the front lines, as one US Army assessment of rampant mental breakdowns put it.[28] The average time given before a soldier was mentally shattered by combat was two hundred days.[29] Some men, of course, were broken in their first minutes under shellfire, while others fought for months on end and appeared mentally unscathed—until it was too late.

Still, Hitler's legions fought on, in defense of their homeland, out of fear and hatred of the fast-approaching Bolshevik hordes. Consumed by anger and the basest of urges, the Red Army's sole rewards for the loss of millions of comrades were German females of almost any age. Brainwashed by Hitler, whose malignancy was all they had known, German teenagers fought with an astonishing fury. In the last three months of the war, more than 300,000 German soldiers would die each month, three-quarters of them on the Eastern Front, where the Wehrmacht had been bled dry after four years of total, industrial slaughter and genocide.

Late that February, the 5th Rangers who had landed on the Dog White sector of Omaha Beach and had somehow survived the long, bloody trek into the fatherland found themselves fifty miles east of Luxembourg, fighting against the 6th SS Mountain Division. In just nine days, Hitler's men with the twin lightning bolts etched on their helmets killed more than half of all the Rangers lost in the entire war.

For Charles "Ace" Parker, who had led his men from Omaha to Pointe du Hoc on D-Day, the battle of Irsch-Zerf, which raged from February 23 to March 4, was worse even than Normandy. In just one incident, near the Saar River, under accurate and high-velocity artillery fire, Parker lost a third of his men—six killed and eighteen wounded. Drenched in sweat despite the freezing mist, taking just one hill from Hitler's finest "broke our hearts," he recalled, as he and his men scrambled at night under the weight of heavy packs through forests so densely packed that each man, terrified of being left alone, was "hanging on the very breath of his pal in front of him."[30]

———

THE PACE OF THE ALLIED drive picked up as spring beckoned and the winter snows began to melt. Advanced armored units rolled toward the banks of the swollen Rhine River, the last major obstacle on the road to Berlin.

On March 24, Colonel Joel Crouch was back at the controls of a C-47, this time as the lead pilot for the 17th Airborne during Operation Varsity, an Allied assault across the Rhine—the largest airborne operation in history to be carried out in one place on one day. At 7:17 A.M., Crouch lifted off from an airfield at Chartres, France, carrying men from the 507th Parachute Infantry Regiment, including its commanding officer, a tough-talking thirty-four-year-old New Yorker called Colonel Edson Raff. Two hours later, leading an armada of C-47s dubbed "Thunder from Heaven," Crouch was approaching the Rhine when Raff, known as "Little Caesar" to his men because of his stocky physique, leaned into his cockpit.

"I'll bet you a case of champagne," said Crouch, who had worked with Raff before, "that we drop you right on the button."

It was too good an offer to refuse. Crouch was a damn fine pilot, but Raff knew only too well, having commanded the first US paratroop unit to jump into combat, in November 1942, how difficult it was to hit a drop zone with real accuracy. Back in North Africa, that first time, he'd been dropped thirty-five miles from his objective, breaking several ribs as he hit the ground.

"You're on!" said Raff.

At 9:51 A.M., Crouch was over the Rhine, the last natural bulwark between the Allies and Berlin, a willow-fringed swirl of brown water that represented the last hope for the German people and which Hitler had, according to one perceptive journalist, "called upon in this climactic hour as if it were the protecting almighty Jehovah of his dark religion."[31]

A red light flashed on—Raff and his fellow jumpers had four minutes until bailout. They stood up and hooked up, each laboring under the weight of ninety pounds of weapons and equipment. Smoke and haze covered the drop zone. Crouch would need all the skill he could muster. The green light glowed.

"Let's go!" Raff shouted, and then jumped. His men followed, clearing the plane in just ten seconds. Before long, parachutes filled the skies above the city of Wesel as far as the eye could see.[32]

Crouch lost his bet. Raff and some five hundred of his men landed two miles from their designated drop zone, and Raff once again found himself marching to where he was supposed to be. Long after the war, Crouch and Raff would cross paths once more and, after a lighthearted argument, Crouch agreed to pay for half a case of champagne.[33] The finest pathfinder pilot of World War II, who had flown the lead plane in operations in Sicily, mainland Italy, Normandy, and Belgium, and finally across the Rhine,[34] Crouch would go on to enjoy a long and successful postwar career in the air, dying in Hawaii in 1997 at the age of eighty-six.[35]

The superb British glider pilot Jim Wallwork also took part in Operation Varsity, his fourth airborne operation of the war. This time Wallwork was not at the controls of a Horsa glider, as on D-Day, but piloting a large Hamilcar carrying an anti-tank gun to support the sixteen thousand Allied paratroopers dropped that morning of March 24 onto the eastern side of the northern

Rhine. According to one account, Wallwork came across a para-trooper who had been killed, removed his parachute, and later sent it to the dead man's pregnant fiancée: "Her mother made a wedding gown from the white nylon and with leftover material made a Christening dress for [the] child."[36] Yet again, Wallwork fought on the ground before finally returning to England as the Germans fell back. Operation Varsity would later be viewed as the most successful airborne operation of the war.

By the time Wallwork was back in England, a traumatized Lieutenant John Spalding had been sent to the United States. On May 5, the day Berlin fell to the Soviets, he entered 250th Station Hospital, Camp Kilmer, New Jersey, to undergo special treatment for severe combat fatigue.

It was just after 8 A.M. on May 7, near a small town in Czechoslovakia, when a colonel from Spalding's regiment, which had suffered almost eight thousand casualties in World War II, listened as a message crackled from a radio set.

"Cease all forward movement."

It was finally, after 443 days of combat, all over.

"It's about goddamn time," blurted one officer who had fought in North Africa and all the way across Europe.[37] "Only one man who came overseas with Company E originally," noted a young lieutenant in a final combat report, "is still with the organization, but all those who are or have ever been a part of it, have a right to be proud."[38]

In capitals around the world, there was ecstatic celebration. Winston Churchill, the leader who had arguably saved Western civilization by standing so strong in the dark days of 1940, addressed a vast crowd in Whitehall, in the heart of London. "This is your victory," he shouted. "It is the victory of the cause of freedom in every land."[39]

As the free world erupted in euphoria, one of the very first to fight to liberate France, Major John Howard, was "coming round from [an] operation," he recalled, "feeling nauseous and very groggy." The operation had followed months of pain since a traffic accident that had mangled his leg the previous November.[40] His wife, Joy, and their two children visited Howard but could not lift his spirits. They departed to go to a party, leaving Howard almost alone on his ward, depressed, "unable to forget all the dear friends I'd lost in the war who had not seen peace restored."[41]

By contrast, for Colonel James Rudder, V-E Day was enormously joyful; he later described it as the greatest of his life other than his wedding day.[42] Now commanding the 109th Regimental Combat Team of the 28th Infantry Division, he celebrated at his headquarters, southwest of Frankfurt on a large country estate, and was photographed with other officers, grinning from ear to ear, a glass raised high. The former high school football coach and teacher had been begged to stay on in the army but would have none of it, preferring to return to his wife, Margaret, and their five children in Texas and civilian life. He had received every possible award for valor in the year since scaling the heights at Pointe du Hoc—all except the Medal of Honor.

In a replacement depot in Le Havre, one of Rudder's finest combat commanders, Ace Parker, heard a radio broadcast of

Churchill's victory speech in London. A loudspeaker had been hung between two trees. Some men listened to the "rotund voice" of Churchill as if being preached to by the Almighty. No one cried tears of joy or cheered. They were just glad to be alive. The overwhelming emotion was relief.

Parker had fought all across Europe, having landed eleven long months before with the 5th Rangers on Bloody Omaha on D-Day. He had slept in smashed farmhouses in the blackened ruins of so many villages. He had crawled day and night, nose often pressed to the shell-ravaged ground of Nazi Europe, where nineteen million civilians now lay dead. For almost a year, he had known its seasons, its beauty, as well as the terrors of its dense, primeval forests, where he'd shivered in snow-crusted foxholes. "I took a long, deep breath," he recalled, "and slowly that small fist of vague tension deep in the viscera loosened its grip." At last, after the deaths of more than 130,000 of his coun- trymen, Europe had been liberated. His job was done.

Parker was confined to camp and therefore forced to cele- brate victory over a desultory dinner of Spam followed by canned fruit salad.

"Is this a meal fit to be set before conquerors on the night of their victory?" asked a smart-ass officer, a Stanford graduate.

"Hell, no!" someone replied. "Not when we just made the world safe for democracy again."

"I wonder what the losers are eating tonight?" asked Parker.

"Probably the same as us, if I know my armies," said the Stanford graduate.

Parker wanted to be in the streets with the people he'd helped set free. He wanted one last night to enjoy the France he had come to love.

"Jesus Christ," someone finally said, "we've got to celebrate tonight."

Parker and several other officers made their escape, jumping a wall and then wending their way through drab working-class suburbs into the heart of the city. Parker looked at the passersby and couldn't help but see the young faces of the men who had been killed and now lay buried in graveyards all across Europe, men who hadn't known what they were fighting for and wouldn't have understood what they'd won even if they'd lived. Being alive, like Parker, would have been more than enough for the men he led on D-Day, who had crouched down in that landing craft as H-Hour neared and the guns started to scream. They had tried to survive with a "zest that only the young have for living." So few had succeeded.

Le Havre was a disappointment. There were no raucous crowds, no crammed bars of GIs and mademoiselles hugging and singing "La Marseillaise." It was as if the heavily bombed port had shut up shop and gone to bed early, wanting to sleep off the trauma and humiliation of the war.

On the way back to camp, Parker came across a bar. He could hear the voices of Americans getting drunk, so he went inside.

"There's a babe who takes guys upstairs," said a GI. "They say she's a marvel. You don't even have to move. She does everything."

"She'd do great in an old man's home," said Parker.

It was a depressing dive. Parker wished he was back in Germany with the 5th Ranger Battalion, with the men he'd fought with, not drinking vile plonk and looking at a middle-aged whore in a gingham dress, hair pulled back in a prim bun. Then the bar jumped to life and his fellow soldiers were running for the doors—military police had arrived. Parker scurried upstairs, leaving his cap on the bar. Then he felt a warm body beside his.

"Pour la victoire," whispered the woman in the gingham dress.

Why not?

Her soft hand held his, and she led him to a room with a lonely bed. "She was France," Parker later recalled, "shabby, war-ravaged, badly used, and importuning. And I loved France."

"Pour la victoire."

Parker and his fellow officers traipsed, tired and dispirited, back to their camp. "The war against Hitler was over," recalled Parker. "No artillery fire grew louder in the distance to chill the marrow of our bones. At the end of the road there was no bloody, godforsaken beach resounding with the cries of mortal agony. There was only a dreary Replacement Depot into which we would have to sneak undetected on the first leg of the long journey home."[43]

BACK IN THE UNITED STATES, two days later, on May 9, Lieutenant John Spalding entered a rehabilitation program.[44] A medical report stated, "He attends calisthenics, orientation classes and group psychotherapy sessions. In the afternoon he plays golf. At the present time his principal symptoms are in the nature of nervousness, anxiety, fatigability, irritability, depression, insomnia and battle dreams. He has feelings of indecisiveness, uncertainty, and insecurity. He attributes the cause of his illness as due to 120-days continuous combat as a Rifle Platoon Leader, worry over heavy casualties in his outfit and provoked by stress of 4-1/2 years of regimentation . . . He feels that he cannot train troops anymore because of his hatred for guns."[45]

The first officer to break out from Omaha Beach would forever be scarred by the trauma of war. He insisted he was no hero. "I didn't do a thing," he told a local reporter in late 1945. "My men did it all. Don't give me the credit." Spalding's marriage fell apart not long after he left the hospital, but then he found love again and remarried in October 1946, had three children, and rose to a management position in a clothing store. It seemed as if he had put the war behind him and found happiness and a sense of purpose again. He was drawn to politics, serving as a Democrat in the Kentucky House of Representatives for two terms beginning in 1947. Tragically, one night in November 1959, while his children were asleep in a nearby room, his second wife picked up a rifle after a fierce argument and shot him from close range in the heart. The .22-caliber bullet was small but lethal. Spalding died at just forty-four years of age, in a pool of his own blood on his bedroom floor.

Spalding's extraordinarily courageous comrade-in-arms, Sergeant Phil Streczyk, suffered an equally sad fate. He had returned to New Jersey after the war, married a local girl with whom he had four children, but was tormented by his wounds and memories of combat, and committed suicide on June 25, 1958. Among his belongings, inexplicably, his family discovered a ribbon for a Medal of Honor, the award he should have received for his actions on June 6, 1944, when he led the first Americans off Omaha Beach.[46]

AFTER PEACE HAD BROKEN OUT, Captain Frank Lillyman chose to stay on in devastated Europe, having won twelve decorations, including the Distinguished Service Cross. He wanted to retain his rank of captain and eagerly accepted a job offered by the Office of Strategic Services, the forerunner of the CIA. Lillyman was told he would be in charge of a three-man unit, complete with jeep and radio, which would aid in the evacuation of British prisoners of war from the ruins of the Third Reich.

Lillyman and his team met one evening in late May 1945, just a few weeks after the end of the war in Europe, at a villa on a farm in southern Bavaria called Gut Krumbach. The farm was a base for an Allied intelligence unit, which was interrogating suspected members of the Gestapo, the Nazis' notoriously brutal secret police.

One of the Allied officers at the interrogation center introduced himself to Lillyman.

"How do you do?" said the officer. "I am Captain Mason, British Intelligence Service, excuse the uniform."

Captain Mason was of medium height, with light hair and close-set eyes.[47] He said that although he was wearing an American lieutenant's uniform, he had recently been promoted to captain. That meant he in fact held the same rank as Lillyman. Mason added that he was in the middle of interrogating a suspect who was refusing to cooperate.

Lillyman got a good look at the suspect, a dentist called

Eugen Krug. He had marks on his face from where Mason had punched him earlier in the evening.

Mason asked if Lillyman wanted to join the interrogation.

Lillyman agreed.

"Doctor Krug," one of the interrogators asked, "do you know how to box?"

A table in the villa's living room was moved to the side. According to one account, Lillyman "began to spar with the helpless dentist." Before long, Krug looked as if he'd gone twelve rounds with the famed heavyweight Joe Louis.

The group of interrogators finished with Krug around 1 A.M., at which point his head wounds were bathed in eau de cologne and he collapsed. He was eventually released, having failed to provide useful information.

Lillyman had no inkling that he had been made complicit in the ever more sadistic actions of an impostor, the most notorious British traitor of the war. Mason was in fact thirty-nine-year-old Harold Cole, a Londoner who had discreetly worked with Nazi intelligence services for more than three years, betraying at least 150 members of the French Resistance, a third of whom were then murdered by the Gestapo. As a biographer of Cole put it, "Everyone who had passed through the unspeakably brutal war just ended had been marked by the experience. But Cole had been to the very dark heart of the evil and returned. His aura had fed upon the violence and grown; Cole thereby drew others into his decaying orbit." Among those drawn into Cole's "dark spiral" was the D-Day hero Captain Frank Lillyman.[48]

Lillyman had been conned by Cole, yet he did have some reservations about him at first. Why was this British captain wearing an American lieutenant's uniform? Then there was the blatant thieving. As Lillyman spent more time with this sup- posed Captain Mason, he noted that he "spent considerable time in seizing anything that struck his fancy—cheese, wines, per- fume, jewelry, and automobiles." Cole also had a nasty penchant for backhanding women who did not cooperate.

Despite his suspicions, Lillyman became more and more in- volved with the sadistic cockney in a borrowed uniform, espe- cially after he secretly checked Cole's papers one morning, while Cole was taking a bath, and found an identification card that appeared to confirm the man's status as a British intelligence officer. To Lillyman, Cole was reminiscent of the calm and cal- culating British pathfinders he had met; Lillyman had even im- itated them from time to time, dropping the odd "bloody" into his conversation.

Mason proved to be a malign influence on the impression- able American captain. Before long Lillyman was copying Cole's mockery of posh British officers, striking a riding crop against his jump boots as he put on a fake accent. Whipping prisoners until they screamed was also par for the course. Lillyman was "still looking for the thrills" he had found in combat and was also, according to one report, "one of those fellows who just couldn't quit when the flag was waved."[49]

It all ended in murder. Late on the night of June 8, 1945, within two days of the anniversary of D-Day, the first American to drop into France was drinking heavily with Mason and two of his accomplices. They then drove a man named Georg Hanft, whom Cole had futilely yet brutally beaten in the hopes of dis- covering the whereabouts of a fortune in gems and gold, toward a forest near Ravensburg. Lillyman was seated up front, beside the driver, armed with a Colt .32 pistol. Hanft continued to deny that he had hidden a fortune. The car pulled off a road and entered a beech forest.

In the beam of the car's headlights, Hanft was put against a tree, and then Cole hit him over the head with the barrel of his pistol.

Lillyman stood and watched. "I can still see the poor little bastard standing there," he later recalled. "He was asked something in German and just threw his arms out in a shrug as if to say, 'What can I say?'"[50]

Again he was pistol-whipped, then a kick in the groin from Lillyman.

It was after midnight.

Cole demanded the truth.

Hanft had nothing to add.

Cole lifted his Sten gun and sprayed Hanft, and then two other men pumped bullets into his doubled-up body. Cole put his pistol to Hanft's temple and finished him off. The group went their separate ways. Cole assumed he would be hunted by British intelligence once they found time to fully investigate his crimes and interview some of his victims. That summer, he was indeed apprehended by the British after a girlfriend in Paris tipped off police, but he managed to escape their custody, this time disguising himself in a GI's uniform. He would finally be shot dead on January 8, 1946, in Paris by a French police detective, a Resistance veteran, and buried in a pauper's grave.[51]

Captain Frank Lillyman probably regretted his liaison with Cole for the rest of his days, for it cast an ugly shadow on what had been a stellar record in combat. He was questioned at length in France before returning to the States, but he steadfastly denied being a murderer. "I did not take part in the shooting," he swore. The other three men who had been present at the murder stated that Lillyman had in fact been involved in the shooting, but no criminal charges were ever brought against him.[52]

When not in combat, Lillyman had often killed time since D-Day by scribbling letters and making sketches and fantasizing about a dream vacation he would take with his wife and daughter. After he returned home to Skaneateles, New York, that fall of 1945, he had a few drinks one night and wrote a letter to the Hotel Pennsylvania, in New York City, after reading an advertisement that promised special treatment for guests who were veterans. "I'd like a suite that will face east," jotted Lillyman, "and English-made tea that will be served to me in bed . . . For breakfast, a fried egg with yolk pink and the white firm, coffee brewed in the room so I can smell it cooking . . . No military title . . . 'Mister' will be music to my ears . . ."[53]

Lillyman also wanted a "grey-haired motherly maid" to look after his daughter while he ate lobster Newburg and filet mignon.

"Can you do it?" he challenged.[54]

They sure could. A few weeks later, in November 1945, a concierge greeted Lillyman and his wife and four-year-old daughter, Susan, and assured them that "everything was set."[55] Lillyman had turned up wearing his twelve wartime decorations, including the Distinguished Service Cross, and before long he was enjoying a five-room suite, complete with a sideboard full of booze and a sunken bathtub. He was even photographed by the press lying in bed with a cooked breakfast, feted by *Life* magazine as the cheeky combat veteran cocky enough to ask for and receive the perfect homecoming, unlike so many of his peers who were struggling silently with trauma and depression.

Lillyman would stay in the army, retiring in 1968 as a lieutenant colonel. He died of a stroke in 1971 at Walter Reed Hospital, aged fifty-five, and was remembered in a *New York Times* obituary as a "dreamer" who had been "much honored as the first American paratrooper to drop behind German lines during the Normandy invasion in World War II."[56]

IN MEMORIAM

I have come to realize, very deeply, that that moment of D-Day marked a turning point of the twentieth century—it was perhaps the most dramatic moment of the twentieth century, because it enabled the freedom of the world. There's something sacred about it.[1]

—CAPTAIN JOSEPH DAWSON,
G Company commander,
US 1st Infantry Division

THE FORTY-FOUR-YEAR-OLD TEXAN had added thirty pounds and four inches to his waist since D-Day. It was a sunny, clear day, and he stood with his son, a fourteen-year-old with bright blue eyes, in a fishing boat plowing through the English Channel. Then it appeared: the unmistakable knife-edged outcrop.

"There it is," said Colonel James Rudder to the boy, Bud. "Pointe du Hoc."

It was May 1954. Rudder was returning to Normandy for the first time since his Rangers had sacrificed so many lives to scale Pointe du Hoc. He found that the clifftops had barely changed, though the moonscape of craters and ugly, singed earth were now covered in grass. There were no crowds of vacationers, no memorial plaques, no parking lots crammed with tour buses full of patriotic children and grandchildren of the "Greatest Generation." The heroics at Pointe du Hoc had yet to become legendary, yet to be commemorated adequately. The war was still too close, too painful in the memories of those who had endured those years.

Rudder walked with his son to where he had set up his command post, weaving between the massive shell holes. He finally arrived at the ruins of a concrete blockhouse, open to the Channel winds, its floor still strewn with rubble.

He called to his son.

"I want you to see this."

The boy came over and followed his father into the concrete command post.

"This is where the shell hit," said Rudder, pointing to a spot on the ceiling where two steel rods were exposed. "They say it wasn't from one of our ships, but when you look at the direction, it had to be. The artillery captain, a nice-looking, black-haired boy—I wish I could remember his name—was killed right here. The navy lieutenant, who was spotting with us, fell right here."[2]

Rudder pointed to a corner.

"It knocked me over right here."

Rudder pulled back his coat sleeve, undid his shirt cuff, rolled it back, and showed his forearm. "Right under that," he said, indicating the red scar, "is a piece of concrete from here . . . You carry it around with you for ten years and you bring it back where it came from."

"I thought you had two pieces in there?" said Bud.

They explored the concrete ruins further.

"I've thought about this a lot," said Rudder. "The way I pictured it, you could just about reach up and touch the place where the shell hit, and you just about can."

They moved outside. The boy stepped close to the edge of the cliffs, looking down the ninety feet to a narrow stone beach below.

"Bud!" cried Rudder.

"Yes?"

"Look, son. I want you to keep away from that edge."

"I'm just looking."

"You could fall off there, and I'd have to go home and face your mother."

Ten years had gone fast. Rudder had returned from the war and thrown himself, as so many of his men had, into hard work and raising a family. For six years he had been mayor of the town of Brady, Texas, and had worked as an executive in manufacturing. Then *Collier's* magazine had come calling, wanting to do a cover story on him for an issue to commemorate the tenth anniversary of D-Day.

"You think of the wonderful kids you had with you," Rudder told the reporter as he walked among the grassed-over shell holes and rusted iron and crumbling concrete of the casemates. "You think that if you could have men like that around you in a peacetime world, men as devoted as that, there wouldn't be anything you couldn't accomplish."[3]

Rudder would prove to be just as effective as a leader away from the battlefield, becoming the most distinguished and trusted president in the history of Texas A&M University. In 1963, five years into his tenure as president, he decided that the university should admit women.[4] "If Texas A&M goes on fighting and resisting this," he declared, "we'll find in ten years from now that we are still about the same size . . . Now is the time to change and move on."[5] Rudder was right. Sadly, he would die in 1970, at the age of just fifty-nine.

The same year that women were admitted to Texas A&M, Rudder's former supreme commander, Dwight Eisenhower, returned to Normandy. Over several days in August 1963, he was filmed visiting Pointe du Hoc, Omaha Beach, and the bocage for a CBS special presented by Walter Cronkite. It was impossible not to be deeply moved by the footage of a somber and pensive Eisenhower walking among the seemingly endless rows of white crosses at Colleville-sur-Mer, where some nine thousand American soldiers had been laid to rest. He was shown seated on a wall, studying the graves of the men he had sent into the invasion, less than a hundred yards from where Lieutenant John Spalding had broken off the Easy Red sector of Omaha Beach.

"You knew many hundreds of boys were going to give their lives or be maimed forever," he told Cronkite. "These men came here . . . to storm these beaches for one purpose only. Not to gain anything for ourselves, not to fulfill any ambitions that America had for conquest, but just to preserve freedom."[6]

The next American president to speak with true eloquence and sincerity about the Allied sacrifice in Normandy was Ronald Reagan. At Pointe du Hoc in 1984, to mark the fortieth anniversary of D-Day, Reagan spoke before a group of world leaders as well as survivors from the 5th and 2nd Rangers.

"We stand on a lonely, windswept point on the northern shore of France," said Reagan, beginning his finest speech as president and the most memorable of any American politician who has ever walked the beaches of Normandy. "The air is soft, but forty years ago at this moment, the air was dense with smoke and the cries of men, and the air was filled with the crack of rifle fire and the roar of cannon."

Reagan then lauded the veterans, seated in rows facing him.

"These are the boys of Pointe du Hoc," he declared. "These are the champions who helped free a continent."

Reagan unveiled two memorials at Pointe du Hoc and reminded the world, then enduring the last decade of the Cold War, that the US had learnt a painful but important lesson in the twentieth century: "It is better to be here ready to protect the peace than to take blind shelter across the sea, rushing to respond only after freedom is lost. We've learned that isolationism never was and never will be an acceptable response to tyrannical governments with an expansionist intent."[7]

The Cold War had ended by 1993, almost fifty years after D-Day, when Lieutenant Colonel Terence Otway returned to the Merville Battery, having enjoyed a long postwar career in business. He was filmed meeting his opposite number, the German commander Raimund Steiner, who had fought him on D-Day. It was an uncomfortable encounter. Otway later confessed that he did not have the "guts" to "refuse" the German's "proffered hand."[8] But he had never forgotten his boys who had been picked off by Steiner's troops as they had dangled helplessly, trapped by their parachutes, in nearby trees.

It was too simplistic to talk of forgiveness and of moving on. So much had been lost. So much deep hatred had been aroused. For Otway and many of his ilk, the battlefields of Normandy would forever be hallowed ground, a place where young men they had led and loved had given their lives upon their every command. During one return visit, Otway spotted several tourists picnicking near the Merville Battery and insisted they leave the area, declaring, "I don't like people eating and drinking where my men died."[9]

The fiftieth anniversary saw the largest commemoration of D-Day since the war ended. Dozens of veterans who had landed in the first wave returned for the first time to where they had fought hardest when the stakes were highest on arguably the most impactful day in modern history. The 4th Division's Leonard Schroeder, believed to be the first American infantryman to wade ashore on D-Day, stood once more on the sands of Utah Beach. Schroeder had remained in the army after the war, serving for thirty years, seeing combat in Korea and Vietnam. "I realize that to be the first man ashore is an immense honor," he told a French magazine, "yet I do not merit it more than anyone else. Five of my men died . . . They alone are the heroes."[10]

Atop the cliffs of Pointe du Hoc, George Kerchner stood proudly beside one of his sons, as well as other veterans from the 2nd Ranger Battalion and their families. One of Kerchner's men from D Company told Kerchner's son how on D-Day he and others had been surrounded and badly outnumbered: "I cried like a baby and your dad held me like a baby."[11]

After the war, Kerchner had become an infantry instructor before being discharged with the rank of captain. He returned to his prewar job at Arundel Ice Cream Company and rose quickly through the ranks to become company president. In 1959, his company's store in the Northwood Plaza Shopping

Center, in Maryland, was picketed by African American students protesting segregation. Kerchner told the students they were more than welcome in his store. "I want you to know that you will have as much right to come in here as anyone else," he said. He sold the company in 1970, and in his retirement he was reportedly "an avid boater and fisherman."[12]

The officer who had achieved as much as any man at Pointe du Hoc died in 2012, at the age of ninety-three, a much loved and admired citizen of his Maryland community. "I didn't think I did anything that heroic," Kerchner told a reporter before his death. "I knew nobody but the Rangers could have done what we did."[13]

A still sprightly Bill Millin, wearing a leather tunic and a green beret, stood close to Pegasus Bridge on June 6, 1994, and in an upbeat brogue told of how he had arrived with Lord Lovat fifty years before. "Lovat was a bit of a critic, so I had to concentrate on my playing," he remembered with a smile as an incredulous reporter marveled at his story. When asked why the Germans hadn't shot him as he played, Millin grinned and tapped his head. "The Germans said I was *dummkopf*—mad," he explained. "But if I was mad, then Lovat was even more mad!"

Lord Lovat was not in Normandy for the fiftieth anniversary, but from his home in Scotland he spoke on television of how "touch and go" the whole D-Day operation had been. "If we hadn't gotten a footing that first day," said Lovat, still pained by his battle wounds yet as elegant and erudite as ever, "the war would have been delayed for a very long time."[14]

After the war, Lovat had returned to his 200,000-acre estate, Beaufort, in Scotland, and had devoted himself to breeding shorthorn cattle and improving the forests on his lands. He wrote a scintillating and deeply affecting memoir, *March Past,* in which he concluded that the "causes of war are falsely represented: its purpose dishonest and the glory meretricious. Yet we remember a challenge to spiritual endurance and the awareness of a common peril endured for a common end." It was the sacred duty of the warriors who had survived the "shattering experience" of combat in Normandy to "enshrine the memory of those brave men who did not return."[15]

Lovat's last years were plagued by tragedy, an utterly undeserved fate.[16] Though he was blessed with good looks, great charm, and courage, the gods cruelly conspired against him at the end, as if to remind other mortals that no men are given everything. His youngest son, Andrew Fraser, was killed by a buffalo on safari in Africa. His eldest son, Simon, died of a heart attack just two weeks later, and after his death it was reported that he had "left large debts on the Beaufort estates that [had] been for so long associated with the name of Lovat." The seventeenth Lord Lovat died not long after, on March 16, 1995. He was survived by two beautiful daughters and his wife, Rosamond, who had waited so patiently for him to return from the greatest commando raids of World War II.[17] A grief-stricken Bill Millin, who would pass away in 2010, played his bagpipes at Lovat's funeral.

In 1998, the blockbuster film *Saving Private Ryan* brought international focus once more to the heroism shown on Omaha Beach. The opening scenes in particular were widely praised by surviving veterans. So visceral was the re-creation of the slaughter, some men were in fact thrust back into the cauldron of war. "It was very realistic," said Dan Farley, of the 5th Ranger

Battalion, "but what is missing are the smells. Smells of burnt flesh and blood, so much blood. You never forget those smells . . . I never understood why I ran on the beach with a man on each side of me and how they could go down but not me. I always wondered why I was spared instead of someone else." When asked what had made the difference between success and failure on D-Day, Farley stressed that during the most critical combat of modern times it was the "heart and mind" that had mattered most.[18]

Arguably the finest British glider pilot of World War II, Jim Wallwork returned to Normandy several times after the war, joining comrades at Pegasus Bridge and raising a glass of champagne at precisely 12:15 A.M. each June 6 to celebrate their extraordinary exploits. He had emigrated to Canada after the war, during which he'd flown in every major Allied airborne operation, and had never piloted a plane again. "We were of that daft age where you believe that you are invincible and are going to live forever—that if a bloke's going to be shot it's going to be the one next to you," he said. "We had not the slightest doubt we were going to pull it off. There's so much going on and there's the fear of what's coming next. There's so much excitement which you repress. It is only afterwards that you think how lucky we were to survive."[19]

On one return visit, Wallwork donated his Distinguished Flying Medal to the museum near Pegasus Bridge where Bill Millin's pipes are also on display today, explaining, "I thought it would be better in the museum than in the top drawer of my dresser under my socks."[20] Wallwork died at the age of ninety-three in 2013. One of his final requests was to have his ashes spread near Pegasus Bridge.[21]

On the seventieth anniversary of D-Day, in 2014, very few men were still alive from the first wave. Sons and daughters were often contacted to speak to the still fascinated press about their fathers. The son of Sergeant Major Stanley Hollis, Britain's sole D-Day recipient of the Victoria Cross, echoed other children of the first wave in stressing that his father had avoided talking in detail about combat: "If it was pigeons you wanted to talk about, you were fine, but not the war."

As a boy, Brian Hollis had gone to Buckingham Palace with his father, a "pleasant, quiet man, and a very good father," to watch him receive the Victoria Cross from King George. "There was my dad, in front of us, talking to the King," recalled Brian, "and he turned round and waved at me to come up. I went up to the stage and the King said, 'You must be very proud of your father.'"

After the war, Stanley Hollis had struggled to find work in grim, austerity-ridden Britain, where rationing continued until 1954. He had reportedly been "reduced to supporting his wife and two children by pushing trolleys of scrap into a blast furnace" but had stubbornly refused to accept government help or even to claim his war pension: "I don't need charity handouts."[22] He had eventually been able to support his family by working as a landlord in a pub in his native Middlesbrough. Drunks who caused trouble were quickly dealt with. Regulars recalled Hollis sometimes standing behind the bar of his pub, appropriately called the Green Howard, pulling pints as blood seeped from old wounds to his feet.

Like Terence Otway, Hollis could not forgive or forget. "Although I am not proud of it," he admitted, "I find it impossible to treat a man as an enemy one minute and then shake his hand. I saw the results of too many of their atrocities ever to trust, or like, the Germans again."[23] Hollis died in 1972, aged fifty-nine, from a stroke. His Victoria Cross was found in a drawer among some discarded bottle tops.[24] "If I hadn't done the things I did," he had often insisted, "somebody else would have done them."[25] He just happened to have done them first.

In 2018, Léon Gautier stood outside the No. 4 Commando Museum, in Ouistreham, surrounded by grateful visitors from the US and Britain who had come to honor him. He was one of only five surviving French commandos out of 177 who had landed in the first wave on D-Day, just a few hundred yards away from the museum on Sword Beach. After surviving the Battle of Normandy, he had kept his promise to his English girl-friend, Dorothy, and they had gotten married and then moved to France, where they eventually settled, of all places, in the sea-side town of Ouistreham, which Gautier had liberated on D-Day.

Each June 6 for several decades, Gautier has left his modest home, half a mile from Sword Beach, and journeyed to a memo-rial where he has laid a wreath in honor of his fallen brothers. It is time now, he says, for a new generation to carry the flame of remembrance, and to ensure that Europe is never again en-slaved, that it remain at peace, after almost seventy-five years— by far the longest period in its history. Time now for others to be "vigilant."[26]

ACKNOWLEDGMENTS

Over twenty years many veterans have helped me in my research on D-Day and the Battle of Normandy. They include Waldo Werft, Bob Slaughter, Fred Glover, Bob Sales, Dan Farley, John Raaen, Hal Baumgarten, John Barnes, Russell Pickett, Ray Nance, Jimmy Green, Roy Stevens, and Léon Gautier. Staff at the following institutions have provided invaluable information and images: the National WWII Museum in New Orleans, the First Division Museum at Cantigny, the Library of Congress, the National Archives in the United States, the Imperial War Museum in London, the National D-Day Memorial in Bedford, Virginia, the Queen's Own Rifles of Canada Regimental Museum in Toronto, the Green Howards Regimental Museum in the United Kingdom, and the Mémorial de Caen in France. A huge thanks to Amy Squiers for transcribing many hours of interviews. John Snowdon provided amazing tips and company and photographs during several visits to Normandy. Sylvain

Kast was a superb guide to the beaches. Michael Edwards sent many oral histories.

I've been very lucky to have had a highly skilled and supportive editor, Brent Howard, ably backed by his assistant, Cassidy Sachs. Thanks also to the production, marketing, and sales teams at Dutton. My agent, Jim Hornfischer, was as usual second to none. My wife, Robin, and son, Felix, were much missed on many trips to the places where the First Wave fought seventy-five years ago.

BIBLIOGRAPHY

Air Force Association. *Air Force Fifty*. Paducah, KY: Turner, 1998.

Ambrose, Stephen. *Pegasus Bridge*. New York: Simon and Schuster, 1985.

Astor, Gerald. *June 6, 1944*. New York: St. Martin's, 1994.

Bailey, Roderick. *Forgotten Voices of D-Day*. London: Random House, 2009.

Balkoski, Joseph. *Beyond the Beachhead: The 29th Infantry Division in Normandy*. Harrisburg, PA: Stackpole Books, 1989.

———. *Omaha Beach: D-Day, June 6, 1944*. Mechanicsburg, PA: Stackpole Books, 2004.

———. *Utah Beach*. Mechanicsburg, PA: Stackpole Books, 2005.

Bando, Mark. *The Screaming Eagles at Normandy*. Minneapolis: Zenith Press, 2011.

Barber, Neil. *The Day the Devils Dropped In*. Barnsley, UK: Pen and Sword Books, 2004.

———. *The Pegasus and Orne Bridges*. Barnsley, UK: Pen and Sword Books, 2014.

Beau-Lofi, Denise. *Il fallait y croire*. Vanves, France: Édition du bout de la rue, 2013.

Black, Robert. *The Battalion*. Mechanicsburg, PA: Stackpole Books, 2006.

Blair, Clay. *Ridgway's Paratroopers: The American Airborne in World War II*. New York: William Morrow, 1985.

Blumenson, Martin. *Battle of the Generals*. New York: William Morrow, 1995.

Botting, Douglas. *The D-Day Invasion*. New York: Time-Life Books, 1978.

Bradley, Omar. *A Soldier's Story*. New York: Henry Holt, 1951.

Bradley, Omar, with Clay Blair. *A General's Life*. New York: Simon and Schuster, 1983.

Breuer, William B. *Geronimo*. New York: St. Martin's, 1989.

Brinkley, Douglas. *The Boys of Pointe du Hoc*. New York: HarperPerennial, 2006.

Buckley, John. *Monty's Men: The British Army and the Liberation of Europe*. New Haven, CT: Yale University Press, 2014.

Bull, Stephen. *Commando Tactics*. Barnsley, UK: Pen and Sword Books, 2011.

Butcher, Harry. *My Three Years with Eisenhower*. New York: Simon and Schuster, 1946.

Capa, Robert. *Slightly out of Focus*. Modern Library ed. New York: Modern Library, 1999. First published 1947 by Henry Holt (New York).

Carell, Paul. *Invasion*. New York: Bantam Books, 1960.

Churchill, Winston. *The Second World War*. New York: Time, Inc., 1959.

Clay, Steven. *Blood and Sacrifice: The History of the 16th Infantry Regiment from the Civil War Through the Gulf War*. Chicago: Cantigny First Division Foundation, 2001.

Collier, Richard. *D-Day*. London: Cassell, 1999.

de la Billière, Sir Peter. *Supreme Courage: Heroic Stories from 150 Years of the Victoria Cross*. London: Little, Brown, 2004.

D'Este, Carlo. *Decision in Normandy*. New York: Dutton, 1983.

Drez, Ronald J., ed. *Voices of D-Day: The Story of the Allied Invasion Told by Those Who Were There*. Eisenhower Center Studies on War and Peace. Baton Rouge: Louisiana State University Press, 1994.

Dunning, James. *The Fighting Fourth: Number 4 Commando at War, 1940–45*. Stroud, UK: History Press, 2010.

Eisenhower, Dwight D. *Crusade in Europe*. New York: Doubleday, 1948.

Eisenhower, John S. D. *Allies*. New York: Da Capo Press, 2002.

Ewing, Joseph. *Twenty-Nine Let's Go!* Washington, DC: Infantry Journal Press, 1948.

Ferguson, Gregor. *The Paras 1940–84*. Oxford: Osprey, 1984.

Fowler, Will. *Pegasus Bridge*. Oxford: Osprey, 2010.

Freeman, Roger. *The Mighty Eighth*. London: Cassell, 2000.

Fuller, Sam. *A Third Face*. New York: Alfred A. Knopf, 2002.

Gavin, James M. *Airborne Warfare*. Washington, DC: Infantry Journal Press, 1947.

———. *On to Berlin*. New York: Viking, 1978.

Gawne, Jonathan. *Spearheading D-Day*. Paris: Histoire et Collections, 1998.

Gilbert, Martin. *Winston Churchill: Road to Victory, 1941–1945*. Boston: Houghton Mifflin, 1986.

Grant, Douglas. *The Fuel of the Fire*. London: Cresset Press, 1950.

Hamilton, Nigel. *Master of the Battlefield: Monty's War Years, 1942–1944*. New York: McGraw-Hill, 1983.

Harrison, Gordon. *Cross-Channel Attack*. Washington, DC: Office of the Chief of Military History, Department of the Army, 1951.

Hastings, Max. *Overlord*. New York: Simon and Schuster, 1984.

Hastings, Robin. *An Undergraduate's War*. London: Bellhouse, 1997.

Hatfield, Thomas. *Rudder*. College Station: Texas A&M University Press, 2011.

Hickey, R. M. *The Scarlet Dawn*. Campbellton, NB: Tribune, 1949.

Holt, Tonie, and Valmai Holt. *Major and Mrs. Holt's Battlefield Guide to the Normandy D-Day Landing Beaches*. Barnsley, UK: Pen and Sword Books, 2009.

Howard, John, and Penny Bates. *The Pegasus Diaries.* Barnsley, UK: Pen and Sword Books, 2008.

Howarth, David. *Dawn of D-Day.* New York: Skyhorse, 2008.

Ingersoll, Ralph. *Top Secret.* New York: Harcourt, Brace, 1946.

Isby, David, ed. *Fighting the Invasion: The German Army at D-Day.* London: Greenhill, 2000.

Jeffers, H. Paul. *Theodore Roosevelt Jr.: The Life of a War Hero.* Novato, CA: Presidio Press, 2002.

Johnson, Garry, and Christopher Dunphie. *Brightly Shone the Dawn.* London: Frederick Warne, 1980.

Kaufman, J. E., and H. W. Kaufman. *The American GI in Europe in World War II: D-Day, Storming Ashore.* Mechanicsburg, PA: Stackpole Books, 2009.

Kershaw, Alex. *Avenue of Spies.* New York: Crown, 2015.

———. *The Liberator.* New York: Crown, 2012.

King, Martin, David Hilborn, and Jason Nulton. *To War with the 4th.* Havertown, PA: Casemate, 2016. Kindle.

Kirkland, William B. *Destroyers at Normandy: Naval Gunfire Support at Omaha Beach.* Washington, DC: Naval Historical Foundation, 1994.

Koskimaki, George. *The Battered Bastards of Bastogne.* New York: Ballantine Books, 1994.

———. *D-Day with the Screaming Eagles.* Havertown, PA: Casemate, 2002.

Lane, Ronald. *Rudder's Rangers.* Altamonte Springs, FL: Ranger Associates, 1994.

Lewis, Jon E. *Voices from D-Day.* New York: Skyhorse, 2014.

Liddell Hart, B. H. *The Rommel Papers.* New York: Da Capo Press, 1953.

Liddle, Peter, ed. *D-Day: By Those Who Were There.* Barnsley, UK: Pen and Sword Military, 2004.

Lieb, Peter. *Konventioneller Krieg oder NS-Weltanschauungskrieg?* Munich: De Gruyter Oldenbourg, 2007.

Lovat, Lord Simon Fraser. *March Past.* London: Weidenfeld and Nicolson, 1978.

Luck, Hans von. *Panzer Commander.* New York: Random House, 1989.

Magdelaine, Yann. *Utah.* Bayeux, France: Orep Éditions, 2012.

Martin, Charlie. *Battle Diary.* Toronto: Dundurn Press, 1997.

Masters, Charles J. *Glidermen of Neptune.* Carbondale: Southern Illinois University Press, 1995.

Mayo, Jonathan. *D-Day, Minute by Minute.* New York: Marble Arch Press, 2014.

McNiece, Jake, and Richard Killblane. *The Filthy Thirteen.* Havertown, PA: Casemate, 2005.

Middlebrook, Martin. *Arnhem 1944: The Airborne Battle.* London: Viking, 1994.

Miller, Russell. *Nothing Less Than Victory.* New York: William Morrow, 1994.

Mills-Roberts, Derek. *Clash by Night.* London: William Kimber, 1969.

Moen, Marcia, and Margo Heinen. *The Fool Lieutenant.* Elk River, MN: Meadowlark Publishing, 2000.

———. *Reflections of Courage on D-Day.* Elk River, MN: DeForest Press, 1999.

Moorehead, Alan. *Eclipse.* New York: Harper and Row, 1945.

Moran, Jeff. *American Airborne Pathfinders in World War II.* Atglen, PA: Schiffer Military History, 2003.

Morgan, Kay Summersby. *Past Forgetting: My Love Affair with Dwight D. Eisenhower.* New York: Simon and Schuster, 1976.

Morgan, Mike. *D-Day Hero.* Stroud, UK: Sutton, 2004.

Morison, Samuel Eliot. *The Invasion of France and Germany.* Edison, NJ: Castle Books, 2001.

Murphy, Brendan. *Turncoat.* San Diego: Harcourt, Brace, Jovanovich, 1987.

O'Donnell, Patrick K. *Dog Company.* Cambridge, MA: Da Capo Press, 2012.

Polk, David. *World War II Army Airborne Troop Carriers.* Paducah, KY: Turner, 1992.

Pogue, Forrest. *Pogue's War.* Lexington: University Press of Kentucky, 2006.

———. *Supreme Command.* Washington, DC: Office of the Chief of Military History, Department of the Army, 1954.

Preisler, Jerome. *First to Jump.* New York: Berkley Caliber, 2014.

Pyle, Ernie. *Brave Men.* Lincoln: University of Nebraska Press, 2001.

Raaen, John C., Jr. *Intact.* St. Louis: Reedy Press, 2012.

Reynolds, David. *Rich Relations.* London: Phoenix Press, 2000.

Saunders, Hilary St. George. *The Green Beret.* London: New English Library, 1975.

Scannell, Vernon. *Arguments of Kings.* London: Robson Books, 1987.

Scott, Desmond. *Typhoon Pilot.* London: Leo Cooper, 1982.

Sevareid, Eric. *Not So Wild a Dream.* New York: Alfred A. Knopf, 1946.

Shilleto, Carl. *Pegasus Bridge and Merville Battery.* Conshohocken, PA: Leo Cooper Combined, 1999.

Shuey, Theodore G. *Omaha Beach Field Guide.* Bayeux, France: Éditions Heimdal, 2014.

Simonnet, Stéphane. *Commandant Kieffer.* Paris: Éditions Tallandier, 2012.

Smith, Jean Edward. *Eisenhower in War and Peace.* New York: Random House, 2012.

Smith, Walter Bedell. *Eisenhower's Six Great Decisions: Europe 1944–1945.* New York: Longmans, Green, 1956.

Stasi, Jean-Charles. *Ennemis et frères.* Bayeux, France: Éditions Heimdal, 2016.

———. *Kieffer Commando.* Bayeux, France: Heimdal, 2014.

Strong, Michael. *Steiner's War: The Merville Battery.* Somerset, UK: Self-published, 2013.

Taylor, Charles. *Omaha Beachhead.* Washington, DC: Center of Military History, 1984.

Taylor, Maxwell. *Swords and Plowshares.* New York: W. W. Norton, 1972.

United States Army Air Forces. *DZ Europe: The Story of the 440th Troop Carrier Group.* Germany: n.p., 1945.

United States Army Historical Division. *Utah Beach to Cherbourg.* Washington, DC: Department of the Army, 1947.

Veitch, Michael. *Fly.* Sydney: Viking, 2006.

Williams, Andrew. *D-Day to Berlin.* London: Hodder and Stoughton, 2004.

Zaloga, Steven J. *D-Day 1944 (2): Utah Beach and the US Airborne Landings.* Oxford: Osprey, 2004.

———. *Rangers Lead the Way.* Oxford: Osprey, 2009.

Zuehlke, Mark. *Juno Beach.* Toronto: Douglas and McIntyre, 2005.

NOTES

PART 1: TWILIGHT OF THE IDOLS

1. "Research Starters: D-Day," National WWII Museum, http://www.nation
   alww2museum.org/learn/education/for-students/ww2-history/d-day
   -june-6-1944.html??referrer=https://www.google.com/.

CHAPTER 1: JUNE 5, 1944

1. Dwight D. Eisenhower, interview by Walter Cronkite, *CBS Reports*, CBS,
   August 1963.
2. Smith, *Eisenhower's Six Great Decisions*, pp. 53–54.
3. Collier, *D-Day*, p. 20.
4. Collier, *D-Day*, p. 29.
5. Reynolds, *Rich Relations*, p. 360.
6. Collier, *D-Day*, p. 21.
7. "I'm sure it wasn't five minutes," Eisenhower told Walter Cronkite in 1963.
   "Five minutes under such conditions would seem like a year." Eisenhower,
   interview by Walter Cronkite.
8. Pogue, *Supreme Command*, p. 170.
9. Tim Rives, "OK, We'll Go," National Archives (US), https://www.archives
   .gov/files/publications/prologue/2014/spring/d-day.pdf.
10. John S. D. Eisenhower, *Allies*, p. 469.
11. Koskimaki, *D-Day with the Screaming Eagles*, p. 27.
12. Moran, *American Airborne Pathfinders*, p. 41. "My commanders figured
    that here was an excellent opportunity to get rid of their right balls by

sending them to my pathfinder group. I had no TO [table of organization] so there was no rank among enlisted men. I had inherited former first sergeants and other NCOs, who were excellent men, but who had been busted to private because they had discipline problems. A few didn't even know what the Morse code was."

13. Moran, *American Airborne Pathfinders,* p. 41.
14. *The Guardian,* May 22, 2004.
15. Howarth, *Dawn of D-Day,* p. 126.
16. In basic training, Howard had had a tough time. "I freely admit I cried my eyes out for the first couple of nights when I was in the barracks room with these toughs and wondered if I'd survive."
17. Barber, *The Pegasus and Orne Bridges,* p. 63.
18. Imperial War Museum (hereafter cited as IWM), Sound Recording no. 11061.
19. http://www.independent.co.uk/news/people/lord-lovat-1611984.html.
20. *The Independent,* March 20, 1995.
21. http://www.pegasusarchive.org/normandy/lord_lovat.htm.
22. Hugh Schofield, "Veteran Feels at Home on D-Day Beach," BBCNews, May 23, 2004, http://news.bbc.co.uk/2/hi/europe/3735307.stm.
23. Stasi, *Ennemis et frères,* p. 91.
24. Simonnet, *Commandant Kieffer,* pp. 339–40.
25. http://www.pegasusarchive.org/normandy/lord_lovat.htm.
26. http://www.pegasusarchive.org/normandy/lord_lovat.htm.
27. Collier, *D-Day,* p. 113.
28. Lovat, *March Past,* p. 304.
29. http://www.pegasusarchive.org/normandy/lord_lovat.htm.
30. Saunders, *The Green Beret,* p. 261.
31. http://content.time.com/time/magazine/article/0,9171,164496,00.html.
32. Miller, *Nothing Less Than Victory,* pp. 148–49.
33. Lovat, *March Past,* p. 299.
34. Léon Gautier, interview with author.
35. Stasi, *Ennemis et frères,* p. 92.
36. Miller, *Nothing Less Than Victory,* p. 190.
37. Saunders, *The Green Beret,* p. 261.
38. Stasi, *Ennemis et frères,* pp. 92–93.
39. http://historyarticles.com/southwick-house/.
40. Barbara Wyden Papers, 1944–1945, Dwight D. Eisenhower Library, Abilene, Kansas.
41. Smith, *Eisenhower in War and Peace,* p. 315.
42. Collier, *D-Day,* p. 27.
43. Dwight D. Eisenhower, *Crusade in Europe,* p. 249.
44. Collier, *D-Day,* p. 27.
45. Eloise Lee, "Here's the Chilling Letter General Eisenhower Drafted in Case the Nazis Won on D-Day," Business Insider, June 6, 2012.
46. Morgan, *Past Forgetting,* pp. 191–92.
47. *Washington Post,* June 6, 1984.

48. Bob Moen, *Sun Journal* (Maine), May 19, 1994.

49. Koskimaki, *D-Day with the Screaming Eagles*, p. 21.

50. Dwight D. Eisenhower, *Crusade in Europe*, p. 251.

51. Morgan, *Past Forgetting*, p. 216.

52. http://www.americandday.org/Documents/1st_SSB-No3_Commando-War%20Diaries.html.

53. Léon Gautier, interview with author.

54. Lovat, *March Past*, p. 305.

55. http://anthem4england.co.uk/anthems/heart-of-oak/.

56. *The Independent*, August 22, 2010.

57. *The Scotsman*, March 11, 2016.

58. Saunders, *The Green Beret*, p. 261.

59. Moorehead, *Eclipse*, p. 107.

60. Lovat, *March Past*, p. 305.

61. Lovat, *March Past*, p. 256.

62. Lovat, *March Past*, p. 9.

63. Lovat, *March Past*, p. 260.

64. Collier, *D-Day*, p. 13.

65. Lovat, *March Past*, p. 277.

66. Lovat, *March Past*, p. 266.

67. Lovat, *March Past*, p. 305.

68. Fuller, *A Third Face*, p. 158.

69. http://www.americandday.org/D-Day/1st_Infantry_Division-Order_of_battle.html.

70. John Spalding, medical record, courtesy of Max Poorthuis, president, 16th Infantry Regiment Historical Society.

71. http://www.ssqq.com/travel/oslo2010dday5.htm.

72. John Spalding questionnaire, Cornelius Ryan Collection of World War II Papers, Mahn Center for Archives and Special Collections, Ohio University Libraries, Box 12, Folder 55. All of E Company had been told several times that a pre-invasion air force bombing would be highly effective, destroying beach defenses and German strongpoints. "We had been led to believe," recalled Spalding, "[that] German troops would be in a state of shock from aerial and naval bombardment. How little we knew, how great our faith! The navy promised us we would be dumped ashore without even getting our shoes wet."

73. Capa, *Slightly out of Focus*, p. 134.

74. Howard and Bates, *The Pegasus Diaries*, p. 115.

75. http://www.pegasusarchive.org/normandy/john_howard.htm.

76. Drez, *Voices of D-Day*, pp. 98–104.

77. Barber, *The Pegasus and Orne Bridges*, p. 64.

78. IWM, SR 11357.

79. Fowler, *Pegasus Bridge*, p. 21.

80. *D-Day: Turning the Tide*, written and presented by Charles Wheeler (Bristol, UK: BBC Bristol, 1994).

81. IWM, SR 11357.

82. *The Independent,* May 30, 2009.
83. Howard and Bates, *The Pegasus Diaries,* p. 118.
84. *Daily Telegraph,* December 16, 2005.
85. Fowler, *Pegasus Bridge,* p. 15.
86. IWM, SR 11357.
87. Fowler, *Pegasus Bridge,* p. 28.
88. http://monologues.co.uk/musichall/Songs-A/A-be-My-Boy.htm.
89. Fowler, *Pegasus Bridge,* p. 28.
90. Howard and Bates, *The Pegasus Diaries,* p. 116.
91. https://www.poets.org/poetsorg/poem/soldier.
92. Howard and Bates, *The Pegasus Diaries,* p. 1.
93. *New York Times,* May 9, 1999.
94. http://www.pegasusarchive.org/normandy/jim_wallwork.htm.
95. *Daily Express,* February 2, 2013.
96. Masters, *Glidermen of Neptune,* p. 40.
97. Johnson and Dunphie, *Brightly Shone the Dawn,* pp. 30–31.
98. http://www.pegasusarchive.org/normandy/jim_wallwork.htm.
99. North Witham was one of twenty-two scattered across England from which some twenty thousand airborne troops would take off in the next few hours.
100. Botting, *The D-Day Invasion,* p. 91.
101. http://paul.rutgers.edu/~mcgrew/wwii/usaf/html/DDay.html.
102. *Air and Space* magazine, June 6, 2014. He would fly 125 missions supporting special forces in Vietnam.
103. Polk, *World War II Army Airborne Troop Carriers,* p. 106.
104. http://legendsofflightnurses.org/TheStoryOfAirEvacuation/FullText.pdf.
105. Air Force Association, *Air Force Fifty,* p. 173.
106. http://www.americanairmuseum.com/person/242977.
107. https://amcmuseum.org/history/troop-carrier-d-day-flights/.
108. Frank L. Lillyman, "Report of D-Day Pathfinder Activities," July 1, 1944, 101st Airborne Division Pathfinder Group, APO 472–US ARMY, National Archives (US), http://www.6juin1944.com/assaut/aeropus/en_page.php?page=after_pathf_101.
109. *The Ninth Flyer* (official newsletter of the Ninth Air Force Association), vol. 2, no. 2 (Summer 1992), p. 22.
110. http://www.americanairmuseum.com/place/271.
111. Lillyman, "Report of D-Day Pathfinder Activities."
112. *Air and Space,* June 6, 2014.
113. Balkoski, *Utah Beach,* p. 102.
114. Kaufman and Kaufman, *The American GI in Europe in World War II,* p. 169.
115. http://paul.rutgers.edu/~mcgrew/wwii/usaf/html/DDay.html.
116. https://amcmuseum.org/history/troop-carrier-d-day-flights/.
117. *Reno Evening Gazette,* June 8, 1944.
118. *Reno Evening Gazette,* June 8, 1944.

119. Moran, *American Airborne Pathfinders in World War II*, p. 54.
120. *Reno Evening Gazette*, June 8, 1944.
121. Koskimaki, *D-Day with the Screaming Eagles*, p. 27.

CHAPTER 2: HAM AND JAM

1. Drez, *Voices of D-Day*, pp. 98–104.
2. *The Ninth Flyer* (official newsletter of the Ninth Air Force Association), vol. 2, no. 2 (Summer 1992), p. 22.
3. Howard and Bates, *The Pegasus Diaries*, pp. 116–17.
4. Jonathan Owen, "Heroes of Pegasus Bridge (Who Also Liberated a Bar)," *The Independent*, May 30, 2009, http://www.independent.co.uk/news/uk /this-britain/heroes-of-pegasus-bridge-who-also-liberated-a-bar -1693512.html.
5. http://www.britisharmedforces.org/pages/nat_jim_wallwork.htm.
6. http://www.pegasusarchive.org/normandy/jim_wallwork.htm.
7. Breuer, *Geronimo*, pp. 202–3.
8. http://www.theguardian.com/uk/2004/may/23/secondworldwar.military.
9. Bando, *The Screaming Eagles at Norm*andy, p. 32.
10. *New York Times*, March 25, 2007. Pedone later "assisted in development of NATO, [was] appointed Chairman of Command and Control Committee for Joint Chiefs of Staff, briefed presidents Johnson and Kennedy. Flew 245 combat missions. Ph.D. in International Affairs. Also survived by his son, Lt. Col. Stephen (retired)."
11. Breuer, *Geronimo*, pp. 202–3.
12. Howard and Bates, *The Pegasus Diaries*, p. 117.
13. Fowler, *Pegasus Bridge*, p. 30.
14. Howard and Bates, *The Pegasus Diaries*, p. 118.
15. While the first airborne troops flew above the English Channel on D-Day, Englishman Lieutenant Norman Poole, an electrician's son and a brilliant pianist, was already leading a six-man SAS team whose mission was to draw German attention from the landings of the American 82nd Airborne, which would begin at 1:15 A.M. As part of Operation Titanic IV, twenty-four-year-old Poole leapt from a plane at 12:10 A.M., his feet touching French soil a minute later. He jumped unarmed, a carrier pigeon strapped to his chest, among two hundred "dummy parachutists," all called "Rupert," each several inches tall and primed with small explosive charges that simulated rifle fire. For several minutes Poole and his men made fake battle noises using special gramophones attached to amplifiers and then went into hiding, having successfully drawn the attention of several hundred Germans in the vicinity. The pigeon Poole carried was one of only several to get back to England, unlike Poole and his comrades, who would become POWs. *Daily Mail*, July 7, 2015.
16. Koskimaki, *D-Day with the Screaming Eagles*, p. 28.
17. Koskimaki, *D-Day with the Screaming Eagles*, p. 28.

18. Breuer, *Geronimo,* p. 205.
19. Breuer, *Geronimo,* p. 205.
20. Frank L. Lillyman, "Report of D-Day Pathfinder Activities," July 1, 1944, 101st Airborne Division Pathfinder Group, APO 472–US ARMY, National Archives (US), http://www.6juin1944.com/assaut/aeropus/en_page.php ?page=after_pathf_101.
21. Lillyman, "Report of D-Day Pathfinder Activities." "First reception was received at approximately 0045," according to one report. "Lights were turned on at 0040."
22. Koskimaki, *D-Day with the Screaming Eagles,* p. 28.
23. Drez, *Voices of D-Day,* pp. 98–104.
24. http://www.britisharmedforces.org/pages/nat_jim_wallwork.htm.
25. http://www.keepitsoaring.com/LKSC/Downloads/Horsa_Glider _Notes.pdf.
26. http://www.pegasusarchive.org/normandy/jim_wallwork.htm.
27. Howard and Bates, *The Pegasus Diaries,* p. 120.
28. Drez, *Voices of D-Day,* pp. 98–104.
29. http://www.pegasusarchive.org/normandy/jim_wallwork.htm.
30. Fowler, *Pegasus Bridge,* p. 35.
31. Howard and Bates, *The Pegasus Diaries,* p. 121.
32. http://www.pegasusarchive.org/normandy/jim_wallwork.htm.
33. http://www.britisharmedforces.org/pages/nat_jim_wallwork.htm.
34. Drez, *Voices of D-Day,* pp. 98–104.
35. Fowler, *Pegasus Bridge,* p. 39.
36. Barber, *The Pegasus and Orne Bridges,* p. 88.
37. Fowler, *Pegasus Bridge,* p. 39.
38. *The Independent,* December 21, 2013.
39. *Daily Telegraph,* June 5, 2004.
40. Hastings, *Overlord,* p. 229.
41. Shilleto, *Pegasus Bridge and Merville Battery,* p. 51.
42. Richard Spalding, "D-Day, Discovering the Father I Never Knew," BBC News, June 3, 2014, http://www.bbc.com/news/uk-england-27610572.
43. Fowler, *Pegasus Bridge,* p. 39.
44. *The Independent,* December 21, 2013.
45. IWM, SR 11073.
46. Shilleto, *Pegasus Bridge and Merville Battery,* p. 59.
47. Fowler, *Pegasus Bridge,* p. 41.
48. Ambrose, *Pegasus Bridge,* p. 104.
49. "Suicide Missions of D-Day," *Dangerous Missions,* episode 28 (History Channel, 2001).
50. Koskimaki, *D-Day with the Screaming Eagles,* p. 28.
51. *Airborne Quarterly,* Summer 2003, pp. 93–95.
52. Lillyman, "Report of D-Day Pathfinder Activities."

Chapter 3: The Cruel Seas

1. *VSD* magazine, June 8, 1994.
2. King, Hilborn, and Nulton, *To War with the 4th,* pp. 1322–35.
3. Balkoski, *Utah Beach,* p. 189.
4. https://umdarchives.wordpress.com/2013/11/11/heroes-on-the-playing-field-and-on-the-battlefield-maryland-athlete-soldiers/.
5. Balkoski, *Utah Beach,* p. 179.
6. *VSD* magazine, June 8, 1994.
7. Theodore Roosevelt Jr. Papers, Box 61, Library of Congress.
8. https://www.archives.gov/historical-docs/todays-doc/?dod-date=606.
9. Balkoski, *Utah Beach,* p. 187.
10. *Washington Post,* March 12, 2012.
11. *Baltimore Sun,* February 20, 2012.
12. *Washington Post,* March 12, 2012.
13. George Kerchner, oral history, Eisenhower Center. "Then medium bombers would plaster the area, and only three minutes before six-thirty, fighters would strafe the Pointe. The attacks were designed to keep the defenders pinned down, so they wouldn't see us approach the Pointe. They would be kept from the edge of the cliff. Otherwise they could cut our ropes before we even managed to get halfway up the cliff."
14. http://www.history.army.mil/books/wwii/smallunit/smallunit-pdh.htm.
15. Zaloga, *Rangers Lead the Way,* p. 16.
16. Moen and Heinen, *The Fool Lieutenant,* p. 63.
17. Lane, *Rudder's Rangers,* pp. 96–97.
18. Black, *The Battalion,* p. 79.
19. Moen and Heinen, *The Fool Lieutenant,* p. 90.
20. Ranger Jack Kuhn remembered that Rudder was far superior to any commanding officer he had encountered: "None of [the] commanders who came before him measured up. He had a steely-eyed look when he was not pleased. There was also a look of pride when we were successful at some training exercise. In spite of his rank, he was always friendly towards the troops. He knew I was married and always asked me how Mary and our baby were doing. One day during a bull session in the field—Rudder made it a habit of holding informal gripe sessions to learn the feelings of the men—a fellow mentioned that the colonel had said every man would be issued a wristwatch. This young Ranger remarked he had never been given one. Col. Rudder declared that would be corrected immediately. He walked over to the soldier, took his own wristwatch off, and gave it to the Ranger." Astor, *June 6, 1944,* p. 65.
21. Lane, *Rudder's Rangers,* p. 97.
22. *Collier's,* June 11, 1954.
23. Collier, *D-Day,* p. 180.
24. Moen and Heinen, *The Fool Lieutenant,* p. 88.
25. Drez, *Voices of D-Day,* pp. 98–104. Jack Kuhn, belonging to D Company of the 2nd Ranger Battalion, waited nervously for the order to board landing

craft. "I could not envision myself going into combat. It seemed so detached from me . . . The one thing I feared was not being able to face the test. I didn't want to coward out. Then everyone else said the same thing, and I was okay. I never had the apprehension that I would be killed or wounded."

26. http://www.legis.state.pa.us/WU01/LI/LI/US/PDF/2004/0/0061.PDF.
27. Collier, *D-Day*, p. 116.
28. http://the-american-catholic.com/tag/father-joe-lacy/.
29. On June 6, 1944, at 7:30 A.M., LCA 1377 landed Rangers on the Dog Green sector of Omaha Beach. According to one report, "Father Lacy was the last man out just before an artillery shell hit the fantail . . . Wounded men were everywhere, both on the beach and in the water feebly trying to get to the beach. Father Lacy did not hesitate. With no thought for his own safety he waded into the water to pull men out of the ocean and onto the beach. He began treating the wounded on the beach and administering the Last Rites to those beyond human assistance . . . Father Lacy continued to tend their wounded and the wounded of other units. For his actions that day Father Lacy was awarded the Distinguished Service Cross, the second highest decoration for valor, after the Medal of Honor, in the United States Army." http://the-american-catholic.com/tag/father-joe-lacy.
30. Brinkley, *The Boys of Pointe du Hoc*, p. 66.
31. http://www.pegasusarchive.org/normandy/terence_otway.htm.
32. IWM, SR 12133.
33. http://www.pegasusarchive.org/normandy/terence_otway.htm.
34. http://warfarehistorynetwork.com/daily/wwii/attack-on-the-merville-gun-battery-during-the-battle-of-normandy/.
35. Howarth, *Dawn of D-Day*, p. 53.
36. *Daily Telegraph*, July 25, 2006.
37. http://www.pegasusarchive.org/normandy/terence_otway.htm.
38. http://warfarehistorynetwork.com/daily/wwii/attack-on-the-merville-gun-battery-during-the-battle-of-normandy/.
39. *D-Day: Turning the Tide*, written and presented by Charles Wheeler (Bristol, UK: BBC Bristol, 1994).
40. "Suicide Missions of D-Day," *Dangerous Missions*, episode 28 (History Channel, 2001).
41. IWM, SR 21061.
42. IWM, SR 12133.
43. Howard and Bates, *The Pegasus Diaries*, p. 125.
44. https://paradata.org.uk/people/nigel-poett.
45. http://www.pegasusarchive.org/normandy/nigel_poett.htm.
46. IWM, SR 11559.

Chapter 4: A Grade-A Stinker

1. Fred Glover, interview with author.
2. http://www.6juin1944.com/en_journee.html.
3. http://www.pegasusarchive.org/arnhem/batt_512.htm.

4. Strong, *Steiner's War,* p. 89.

5. http://www.6juin1944.com/espace/merville/cartmerv_e.php.

6. Johnson and Dunphie, *Brightly Shone the Dawn,* p. 42.

7. http://www.pegasusarchive.org/normandy/terence_otway.htm.

8. Howarth, *Dawn of D-Day,* pp. 53–54.

9. http://warfarehistorynetwork.com/daily/wwii/attack-on-the-merville -gun-battery-during-the-battle-of-normandy/.

10. http://www.pegasusarchive.org/normandy/terence_otway.htm.

11. No married men had been selected for the mission, described as "a grade A stinker of a job" by one senior officer. Collier, *D-Day,* p. 68.

12. http://www.pegasusarchive.org/normandy/terence_otway.htm.

13. 9th Parachute Battalion, "Capture of the Merville Battery," after-action report, 6th Airborne Division, National Archives (UK).

14. http://www.pegasusarchive.org/normandy/terence_otway.htm.

15. http://www.pegasusarchive.org/normandy/terence_otway.htm.

16. IWM, SR 12133.

17. Howarth, *Dawn of D-Day,* p. 57.

18. IWM, SR 12133.

19. IWM, SR 13723.

20. IWM, SR 12133.

21. IWM, SR 13143.

22. 9th Parachute Battalion, "Capture of the Merville Battery," after-action report, 6th Airborne Division, National Archives (UK).

23. IWM, SR 13143.

24. IWM, SR 12133.

25. 9th Parachute Battalion, "Capture of the Merville Battery," after-action report, 6th Airborne Division, National Archives (UK).

26. IWM, SR 12133.

27. *Stars and Stripes,* June 7, 1944.

28. http://www.af.mil/News/Article-Display/Article/485137/allied-air-forces -paved-way-for-d-day/.

29. According to an official after-action report, "The excited babbling of the crewmen betrayed their eagerness for the start of the all-important invasion mission, when they gathered in the crew room for the 0200 briefing on the morning of June 6, 1944. The Group, using fifty-four planes, rather than the usual thirty-six, took off at 0415 and assembled in the early morning darkness. After the long trip over the ship infested Channel to the Cherbourg Peninsula the three boxes of the Group blasted their separate targets. The bombs were away at 0617, just a few short minutes before the first wave of assault troops dashed onto the enemy shore. No planes were lost and only slight enemy opposition, in the form of light to heavy flak was encountered. The results of the bombing were classed as fair to good." http://www.b26.com/page/historyofthe323rdbombgroup.htm.

30. Howarth, *Dawn of D-Day,* p. 127.

31. "Operations by IX Bomber Command," Army Air Force Historical Study no. 36, Military History Institute, Ninth Air Force (October 1945), pp. 71–74.

32. http://www.b26.com/page/historyofthe323rdbombgroup.htm.
33. *Stars and Stripes*, June 7, 1944.
34. https://stanleyehollisvcmemorial.co.uk/biography/.
35. IWM, SR 1648.
36. http://www.patricktaylor.com/war-diary-1.
37. According to one account, "away from exploding shells, the threat of anti-personnel mines and the stammer of German machine guns, Hollis was a quiet, likeable Englishman—just the sort with whom to enjoy a pint in the local." De la Billière, *Supreme Courage,* p. 40.
38. http://www.patricktaylor.com/war-diary-1.
39. http://warfarehistorynetwork.com/daily/wwii/sergeant-major-stan-hollis-the-victoria-cross-on-d-day/.
40. Hastings, *An Undergraduate's War,* p. 116.
41. IWM, SR 1648.
42. Collier, *D-Day,* p. 128.
43. *Daily Mail*, December 26, 2012.
44. IWM, SR 1648.
45. Hastings, *An Undergraduate's War,* p. 150.
46. Hastings, *An Undergraduate's War,* pp. 119–20.
47. IWM, SR 1648.
48. *The Independent*, May 12, 1994.
49. Morgan, *Past Forgetting,* pp. 191–92.
50. Morgan, *Past Forgetting,* pp. 191–92.
51. http://paul.rutgers.edu/~mcgrew/wwii/usaf/html/DDay.html.
52. *The Ninth Flyer* (official newsletter of the Ninth Air Force Association), vol. 2, no. 2 (Summer 1992), p. 22.
53. http://paul.rutgers.edu/~mcgrew/wwii/usaf/html/DDay.html. "You think about the people in your plane and do your job," recalled Pedone. "There's no time to be scared. But if you are afraid, you might as well get right out of the airplane and go back to [base] because you must take control of your senses."
54. http://paul.rutgers.edu/~mcgrew/wwii/usaf/html/DDay.html.
55. Fewer than a third of the pathfinders had landed on their drop zones.
56. Collier, *D-Day,* p. 157.
57. *Sun Journal* (Lewiston, Maine), May 19, 1994.
58. *Sun Journal* (Lewiston, Maine), May 19, 1994.
59. Gavin, *On to Berlin,* p. 105.
60. According to Major General Matthew Ridgway, commander of the 82nd Airborne Division, "We couldn't get in touch with anybody—neither the troops that were supposed to be coming in over the beaches by now, nor with anybody back in England, nor with anybody afloat. In short, we were in the typical situation for which you must be prepared when an airborne division goes into battle . . . For thirty-six hours we had no means of knowing how well or badly we were faring." Balkoski, *Utah Beach,* p. 306.
61. Collier, *D-Day,* p. 160.
62. Frank L. Lillyman, "Report of D-Day Pathfinder Activities," July 1, 1944, 101st Airborne Division Pathfinder Group, APO 472–US ARMY, National

Archives (US), http://www.6juin1944.com/assaut/aeropus/en_page.php
?page=after_pathf_101.

63. http://www.history.army.mil/documents/WWII/Cassidy/cassidy.htm.
64. Preisler, *First to Jump*, p. 91.
65. https://history.army.mil/documents/WWII/Cassidy/cassidy.htm.
66. http://www.dday-overlord.com/bataille-normandie/after-action-reports
/101st/pathfinders.

CHAPTER 5: BLOODY LUCKY

1. https://www.brainyquote.com/quotes/theodore_roosevelt_380703.
2. Jeffers, *Theodore Roosevelt Jr.*, p. 246.
3. *VSD* magazine, June 8, 1994.
4. Collier, *D-Day*, p. 184.
5. Howarth, *Dawn of D-Day*, p. 114. The landing craft started toward the beach.
Roosevelt recalled: "Suddenly [at 6:10 A.M.] we heard the drone of planes and
silhouetted against the colored clouds of dawn, formations of planes swept by
and passed toward shore. Flight after flight dropped its bombs on the German emplacements. There'd be a ripple of thunder, blazes of light, clouds of
dust, and the planes would pass us again on the way home. One fell by me,
flaming like a meteor." Theodore Roosevelt Jr. to wife Eleanor Roosevelt, June
11, 1944, Theodore Roosevelt Jr. Papers, Box 61, Library of Congress.
6. George Kerchner, diary entry, Eisenhower Center. He later noted in his
diary: "Heavy seas, began bailing immediately. Motor launch led us to
wrong point. Sailed along under machine gun fire, bailing all the time."
7. https://www.poetryfoundation.org/poems/45319/the-charge-of-the-light
-brigade.
8. Astor, *June 6, 1944*, pp. 212–15.
9. Zaloga, *Rangers Lead the Way*, p. 27.
10. *Daily Mail*, October 1, 2012.
11. Jack Kuhn belonged to D Company and stood in one of its three boats.
One was commanded by Slater, another by Kerchner, and yet another by
Len Lomell. "I noticed that Captain Slater's boat was very low in the water," remembered Kuhn, "in danger of foundering. It was losing speed and
dropping back from the formation . . . We saw the boat start to go down. I
don't know if anyone else was aware that the Duke was now out of the invasion. I wondered whether we should try to rescue him, but the time lost
would have made us late. Len [Lomell] and I agreed the mission came first.
It was his decision to make; personally I felt I was deserting our commander." Astor, *June 6, 1994*, p. 170.
12. George Kerchner, "Memoir," typescript in Eisenhower Center, University
of New Orleans.
13. Astor, *June 6, 1944*, pp. 212–15.
14. Brinkley, *The Boys of Pointe du Hoc*, p. 69.
15. http://www.uss-corry-dd463.com/d-day_u-boat_photos/d-day_pho
tos.htm.

16. http://www.worldwar2history.info/D-Day/Pointe-Du-Hoc.html.
17. Black, *The Battalion,* p. 106.
18. Parry was one of four brothers. Two lost their lives in WWII. One of them, Captain George Parry, was actually killed on D-Day.
19. Collier, *D-Day,* p. 168.
20. IWM, SR 12133.
21. Barber, *The Day the Devils Dropped In,* p. 81.
22. Collier, *D-Day,* p. 169.
23. IWM, SR 21061.
24. Collier, *D-Day,* p. 169.
25. IWM, SR 21061.
26. IWM, SR 17309.
27. *D-Day: Turning the Tide,* written and presented by Charles Wheeler (Bristol, UK: BBC Bristol, 1994).
28. IWM, SR 17309.
29. IWM, SR 21061.
30. IWM, SR 12133.
31. Shilleto, *Pegasus Bridge and Merville Battery,* p. 104.
32. *D-Day: Turning the Tide,* written and presented by Charles Wheeler (Bristol, UK: BBC Bristol, 1994).
33. Barber, *The Day the Devils Dropped In*, p. 88
34. IWM, SR 17309.
35. IWM, SR 12133.
36. Barber, *The Day the Devils Dropped In*, p. 90
37. Liddle, *D-Day: By Those Who Were There,* p. 75.
38. IWM, SR 12133.
39. Barber, *The Day the Devils Dropped In*, p. 218.
40. Shilleto, *Pegasus Bridge and Merville Battery,* p. 107.
41. IWM, SR 12133.
42. 9th Parachute Battalion, "Capture of the Merville Battery," after-action report, 6th Airborne Division, National Archives (UK).
43. IWM, SR 13143. "My orders were to destroy or neutralize the battery before the rest came ashore," recalled Otway. "And that is what we did. Because of the efforts of my men the first waves arrived without a single shell being fired from Merville." *London Illustrated News,* June 4, 1994.
44. Barber, *The Day the Devils Dropped In,* p. 97.
45. Barber, *The Day the Devils Dropped In,* p. 95.

PART 2: THE DAY

1. Lovat, *March Past,* p. 360.

CHAPTER 6: BY DAWN'S FAINT LIGHT

1. http://www.d-daytanks.org.uk/diary/june6.html.
2. Léon Gautier, interview with author.

3. Saunders, *The Green Beret,* p. 263.
4. Léon Gautier, interview with author.
5. Dunning, *The Fighting Fourth,* p. 129.
6. Collier, *D-Day,* p. 114.
7. Dunning, *The Fighting Fourth,* p. 1.
8. Léon Gautier, interview with author.
9. Stasi, *Ennemis et frères,* pp. 17–18.
10. Stasi, *Ennemis et frères,* p. 21.
11. IWM, SR 34422.
12. Lovat, *March Past,* p. 305.
13. Mayo, *D-Day, Minute by Minute,* p. 141.
14. Stasi, *Ennemis et frères,* p. 97.
15. Lovat, *March Past,* p. 306.
16. http://www.pegasusarchive.org/normandy/gondree.htm. According to one account, the Gondrées had always greatly resented the German occupation. They had not allowed the Germans to use their home. By early 1944, they had begun to help the Resistance. According to one account, "The information collected by the Gondrée family did much to give Major Howard and his Coup de Main force a thorough understanding of the defences around the bridges. Amongst the details that Thérèse discovered was the precise location, in a pillbox housing machine-guns, for the trigger mechanism for the explosives which were to demolish Bénouville Bridge in the event of an attack. Georges Gondrée was known to British Intelligence, and even Major Howard had heard his name during the planning stages of the Invasion. The great contribution that the family made to the success of the operations around Bénouville is perhaps best demonstrated by the example of early May, when Generalfeldmarschall Rommel inspected the bridges and ordered that an anti-tank gun emplacement be established next to Bénouville Bridge. Within two days, Major Howard had been warned that some new structure was being built next to the Bridge, and within a week Georges Gondrée's observations had confirmed both its purpose and the completion of the position." Source: http:www.pegasusarchive.org/normandy/gondree.htm.
17. Fowler, *Pegasus Bridge,* p. 40.
18. "As we got to the Café Gondrée," recalled Wally Parr, "we paused for breath and I heard a noise. Outside the Café Gondrée, there was a grill. I think possibly it was used to lower crates down. We tiptoed over there in the moonlight and looked down and to my surprise I was looking at a woman who was obviously Madame Gondrée and two little children, apparently girls. She was nestled with the one on her left arm in her bosom. The one on the right was staring up at me. I found out later, many years later, that the younger one was Arlette and the older one was Georgette Gondrée. So, I looked down at them and my one fear was that a grenade was going to roll down there and blow them to smithereens. I'm shouting, 'Madame, go in for god's sake! . . . It's the invasion!' She's just staring up at me. She did not speak any English. So I'm shouting my head off to her, 'Go

in!' Those poor little children. I reached in my pocket, pulled out a bar of chocolate, and handed it down. Georgette, the oldest one, took hold of that bar of chocolate. And to this day those two girls are still known as the first two children to be liberated in the invasion of Europe and by a company soldier with a bar of chocolate. I did find out many years later that Madame Gondrée was not convinced that we were British troops. She thought we were Germans trying to rest up, and furthermore . . . she was also convinced that that bar of chocolate was poisoned, so she wouldn't let the girls eat it until finally, the next day, when they realized that it was a true invasion, then the girls had their first decent bar of chocolate in their lives." IWM, SR 11073.

19. Collier, *D-Day*, p. 153.
20. Fowler, *Pegasus Bridge*, p. 41.
21. Ambrose, *Pegasus Bridge*, p. 129.
22. Howard and Bates, *The Pegasus Diaries*, p. 131.
23. Ambrose, *Pegasus Bridge*, p. 131.
24. Hatfield, *Rudder*, p. 121.
25. Hatfield, *Rudder*, p. 122.
26. Raaen, *Intact*, p. 26.
27. http://discerninghistory.com/2016/06/rangers-lead-the-way-how-the-rangers-at-pointe-du-hoc-turned-disaster-into-victory-during-the-d-day-invasion/.
28. Lane, *Rudder's Rangers*, p. 79.
29. Morrison, *The Invasion of France and Germany*, p. 125.
30. Hatfield, *Rudder*, p. 123.
31. General John Raaen, interview with author.
32. Black, *The Battalion*, p. 95.
33. Raaen, *Intact*, p. 27.
34. Carell, *Invasion*, pp. 78–79.
35. Collier, *D-Day*, p. 176.
36. http://histomil.com/viewtopic.php?t=14165.
37. *Daily Telegraph*, May 30, 2004.
38. http://www.tracesofwar.com/persons/22284/Streczyk-Philip.htm.
39. http://www.tracesofwar.com/persons/22284/Streczyk-Philip.htm.
40. http://www.ssqq.com/travel/oslo2010dday5.htm.
41. Forrest C. Pogue, "John Spalding D-Day Narrative," E Co., 16th Inf., Lt. Spalding combat interview, Military History Institute, Carlisle Barracks, PA.
42. E Company, 16th Infantry Regiment, After Action Report, June 1944, National Archives (US).
43. Bob Sales, interview with author.
44. Pogue, "John Spalding D-Day Narrative."
45. Pogue, "John Spalding D-Day Narrative."
46. John Spalding questionnaire, Cornelius Ryan Collection of World War II Papers, Mahn Center for Archives and Special Collections, Ohio University Libraries.

47. Bob Sales, interview with author.
48. Shuey, *Omaha Beach Field Guide,* p. 62.
49. Rommel had written to General Alfred Jodl on April 11, "If in spite of the enemy's air superiority, we succeed in getting a large part of our mobile force into action in the threatened coast defense sectors in the first few hours, I am convinced that the enemy attack on the coast will collapse completely on its first day." Liddell Hart, *The Rommel Papers,* p. 468.
50. https://www.lapetitemusette.com/2017/01/arthur-jahnke-german -veteran-of-23-years-old/?lang=en.
51. Holt and Holt, *Major and Mrs. Holt's Battlefield Guide,* p. 25.
52. Howarth, *Dawn of D-Day,* p. 129.
53. Balkoski, *Utah Beach,* p. 343.
54. Theodore Roosevelt Jr. Papers, Box 61, Library of Congress.
55. Arthur Jahnke, oral history, Eisenhower Center.
56. Just four of thirty-two failed to reach the beach.
57. Zaloga, *D-Day 1944,* p. 55.
58. Arthur Jahnke, oral history, Eisenhower Center.
59. Carell, *Invasion,* p. 49.
60. Arthur Jahnke, oral history, Eisenhower Center.
61. Ellison Parfitt, oral history, Library of Congress.
62. King, Hilborn, and Nulton, *To War with the 4th,* pp. 1502–16.
63. Theodore Roosevelt Jr. to wife Eleanor Roosevelt, June 11, 1944, Theodore Roosevelt Jr. Papers, Box 61, Library of Congress.
64. http://www.4thinfantry.org/content/division-history.
65. Zaloga, *D-Day 1944,* p. 55.
66. Magdelaine, *Utah,* p. 3 (quoting Howard Vander Beek, LCC 60).
67. "Maryland's WWII Profiles in Courage," University of Maryland alumni magazine, November 11, 2004, https://umdarchives.wordpress.com/2013 /11/11/heroes-on-the-playing-field-and-on-the-battlefield-maryland -athlete-soldiers/.
68. *VSD* magazine, June 2–8, 1994.
69. Theodore Roosevelt Jr. to wife Eleanor Roosevelt, June 11, 1944, Theodore Roosevelt Jr. Papers, Box 61, Library of Congress.
70. *VSD* magazine, June 2–8, 1994.

CHAPTER 7: AN ANGEL ON EACH SHOULDER

1. Clay, *Blood and Sacrifice,* p. 185.
2. Forrest C. Pogue, "John Spalding D-Day Narrative," E Co., 16th Inf., Lt. Spalding combat interview, Military History Institute, Carlisle Barracks, PA.
3. Clay, *Blood and Sacrifice,* p. 186.
4. Carell, *Invasion,* pp. 80–81.
5. Pogue, "John Spalding D-Day Narrative."
6. Clay, *Blood and Sacrifice,* p. 186.
7. Clay, *Blood and Sacrifice,* p. 186.

8. Pogue, "John Spalding D-Day Narrative."
9. Cornelius Ryan Collection of World War II Papers, "Wozenski Question-naire," Box 12, Folder 55, Ohio University.
10. Miller, *Nothing Less Than Victory*, p. 335. The officer Spalding was trying to reach was Captain Wozenski, who had made it out of the water and onto the beach and was now lying on shale beside a sergeant, under heavy fire from a strongpoint, WN62, which had several machine guns. "For God's sake get a packet of cigarettes out," he ordered the sergeant, who franti-cally emptied handfuls of sand from a pocket before he found a packet.
11. Pogue, "John Spalding D-Day Narrative."
12. E Company, 16th Infantry Regiment, After Action Report, June 1944, Na-tional Archives (US).
13. Pogue, "John Spalding D-Day Narrative."
14. E Company, 16th Infantry Regiment, After Action Report, June 1944, Na-tional Archives (US).
15. Pogue, "John Spalding D-Day Narrative."
16. Miller, *Nothing Less Than Victory*, p. 334.
17. Carell, *Invasion*, pp. 66–69.
18. Theodore Roosevelt Jr. to wife Eleanor Roosevelt, June 11, 1944, Theodore Roosevelt Jr. Papers, Box 61, Library of Congress.
19. Balkoski, *Utah Beach*, p. 231.
20. http://warfarehistorynetwork.com/daily/wwii/rangers-at-the-pointe/.
21. Lewis, *Voices from D-Day*, p. 121.
22. George Kerchner, "Memoir," typescript in Eisenhower Center, University of New Orleans.
23. https://www.ibiblio.org/hyperwar/USA/USA-A-Small/USA-A-Small-1.html.
24. Zaloga, *Rangers Lead the Way*, p. 31.
25. Kerchner, "Memoir."
26. Kerchner, "Memoir."
27. Collier, *D-Day*, p. 180.
28. Len Lomell, oral history, Eisenhower Center.
29. Len Lomell, oral history, Eisenhower Center.
30. Kerchner, "Memoir."
31. Collier, *D-Day*, p. 180.
32. Morison, *The Invasion of France and Germany*, pp. 125–26.
33. Bailey, *Forgotten Voices of D-Day*, p. 259.
34. IWM, SR 1648.
35. Bailey, *Forgotten Voices of D-Day*, p. 266.
36. IWM, SR 1648.

CHAPTER 8: LA BELLE FRANCE

1. Leonard Lomell, oral history, Eisenhower Center.
2. Astor, *June 6, 1944*, pp. 212–15.
3. Lane, *Rudder's Rangers*, p. 121.

4. "There was an anti-aircraft position off to our right several hundred yards," recalled Lomell. "And machine guns off to the left of us. Maybe a hundred, two hundred yards away. And there was another machine gun that we destroyed on our way in. But we did not waste time, we did have some fire fights, or little skirmishes, if the Germans had a patrol, or half a dozen of them would pop out of an underground tunnel, you know, they had a lot of tunnels there underground and through hedgerows. Well, when we were confronted, we'd drive them out and fight them and they'd run like rabbits, you know, right into their holes, and out they went. But we never stopped. We kept firing and charging all the way through their buildings area, where they came out of their billets . . . We were confronted with them there on our way up the road from the Pointe to the coast road. The coast road ran between Utah Beach and Omaha Beach. Our orders were to set up a roadblock and keep the Germans from going to Omaha Beach. We were to also destroy all communications visible along the coast road. Find the guns, was our big objective." Leonard Lomell, oral history, Eisenhower Center.
5. Drez, *Voices of D-Day.*
6. http://warfarehistorynetwork.com/daily/wwii/rangers-at-the-pointe/.
7. Lomell, oral history.
8. George Kerchner, "Memoir," typescript in Eisenhower Center, University of New Orleans.
9. Hatfield, *Rudder,* p. 144.
10. http://www.cnn.com/books/beginnings/9901/the.victors/.
11. Lane, *Rudder's Rangers,* p. 140.
12. Miller, *Nothing Less Than Victory,* p. 199.
13. *Daily Telegraph,* June 4, 2004.
14. Stasi, *Ennemis et frères,* pp. 99–100.
15. Léon Gautier, interview with author.
16. "Rapport du lieutenant de vaisseau Kieffer," Service Historique de la Défense, Département Marine—TTH2.
17. Lewis, *Voices from D-Day,* p. 128.
18. Beau-Lofi, *Il fallait y croire,* p. 243.
19. Léon Gautier, interview with author.
20. Colonel Philippe Kieffer, After Action Report, June 14, 1944, National Archives (UK).
21. Dunning, *The Fighting Fourth,* p. 128.
22. Colonel Kieffer, After Action Report, June 14, 1944, National Archives (UK).
23. Stasi, *Kieffer Commando,* p. 38.
24. Léon Gautier, interview with author.
25. Stasi, *Kieffer Commando,* p. 41.
26. The official after-action report noted, "A fiercely opposed beach landing during which No. 4 Commando took over the role previously allotted to an earlier wave of Infantry which had been pinned down by enemy fire . . . The Commando, five hundred strong . . . landed in two waves from the HMS Princess Astrid and SS Maid of Orleans . . . touched down on Red

Queen beach, a mile to the west of Ouistreham, at La Beche . . . No. 4 Commando's first wave of LCAs went in at 0820 hrs . . . Mortar bombs were falling in and around the LCAs and as the Commando landed there were 40 casualties, including the Commanding Officer, Lt. Colonel R.W.P. Dawson, who was wounded in the leg. Rapidly forming up under concentrated fire, Number 4 Commando fought their way from the beach to the forming up area . . . putting out of action several of the enemy positions . . . Dawson moved forward to contact 2nd Bn. East Yorks Regt. and was wounded in the head . . ." His second in command took over, and Gautier and others moved into Ouistreham—so began "street fighting through areas infested with snipers." DEFE 2/40, Intelligence/War Diary, No. 4 Commando, National Archives (UK).

27. Dunning, *The Fighting Fourth*, p. 133.
28. Léon Gautier, interview with author.
29. Colonel Kieffer, After Action Report, June 14, 1944, National Archives (UK).
30. Colonel Kieffer, After Action Report, June 14, 1944, National Archives (UK).
31. Stasi, *Kieffer Commando*, p. 47.
32. Beau-Lofi, *Il fallait y croire*, pp. 244–45.
33. "It was thanks to our discipline," Gautier explained, sixty years later. "In the commandos, you had to be disciplined." Hugh Schofield, "Veteran Feels at Home on D-Day Beach," BBC News, May 23, 2004, http://news .bbc.co.uk/2/hi/europe/3735307.stm. Commander Kieffer had told Gautier and others the previous day to expect to lose one out of every two comrades. That grim prediction had not come true. Among all the units belonging to Lord Lovat's commandos, nevertheless, the French had paid the highest price, suffering ten fatalities. Thirty had also been wounded, out of 177 who landed on Sword Beach "in the twilight of the morning," as one nineteen-year-old from Brittany remembered the time of arrival of the first wave. Stasi, *Kieffer Commando*, p. 34.
34. http://www.qor.com/community/cenotaph/dalton.html.
35. Martin, *Battle Diary*, p. 4.
36. http://www.qor.com/community/cenotaph/dalton.html.
37. Charles would later recall "standing on the deck of the SS Monowai with his brother, and trying to think of what to say to your sibling on what might be the last night of both of their lives. As they parted company to prepare for a 0315 reveille to board the assault craft, Charles simply shook his brother's hand and said 'See you on the beach!'" John Fotheringham, "See You on the Beach!," April 2, 2014, Juno Beach Centre, https://www .junobeach.org/see-you-on-the-beach/.
38. http://en.ww2awards.com/person/44752.
39. *Toronto Globe and Mail*, March 24, 1999.
40. https://qormuseum.org/soldiers-of-the-queens-own/dalton-charles -osborne/.
41. *Battle Diary, A Day in the Life of Charlie Martin*, directed by Martyn Burke (Canadian Broadcasting Company, 1994).

42. *The Rifleman: A Journal of the Queen's Own Rifles of Canada,* July 1978, p. 7.
43. Martin, *Battle Diary,* p. 5.
44. WO 179/2958, Intelligence/War Diary, the Queen's Own Rifles of Canada, National Archives (UK).
45. https://qormuseum.org/soldiers-of-the-queens-own/dalton-charles -osborne/.
46. Zuehlke, *Juno Beach,* p. 214.
47. Martin, *Battle Diary,* p. 6.
48. Martin, *Battle Diary,* pp. 4–5.
49. WO 179/2958, Intelligence/War Diary.
50. Zuehlke, *Juno Beach,* p. 210.
51. https://qormuseum.org/soldiers-of-the-queens-own/dalton-charles -osborne/.
52. Zuehlke, *Juno Beach,* p. 210.
53. Zuehlke, *Juno Beach,* p. 211.
54. https://qormuseum.org/soldiers-of-the-queens-own/dalton-charles -osborne/.
55. Zuehlke, *Juno Beach,* p. 212.
56. https://qormuseum.org/soldiers-of-the-queens-own/dalton-charles -osborne/.
57. https://qormuseum.org/soldiers-of-the-queens-own/dalton-charles -osborne/.
58. Zuehlke, *Juno Beach,* p. 218.
59. *The Rifleman: A Journal of the Queen's Own Rifles of Canada,* July 1978, p. 8.
60. Martin, *Battle Diary,* p. 9.
61. https://qormuseum.org/tag/d-day/.
62. Hickey, *The Scarlet Dawn,* p. 196.
63. Of the fourteen thousand Canadians who landed on D-Day, 340 were killed, 574 wounded, and 47 taken prisoner. http://www.junobeach.info /Juno-quick-facts.htm.
64. Lovat, *March Past,* p. 309.
65. http://www.pegasusarchive.org/normandy/war_6cdo.htm#Appendix%20 'A'.
66. http://ojs.victoria.ac.nz/kotare/article/viewFile/716/527.
67. Collier, *D-Day,* p. 188.
68. *The Economist,* August 26, 2010.
69. IWM, SR 3442.
70. IWM, SR 3442.
71. Miller, *Nothing Less Than Victory,* p. 356.
72. IWM, SR 3442.
73. http://www.pegasusarchive.org/normandy/lord_lovat.htm.
74. IWM, SR 11614.
75. *The Independent,* August 22, 2010.
76. IWM, SR 11614.
77. http://www.pegasusarchive.org/normandy/lord_lovat.htm.
78. *Daily Telegraph,* June 6, 2014.
79. IWM, SR 11614.

80. Collier, *D-Day*, p. 190.
81. *New York Times*, August 19, 2010. One commando recalled, "I shall never forget hearing the skirl of Bill Millin's pipes. As well as the pride we felt, it reminded us of home, and why we were fighting there for our lives and those of our loved ones."
82. IWM, SR 11614.
83. *The Independent*, August 22, 2010.
84. *The Independent*, March 20, 1995.
85. Kim Masters, "My Father, the Inglourious Basterd," *Daily Beast*, September 8, 2009.
86. Peter Masters, oral history, Eisenhower Center.
87. *The Independent*, March 20, 1995.
88. Lovat, *March Past*, p. 316.
89. Lovat, *March Past*, p. 311.
90. Lovat, *March Past*, p. 317.
91. DEFE 2/40, Intelligence/War Diary, No. 4 Commando, June 6, 1944, National Archives (UK).
92. Colonel Kieffer, After Action Report, June 14, 1944, National Archives (UK).
93. http://www.pegasusarchive.org/normandy/lord_lovat.htm.
94. Barber, *The Day the Devils Dropped In*, pp. 107–8.
95. http://www.pegasusarchive.org/normandy/terence_otway.htm.
96. According to one subsequent report, "In the early afternoon, the sound of gunfire was heard from the direction of Le Plein and it was clear that it was not aimed at the 9th Battalion. Otway believed that this could only be the Commandos, and so he immediately left the Chateau and ran down the hill to find out what was going on. At the Ecarde crossroads he found elements of No.3 Commando and Brigadier The Lord Lovat. Otway explained the situation to Lovat, who then asked him to escort Captain Westley, one of No.3's troop commanders, on a reconnaissance in preparation for an attack on Amfreville, which the 9th Battalion was asked to support with covering fire. Otway returned to the 9th Battalion and at 15:30 it was obvious that the attack was in progress. After a time, the sound of firing drifted away eastwards and, believing Amfreville to have been taken, Otway decided to head over there to find out what was happening. I said to [Corporal Joe] Wilson, 'We're going down there.' Everybody said, 'You're mad, you'll get killed,' but I said, 'It's a risk I've got to take,' I hadn't got any alternative. Wilson had got hold of a motorbike, so Wilson drove the motorbike, I sat in the sidecar, and we went down there. They passed several dead Commandos on the way and arrived at the Ecarde crossroads in time for a particularly heavy bout of enemy mortaring, which prompted them to seek shelter in a ditch. Brigadier Lovat was nearby with No.6 Commando, Otway called out to him, 'One of your Commando units has just had a sticky time. If you wish to talk to me, come down here, because I'm not bloody well coming up there!' Lovat came over and informed him that No.6 Commando had taken Le Plein, but he wouldn't be able to relieve the

9th Battalion until No.4 Commando arrived and put in a night-attack on Hauger. By the following morning, the 9th Battalion had been relieved at the Chateau d'Amfreville and so they moved into Le Plein." http://www.pegasusarchive.org/normandy/terence_otway.htm.

97. Mayo, *D-Day, Minute by Minute*, pp. 200–1.
98. Luck, *Panzer Commander*, p. 178.
99. Collier, *D-Day*, p. 199.

CHAPTER 9: ALL THE BLUE BONNETS

1. Forrest C. Pogue, "John Spalding D-Day Narrative," E Co., 16th Inf., Lt. Spalding combat interview, Military History Institute, Carlisle Barracks, PA.
2. Morison, *The Invasion of France and Germany*, p. 143.
3. Hatfield, *Rudder*, p. 140.
4. William Puntenney, undated memoir, pp. 40–41, 29th Infantry Division archives, Maryland Military Department, Fifth Regiment Armory, Baltimore.
5. Blumenson, *Battle of the Generals*, p. 37.
6. Bradley, *A General's Life*, p. 251.
7. Edward Wozenski, interview with Thames Television (1972). IWM, SR 3014.
8. Morison, *The Invasion of France and Germany*, p. 137.
9. https://www.backtonormandy.org/personal-stories/3420-waldo-werft.html.
10. "I remembered a lot of wounds from shrapnel," recalled Werft. "Basic medical supplies like bandages, morphine. Main treatment was stopping the bleeding. Plasma was given but not available to me on D-Day. Common wounds were from artillery and mortars' shrapnel. A lot of the tragedies I observed are now a blur that, after seventy-two years, are dim memories. After all, I didn't think or talk about these experiences for over sixty years. Thank goodness a lot of guys recorded their experiences in their young days and wrote books. I still have a lot of memories I have shared on Facebook and remember specific happenings more than specifics on treating the wounded. I don't remember running out of supplies, but there were other medics close by. I am sure we helped each other and worked together treating the wounded and litter bearing. My greatest fear was being severely wounded. I was always scared!" Waldo Werft, interview with author.
11. https://www.backtonormandy.org/personal-stories/3420-waldo-werft.html.
12. Fuller, *A Third Face*, pp. 162–65.
13. Taylor's citation for the DSC, which he earned for his actions on D-Day, reads: "Colonel Taylor landed during the most crucial and threatening period of the invasion operation. Thousands of men lay huddled on a narrow beachhead, their organizations and leaders cut down by the disastrous

enemy fire. Without hesitation, unmindful of the sniper and machine gun fire which was sweeping the beach, Colonel Taylor began to reorganize the units. While continuously exposed to this murderous fire, Colonel Taylor never slackened in his efforts in directing and coordinating the attack. By his initiative and leadership, he was able to clear an exit from the beach and begin moving groups of men from the crowded beachhead. This was the only exit opened in the early part of the assault and subsequent events proved it to be one of the most vital points contributing to the success of this operation. The high professional skill and outstanding courage exhibited by Colonel Taylor exemplify the highest traditions of the military forces of the United States and reflect great credit upon himself, the 1st Infantry Division, and the United States Army." http://www.homeofhe roes.com/members/02_DSC/citatons/03_wwii-dsc/army_tuv.html.

14. *Politico,* June 5, 2014.
15. E Company, 16th Infantry Regiment, After Action Report, June 6, 1944, National Archives (US).
16. Pogue, "John Spalding D-Day Narrative."
17. Pogue, "John Spalding D-Day Narrative."
18. http://www.navsource.org/archives/05/494.htm.
19. Kirkland, *Destroyers at Normandy,* p. 46.
20. Pogue, "John Spalding D-Day Narrative."
21. Pogue, "John Spalding D-Day Narrative."
22. E Company, 16th Infantry Regiment, After Action Report, June 6, 1944, National Archives (US).
23. Pogue, "John Spalding D-Day Narrative."
24. The last remaining holdout on Omaha Beach was the "D-1" Vierville draw, overlooking Dog Green sector, at the far western end of the beach. By midmorning, as Spalding led his platoon toward Colleville, 102 men of the 180 in A Company of the 116th Infantry Regiment who had landed in the first wave lay dead on Dog Green—the largest number of casualties of any Allied infantry company. Those killed included the company commander, twenty-nine-year-old Captain Taylor Fellers, and eighteen other men from rural Bedford, Virginia, which had suffered the highest per capita loss of any Allied community on D-Day. In just a few minutes, German machine gunners had broken the small town's heart. Alex Kershaw, *The Bedford Boys* (Cambridge, MA: Da Capo Press, 2003), p. 208.
25. Collier, *D-Day,* p. 182.
26. Balkoski, *Utah Beach,* p. 196.
27. George Mabry interview, Rowe Papers, Military History Institute, Carlisle Barracks, PA.
28. *New York Times,* April 21, 1987.
29. Taylor, *Swords and Plowshares,* p. 81. Mabry would receive the Distinguished Service Cross for his actions on D-Day and would soon assume command of the 2nd Battalion, replacing MacNeely, and would go on to be awarded the Medal of Honor, becoming one of very few Americans in WWII to receive the two highest decorations for bravery.

30. *VSD* magazine, June 2–8, 1994.
31. *Baltimore Sun*, June 4, 2006.
32. Number 6 Commando, After Action Report, June 6, 1944, WO 218/68, National Archives (UK).
33. Lovat, *March Past*, pp. 319–21.
34. Howard and Bates, *The Pegasus Diaries*, p. 136.
35. IWM, SR 11614.
36. Fowler, *Pegasus Bridge*, p. 55.
37. Howard and Bates, *The Pegasus Diaries*, p. 136.
38. Astor, *June 6, 1944*, p. 265.
39. IWM, SR 11614.
40. Howard and Bates, *The Pegasus Diaries*, p. 136.
41. IWM, SR 11614.
42. IWM, SR 11614.
43. Howard and Bates, *The Pegasus Diaries*, p. 136.
44. IWM, SR 11614.
45. Lovat, *March Past*, p. 322.
46. IWM, SR 11614.
47. Fowler, *Pegasus Bridge*, p. 57.
48. IWM, SR 11614.
49. Lovat, *March Past*, p. 324.
50. Hastings, *An Undergraduate's War*, p. 124.
51. IWM, SR 1648.
52. Stanley Hollis, oral history transcript, Green Howards Regimental Museum, Richmond, North Yorkshire, UK.
53. Liddle, *D-Day: By Those Who Were There*, pp. 138–42.
54. *Daily Telegraph*, June 16, 2005.
55. The citation reads: "During the assault on the beaches and the Mont Fleury battery, CSM Hollis's company commander noticed that two of the pill boxes had been bypassed, and went with CSM Hollis to see that they were clear. When they were 20 yards from the pillbox a machine-gun opened fire from the slit, and CSM Hollis instantly rushed straight to the pillbox, recharged his magazine, threw a grenade through the door and fired his Sten gun into it, killing two Germans and taking the remainder prisoner. He then cleared several Germans from a neighboring trench. By his action he undoubtedly saved the company from being heavily fired on from the rear, and enabled them to open the main beach exit. Later the same day, in the village of Crepon, the company encountered a field gun and crew, armed with Spandaus, at a hundred yards' range. CSM Hollis was put in command of a party to cover an attack on the gun, but the movement was held up. Seeing this, CSM Hollis pushed right forward to engage the gun with a PIAT [Projector, Infantry, Anti-Tank] from a house at 50 yards range. He was observed by a sniper who fired and grazed his right cheek, and at the same time the gun swung round and fired at point blank range into the house. To avoid the falling masonry CSM Hollis moved his party to an alternative position. Two of the enemy gun crew had by this time

been killed, and the gun was destroyed shortly afterwards. He later found that two of his men had stayed behind in the house, and immediately volunteered to get them out. In full view of the enemy, who were continually firing at him, he went forward alone using only a Bren gun to distract their attention from the other men. Under cover of his diversions the two men were able to get back. Wherever fighting was heaviest CSM Hollis appeared, and in the course of a magnificent day's work he displayed the utmost gallantry, and on two separate occasions his courage and initiative prevented the enemy from holding up the advance at critical stages. It was largely through his heroism and resource that the company's objectives were gained and casualties were not heavier and, by his own bravery, he saved the lives of many of his men." Hastings, *An Undergraduate's War,* pp. 124–25.

56. Number 6 Commando After Action Report, June 6, 1944, WO 218/68, National Archives (UK).

57. Lovat, *March Past,* p. 328.

58. IWM, SR 11614.

59. Stan Scott, interview, National Army Museum, UK, 2011.

60. Scott's Number 3 Commando numbered seventy-five men on D-Day. He would be one of just nineteen men still able to fight when pulled off the line in August 1944.

61. Luck, *Panzer Commander,* p. 178.

62. Lovat, *March Past,* pp. 229–30.

63. Pogue, "John Spalding D-Day Narrative."

64. Major Joseph Dawson, interview by Dr. John F. Votaw, April 16, 1991, Dawson file, McCormick Research Center, First Division Museum at Cantigny, Wheaton, Illinois.

65. Pogue, "John Spalding D-Day Narrative."

66. Joseph Dawson interview.

67. Pogue, "John Spalding D-Day Narrative."

68. John Spalding questionnaire, Box 12, Folder 40, Cornelius Ryan Collection of World War II Papers, Mahn Center for Archives and Special Collections, Ohio University Libraries.

69. Pogue, "John Spalding D-Day Narrative."

70. Spalding's DSC citation reads: "The President of the United States takes pleasure in presenting the Distinguished Service Cross to John M. Spalding (0-1317433), Second Lieutenant, U.S. Army, for extraordinary heroism in connection with military operations against an armed enemy while serving with Company E, 2d Battalion, 16th Infantry Regiment, 1st Infantry Division, in action against enemy forces on 6 June 1944, near Colleville-sur-Mer in France. Upon reaching the beach in the initial landing on the coast of France, Second Lieutenant Spalding, completely disregarding his own personal safety, led his men up the beach to the slight cover of a shale shelf. Having suffered numerous casualties, he hesitated only long enough to reorganize his unit. He then led his men over an

embankment, through barbed wire and across a thickly sown minefield. Second Lieutenant Spalding led his men in the attack on a series of enemy strongpoints and successfully destroyed them. Constantly ignoring heavy enemy fire, he at all times continued in the advance and personally destroyed an anti-tank gun which had been firing on beach targets with deadly effect. The personal bravery and superior leadership demonstrated by Second Lieutenant Spalding exemplify the highest traditions of the military forces of the United States and reflect great credit upon himself, the 1st Infantry Division, and the United States Army." Headquarters, First U.S. Army, General Orders No. 31 (July 1, 1944), National Archives (US).

71. John Spalding questionnaire, Cornelius Ryan collection. See also 16th Infantry Regiment's After Action Report, courtesy of Max Poorthius, president of the 16th Infantry Regiment Historical Society.

72. John Spalding, medical record, courtesy of Max Poorthuis, president, 16th Infantry Regiment Historical Society.

73. E Company, 16th Infantry Regiment, After Action Report, June 1944, National Archives (US).

74. Edward Wozenski, interview with Thames Television (1972).

75. Balkoski, *Omaha Beach*, p. 350.

76. Balkoski, *Omaha Beach*, p. 96.

77. Pogue, "John Spalding D-Day Narrative."

78. http://www.ddaymuseum.co.uk/d-day/d-day-and-the-battle-of-normandy-your-questions-answered.

79. D-Day awards for 1st Section, 1st Platoon, Company E, 2nd Battalion, 16th Infantry Regiment, 1st Infantry Division, First Infantry Division Museum.

80. Balkoski, *Omaha Beach*, p. 359.

81. Only four Medals of Honor were awarded to Americans on D-Day.

82. "The Normandy Invasion: Medal of Honor Recipients," US Army Center of Military History, https://history.army.mil/html/reference/Normandy/nor-moh.html. The recipients were John Pinder, Jimmie Monteith, and Carlton Barrett. Only Barrett would survive, living until 1986. Barrett's citation reads: "For gallantry and intrepidity at the risk of his life above and beyond the call of duty on 6 June 1944, in the vicinity of St. Laurent-sur-Mer, France. On the morning of D-day Pvt. Barrett, landing in the face of extremely heavy enemy fire, was forced to wade ashore through neck-deep water. Disregarding the personal danger, he returned to the surf again and again to assist his floundering comrades and save them from drowning. Refusing to remain pinned down by the intense barrage of small-arms and mortar fire poured at the landing points, Pvt. Barrett, working with fierce determination, saved many lives by carrying casualties to an evacuation boat lying offshore. In addition to his assigned mission as guide, he carried dispatches the length of the fire-swept beach; he assisted the wounded; he calmed the shocked; he arose as a leader in the

stress of the occasion. His coolness and his dauntless daring courage while constantly risking his life during a period of many hours had an inestimable effect on his comrades and is in keeping with the highest traditions of the U.S. Army." Medal of Honor Recipients, World War II [Recipients A–F], US Army Center of Military History, https://history.army.mil/html /moh/wwII-a-f.html.

CHAPTER 10: TALLYHO!

1. Shilleto, *Pegasus Bridge and Merville Battery,* pp. 74–75.
2. Howard and Bates, *The Pegasus Diaries,* p. 137.
3. Shilleto, *Pegasus Bridge and Merville Battery,* pp. 74–75.
4. Captain Frank Lillyman, 502nd PIR 101st Airborne Pathfinder activities, After Action Report, 1944, National Archives (US).
5. Preisler, *First to Jump,* pp. 130–32.
6. "D-Day, état des lieux," US Airborne in Cotentin Peninsula, Statistical Tables—Operation Neptune, June 5–13, 1944, http://www.6juin1944.com /assaut/aeropus/en_page.php?page=casualties.
7. Balkoski, *Utah Beach,* pp. 255–56.
8. Astor, *June 6, 1944,* p. 271.
9. Dan Farley, interview with author.
10. "A Hall of Fame for Heroes," reported by Byron Pitts, *CBS Evening News,* September 2, 1998.
11. Moen and Heinen, *Reflections of Courage on D-Day,* p. 4.
12. U.S. Army Historical Division, interviews with various Company A, 5th Rangers, July 1944, National Archives (US).
13. Moen and Heinen, *Reflections of Courage on D-Day,* pp. 98–99.
14. Astor, *June 6, 1944,* pp. 212–15.
15. Balkoski, *Omaha Beach,* p. 281.
16. Moen and Heinen, *Reflections of Courage on D-Day,* p. 101.
17. Moen and Heinen, *Reflections of Courage on D-Day,* p. 105.
18. Kirkland, *Destroyers at Normandy,* p. 62.
19. George Kerchner, diary entry, June 6, 1944, Eisenhower Center.
20. Johnson and Dunphie, *Brightly Shone the Dawn,* p. 133.
21. Martin, *Battle Diary,* pp. 14–15.
22. *The Rifleman: A Journal of the Queen's Own Rifles of Canada,* July 1978, p. 8.
23. http://www.dday-overlord.com/en/d-day/figures.
24. IWM, SR 11614.
25. War Office Records, 171/1302, Intelligence/War Diary, 6th Battalion, the Green Howards, National Archives (UK).
26. The fighting and dying that June 6 were not yet over for the Green Howards. "Drinking champagne when disturbed again by Jerry," noted one officer in his diary. "Saw 4 of our tanks blazing. Put in final attack [south] of St Gabriel and stopped in [a] wood . . . We are the furthest forward troops of the whole invasion and fairly near our objective. The morale was

very high and we have moved very quickly, by-passing any opposition where possible." http://www.patricktaylor.com/war-diary-1.

27. http://greenhowards.org.uk/d-day-and-vc/.
28. War Office Records, 171/1302, Intelligence/War Diary, 6th Battalion, the Green Howards.
29. Hastings, *An Undergraduate's War*, p. 126.
30. Mills-Roberts, *Clash by Night*, p. 103.
31. Léon Gautier, interview with author.
32. Dunning, *The Fighting Fourth*, p. 144.
33. Dunning, *The Fighting Fourth*, p. 145.
34. Astor, *June 6, 1944*, p. 292.
35. Collier, *D-Day*, p. 93.
36. Hugh Schofield, "Veteran Feels at Home on D-Day Beach," BBC News, May 23, 2004, http://news.bbc.co.uk/2/hi/europe/3735307.stm.
37. Astor, *June 6, 1944*, pp. 212–15.
38. Undated press clippings, Dalton scrapbooks, the Queen's Own Rifles Regimental Museum and Archives.
39. *Toronto Globe and Mail*, June 22, 1944. See also undated press clippings, Dalton files, the Queen's Own Rifles Regimental Museum and Archives, Toronto.
40. At 21st Panzer Division HQ, near Caen, around midnight, the 12th SS Panzer Division's notorious Kurt Meyer arrived, having spent most of the day avoiding Allied aircraft. He looked at a map, showing the strength of Allied forces, and declared, "Little fish! We'll throw them back into the sea in the morning." Lewis, *Voices from D-Day*, p. 174.

CHAPTER 11: THE BOCAGE

1. Miller, *Nothing Less Than Victory*, p. 474.
2. *Collier's*, June 11, 1954.
3. *Saturday Evening Post*, August 19, 1944.
4. Howard and Bates, *The Pegasus Diaries*, pp. 142–43.
5. WO 171/1357, Intelligence/War Diary, 2nd Battalion, the Ox and Bucks Light Infantry, National Archives (UK).
6. http://www.pegasusarchive.org/normandy/john_howard.htm.
7. Howard and Bates, *The Pegasus Diaries*, pp. 142–43.
8. Howard and Bates, *The Pegasus Diaries*, pp. 142–43.
9. https://history.army.mil/books/wwii/smallunit/smallunit-pdh.htm.
10. Hatfield, *Rudder*, p. 153.
11. "Either General Cota or Col. Canham felt the Omaha Dog beachhead was too fragile to allow Ranger Force C to leave the beachhead and proceed to PdHoc," recalled Raaen. "One of the two ordered Lt. Col. Schneider to cancel his plans to continue from Vierville to PdHoc and remain in defensive positions on the west end of the beachhead perimeter for the night of D-Day. About midnight of D-Day, a joint meeting was held at the

headquarters of Ranger Force C. Plans were made for the relief of Ranger Force A on D+1. Task Force Metcalf, containing the remnants of the 1st Battalion, 116th Infantry, Ranger Force C, remnants of Ranger Force B and about eight tanks of the 743rd Tank Bn, was to be the advanced guard for the 116th's move to seize Grandcamps-les-Bains on the way to Isigny. Ranger Force C would peel off from TF Metcalf at St. Pierre du Mont and relieve Ranger Force A at PdHoc. Didn't happen that way. A German counter attack early on D+1, caused Lt. Col. Schneider a dilemma. Should he stop the column or continue. He chose to let the three Ranger Companies that had passed the IP to continue toward PdHoc with rest of Force C remaining to help defend the beachhead. I am sure Schneider consulted with Cota, Canham and Metcalf before making such a bold decision. TF Metcalf ran into strong artillery fire beyond St. Pierre. The tanks had actually gotten past the road to PdHoc when they and the Provisional Ranger Company (the remnants of A, B and C Companies, 2nd RIB were combined into a single Ranger Company before entering the bocage) were forced to withdraw to St. Pierre du Mont. At that point, the 29th Division ordered the tanks of the 743rd and Lt. Col. Metcalf and Maj. Sullivan to return to the beachhead to help in its defense and I found myself in command of a ragtag force consisting of C Co, 116th, other remnants of the 1st Bn, 116th, the Prov Co, 2nd Rangers, Cos C and D, 5th Rangers and other divisional units I knew not what. We set up a perimeter defense around the hamlet, expecting an armored counter attack. I also sent out a two man patrol to find Colonel Rudder and his Ranger Force A. They did. The Germans did not attack. The next morning, Lt. Col. Schneider and the remainder of the 5th RIB arrived with essentially the same plan for the attack to relieve PdHoc as I had worked up the night before." General John Raaen, email to author, March 20, 2018.

12. George Kerchner, diary entry, Eisenhower Center.
13. O'Donnell, *Dog Company*, p. 124.
14. George Kerchner, diary entry, Eisenhower Center.
15. General John Raaen, interview with author.
16. 5th Ranger Battalion, After Action Report, A.P.O. 655 US Army, July 2, 1944, National Archives (US).
17. Pogue, *Pogue's War*, p. 122.
18. 2nd Ranger Battalion, After Action Report, June 8, 1944, National Archives (US).
19. Alfred E. Baer, "D-for-Dog: The Story of a Ranger Company" (unpublished manuscript), p. 47.
20. https://history.army.mil/books/wwii/smallunit/smallunit-pdh.htm.
21. In his diary, Lieutenant Kerchner jotted on June 11, 1944, "Went to Mass. Thanked God. First chance to count noses. 'D' Co. has eight dead, 13 wounded, 32 missing, 15 present . . . Ate good. Shaved at last. Make out report." George Kerchner, diary entry, Eisenhower Center.
22. https://armyhistory.org/rudders-rangers-and-the-boys-of-pointe-du-hoc
-the-u-s-army-rangers-mission-in-the-early-morning-hours-of-6-june

-1944/. Kerchner's citation reads: "By his determined leadership and outstanding heroism, he led his company in the successful assault upon and captured 155 mm enemy gun positions. He tenaciously and courageously held his position until relieved and was a constant inspiration and source of encouragement to his troops."

23. Hatfield, *Rudder,* p. 157.
24. http://warfarehistorynetwork.com/daily/wwii/blue-and-gray-at-omaha-beach/.
25. Pyle, *Brave Men,* p. 391.
26. Pyle, *Brave Men,* p. 390.
27. https://qormuseum.org/soldiers-of-the-queens-own/dalton-charles-osborne/.
28. Botting, *The D-Day Invasion,* p. 188.
29. Grant, *The Fuel of the Fire,* p. 186.
30. Scannell, *Arguments of Kings,* p. 165.
31. Lovat, *March Past,* p. 346.
32. Lovat, *March Past,* p. 347.
33. Botting, *The D-Day Invasion,* p. 193.
34. Hastings, *Overlord,* p. 125.
35. Martin, *Battle Diary,* p. 21.
36. https://qormuseum.org/history/timeline-1925-1949/the-second-world-war/war-diaries-1944/.
37. *The Rifleman: A Journal of the Queen's Own Rifles of Canada,* July 1978, p. 8.
38. Martin, *Battle Diary,* p. 21.
39. According to Ian Dalton, Charles Dalton's son, "Elliot was 5 years younger than Charles but they were quite close despite being of different temperaments. Charles was the more serious older brother, a natural leader and great public speaker. He loved standing up and holding forth. Elliot was the party animal extremely handsome and a lady killer as they used to say. The men loved him as one of theirs. Charles was respected but more distant. Charles was married to Helen for several years prior to the war with one child a girl named Jane who still lives in Oakville. Elliot was single and lived with Charles, Helen and Jane on Castlefield Avenue in Toronto in the pre-war years. Dad said Elliot often did not come home at night. He said Elliot used the house as 'his operational base.' This led to some confusion after D-Day. 2 Major Daltons with the QOR at the same address were wounded within days. Mum got confused telegrams saying Charles was wounded in the leg (actually Elliot), then one saying ignore the last telegram Charles was dead. Then another saying ignore last telegram he was wounded in the head but recovering. Helen and Jane spent summers at a summer camp for girls in Muskoka area. Elliot came back to Canada in 1945 and met Marie a New Zealand nurse. He married and had 3 children." Ian Dalton, email to author, April 5, 2018.
40. *The Rifleman: A Journal of the Queen's Own Rifles of Canada,* July 1978, p. 8.
41. Undated press clipping, Dalton files, the Queen's Own Rifles Regimental Museum and Archives, Toronto.

42. *Toronto Globe and Mail*, March 24, 1999.

43. *The Rifleman: A Journal of the Queen's Own Rifles of Canada*, July 1978, p. 8.

44. Johnson and Dunphie, *Brightly Shone the Dawn*, p. 80.

45. Max Hastings, *Overlord*, p. 66.

46. According to one account, the hill was of great significance: "Had the Green Howards been able to capture [it], and they so nearly did, the entire German position in the area west of Caen would have been extremely unpleasant." The British belatedly understood the hill's strategic value when it was finally captured on June 25. "It then became immediately clear why Rommel, after a visit to the area, had so hurriedly moved in one of his crack formations, the 12th SS Panzer Division. By an evil chance the leading element of the division moved into the area during the few hours between the relatively unopposed reconnaissance and the Green Howards' attack." Johnson and Dunphie, *Brightly Shone the Dawn*, p. 89.

47. Liddle, *D-Day: By Those Who Were There*, pp. 138–42.

48. Liddle, *D-Day: By Those Who Were There*, pp. 138–42.

49. Hastings, *An Undergraduate's War*, pp. 132–33.

50. Hastings, *An Undergraduate's War*, p. 134.

51. Hastings, *Overlord*, pp. 136–37.

52. Lovat, *March Past*, p. 349.

53. *The Independent*, March 20, 1995.

54. Lovat, *March Past*, p. 358.

55. Barber, *The Day the Devils Dropped In*, pp. 200–1.

56. For his actions at Merville, Otway would receive the Distinguished Service Order. Otway's DSO citation reads: "For conspicuous bravery and outstanding leadership. This officer led 150 men of his bn on the successful attack of the Sallenelles battery. He personally directed the attack and organised the successful cleaning up of the enemy strong points under heavy enemy mortar and machine gun fire. He led the attack on and successfully held Le Plein until relieved by another formation. On arrival in the Le Mesnil area he succeeded in beating off two major enemy attacks of several hours duration by his magnificent leadership of his numerically very weak and tired bn. His utter disregard of personal danger has been an inspiration for all his men." http://www.pegasusarchive.org/normandy/ter ence_otway.htm.

57. Barber, *The Day the Devils Dropped In*, p. 202.

CHAPTER 12: A DIRTY BUSH WAR

1. Morgan, *Past Forgetting*, p. 194.

2. Murphy, *Turncoat*, pp. 225–26.

3. Dwight D. Eisenhower, *Crusade in Europe*, p. 267.

4. Bob Slaughter, interview with author.

5. Moorehead, *Eclipse*, p. 140.

6. http://www.normandythenandnow.com/caen-before-and-after-the -battle-of-1944/.

7. Hastings, *An Undergraduate's War*, p. 134.

8. Hastings, *Overlord*, p. 213.

9. Lieb, *Konventioneller Krieg oder NS-Weltanschauungskrieg?*, p. 176.

10. Morgan, *D-Day Hero*, p. 93.

11. Moorehead, *Eclipse*, pp. 142–43.

12. Roosevelt would posthumously receive the Medal of Honor: "For gallantry and intrepidity at the risk of his life above and beyond the call of duty on 6 June 1944, in France. After two verbal requests to accompany the leading assault elements in the Normandy invasion had been denied, Brig. Gen. Roosevelt's written request for this mission was approved, and he landed with the first wave of the forces assaulting the enemy-held beaches. He repeatedly led groups from the beach, over the seawall, and established them inland. His valor, courage, and presence in the very front of the attack and his complete unconcern at being under heavy fire inspired the troops to heights of enthusiasm and self-sacrifice. Although the enemy had the beach under constant direct fire, Brig. Gen. Roosevelt moved from one locality to another, rallying men around him, directed and personally led them against the enemy. Under his seasoned, precise, calm, and unfaltering leadership, assault troops reduced beach strongpoints and rapidly moved inland with minimum casualties. He thus contributed substantially to the successful establishment of the beachhead in France." Supernumerary General Officer, 4th Division, General Orders, September 28, 1944, National Archives (US).

13. Jeffers, *Theodore Roosevelt Jr.*, p. 261.

14. Buckley, *Monty's Men*, pp. 109–10.

15. Moorehead, *Eclipse*, p. 134.

16. Bradley, *A General's Life*, p. 280.

17. Dwight D. Eisenhower, *Crusade in Europe*, p. 272.

18. The Americans were as bogged down as their Allied comrades. The ancient hedgerows had robbed the armored units of mobility. One day late that July, a captain in the 102nd Cavalry Reconnaissance asked his men for ideas as to how to deal with the infernal bocage. One man spoke up. "Why don't we get some saw teeth and put them on the front of the tank and cut through these hedges?" Several men laughed, but not Sergeant Curtis Culin, soon to be celebrated as a national hero in America as the man who got the Yank tanks rolling again. "Hang on a minute," said Culin, "he's got an idea there." Before long, the famed "Rhino" was born—a Sherman tank modified to carry saw teeth and able to burst through a hedgerow, providing mobility at last. Hastings, *Overlord*, p. 252.

19. D'Este, *Decision in Normandy*, p. 414.

20. Grant, *The Fuel of the Fire*, p. 193.

21. John Spalding, medical record, courtesy of Max Poorthuis, president, 16th Infantry Regiment Historical Society.

22. Captain Edward Wozenski was still E Company commander. He recalled the following incident: "We were all so secretive, sworn to such secrecy, about these famous 'DD tanks.' Everyone knew those tanks were terrible!

They were supposed to be these incredible tanks, but they performed so badly in tests we called them 'Donald Ducks.' We pleaded with the tank guys to use the British model, the Hobart Funnies, because they were proven to be successful in combat, but they didn't listen to a thing we said. Those idiots almost cost us the invasion. So now here we are in Normandy, the day after the attack, and Sergeant Streczyk, what a sense of humor that man had, calls me over for a look-see into a bunker. The guy has a grin a mile wide. I frowned. Uh oh, here we go again. Now what? Was he going to fake blowing us both to pieces again? So he drags me inside this massive bunker and points. There on the wall the damn Germans had painted a picture of one of our precious secret Donald Duck tanks just so they would recognize it. The painting was so pretty it reminded me of a Betty Grable pin-up! I am surprised they didn't add a big bosomed Fraulein sitting on the muzzle with a big smile on her face. Heck, that's what our guys would have done. Good Lord, the Jerries had known about our vaunted secret weapon the whole time! All that secrecy! [Laughs] Streczyk and I howled over that one. Those idiot tank guys didn't have a clue what they were doing." Edward Wozenski, interview with Thames Television (1972).

23. John Spalding, medical record, courtesy of Max Poorthuis, president, 16th Infantry Regiment Historical Society.
24. Scott, *Typhoon Pilot*, p. 129.
25. Williams, *D-Day to Berlin*, p. 197.
26. Clay, *Blood and Sacrifice*, p. 207.
27. Hastings, *Overlord*, p. 313.
28. Lewis, *Voices from D-Day*, p. 282.
29. http://warfarehistorynetwork.com/daily/wwii/the-hawker-typhoon-1a-1b -worst-raf-fighters-in-wwii/.
30. Veitch, *Fly*, p. 113.
31. Scott, *Typhoon Pilot*, p. 129.
32. Morgan, *D-Day Hero*, p. 102.
33. Dwight D. Eisenhower, *Crusade in Europe*, p. 279.
34. Hastings, *Overlord*, p. 315.
35. Kershaw, *Avenue of Spies*, p. 172.
36. Alex Kershaw, "From D-Day to Paris: The Story of a Lifetime," *World War II Magazine*, April/May 2012.
37. Williams, *D-Day to Berlin*, p. 205.
38. Hastings, *Overlord*, p. 313.
39. http://www.ddaymuseum.co.uk/d-day/d-day-and-the-battle-of-normandy -your-questions-answered.

Chapter 13: Defeating Hitler

1. https://www.ibiblio.org/hyperwar/USA/USA-E-Breakout/USA-E -Breakout-30.html.
2. Phil Davison, "Lieutenant George Kerchner: Veteran of the D-Day Landings," *The Independent*, March 10, 2012. That July 1944, Kerchner had been

informed that R. J. Reynolds Tobacco Co. had announced on a radio show that in his honor, "the makers of Camel cigarettes are sending to our fighters overseas 400,000 Camel cigarettes"; *Baltimore Sun,* February 20, 2012.

3. Howard and Bates, *The Pegasus Diaries,* p. 157.

4. Ambrose, *Pegasus Bridge,* p. 164.

5. Ferguson, *The Paras 1940–84,* p. 26.

6. *The Independent,* January 30, 2013.

7. Middlebrook, *Arnhem 1944,* p. 439.

8. http:// warfarehistorynetwork.com/daily/wwii/101st-in-operation -market-garden-taking-the-bridge-at-best/.

9. http://www.ww2-airborne.us/units/502/502.html. The other recipient was Lieutenant Colonel Robert G. Cole, also of the 502nd PIR.

10. http://www.101airborneww2.com/warstories2.html.

11. http://www.lonesentry.com/gi_stories_booklets/101stairborne/.

12. E Company, 16th Infantry Regiment, 1st Division, "A History of Company E from June 1942," After Action Report, National Archives (US).

13. John Spalding, medical record, courtesy of Max Poorthuis, president, 16th Infantry Regiment Historical Society.

14. *Pike County Courier,* May 24, 2017.

15. *World War II Magazine,* June 12, 2006.

16. Preisler, *First to Jump,* p. 238.

17. Jake McNiece, 506th PIR, 101st Airborne, oral history, Pathfinder, Witness to War Foundation, witnesstowar.org.

18. McNiece, oral history.

19. Preisler, *First to Jump,* p. 238.

20. Jack Agnew, "Live from Bastogne," *The Pathfinder* (9th TC Command Pathfinder Association), vol. 1, no. 4 (1986), p. 4. See also McNiece and Killblane, *The Filthy Thirteen,* p. 276.

21. Preisler, *First to Jump,* p. 242.

22. Interview with Staff Sergeant Jake McNiece, 506th Parachute Infantry, 101st Airborne Division, http://www.witnesstowar.org/search_result/videos/10.

23. *World War II Magazine,* June 12, 2006.

24. Koskimaki, *The Battered Bastards of Bastogne,* p. 507.

25. Hastings, *Overlord,* p. 193.

26. E Company, 16th Infantry Regiment, 1st Division, "A History of Company E from June 1942," After Action Report, National Archives (US), p. x.

27. Hastings, *Overlord,* p. 247.

28. Bruce C. Clarke, "Study of AGF Battle Casualties," September 1946, National Archives (US).

29. In all there were 929,307 individual cases in WWII of men who were treated for what became an epidemic problem. More than one in four men in US combat divisions in Europe had become such casualties since D-Day.

30. Moen and Heinen, *Reflections of Courage on D-Day,* p. 172. By the end of the battle, only twelve of the seventy-two men who had landed on Omaha Beach with Parker were still able to fight.

31. Sevareid, *Not So Wild a Dream,* p. 497.

32. Breuer, *Geronimo*, p. 545.
33. Breuer, *Geronimo*, p. 598.
34. http://www.americanairmuseum.com/person/242977.
35. https://www.airspacemag.com/daily-planet/pilot-who-led-d-day-invasion-180951679/.
36. http://theprovince.com/opinion/letters-d-day-pilot-diwali-lincoln-burnaby-hospital-haida-gwaii-rats-romney-obama-amanda-todd-bullying-gas-tax.
37. Clay, *Blood and Sacrifice*, p. 238.
38. E Company, 16th Infantry Regiment, 1st Division, "A History of Company E from June 1942," After Action Report, National Archives (US), p. xii.
39. Kershaw, *The Liberator*, p. 324.
40. Howard and Bates, *The Pegasus Diaries*, p. 157.
41. Howard and Bates, *The Pegasus Diaries*, p. 157.
42. Brinkley, *The Boys of Pointe du Hoc*, p. 97.
43. Moen and Heinen, *Reflections of Courage on D-Day*, pp. 197–204.
44. John Spalding, medical record, courtesy of Max Poorthuis, president, 16th Infantry Regiment Historical Society.
45. John Spalding, medical record, courtesy of Max Poorthuis, president, 16th Infantry Regiment Historical Society.
46. *Warwick Advertiser*, 25 May 2017.
47. http://2ndww.blogspot.fr/2013/07/the-wartime-treachery-of-harold-cole.html.
48. Murphy, *Turncoat*, p. 222.
49. Murphy, *Turncoat*, p. 229.
50. Murphy, *Turncoat*, p. 245.
51. Harold Cole, Security Service personal files, August 21, 1945–December 23, 1946, files KV 2/415–KV 2/417, National Archives (UK).
52. Murphy, *Turncoat*, p. 222.
53. Preisler, *First to Jump*, p. 142.
54. Preisler, *First to Jump*, p. 142.
55. *Life*, December 3, 1945.
56. *New York Times*, March 8, 1971.

EPILOGUE: IN MEMORIAM

1. Lewis, *Voices from D-Day*, p. 296.
2. *Collier's*, June 11, 1954.
3. *Collier's*, June 11, 1954.
4. http://www.myaggienation.com/aggie_profiles/gen-james-earl-rudder-led-texas-a-m-through-immense/article_c8ad387e-0f43-11e3-824c-0019bb2963f4.html.
5. Brinkley, *The Boys of Pointe du Hoc*, p. 97.
6. *D-Day Plus 20 Years: Eisenhower Returns to Normandy*, presented by Walter Cronkite, *CBS Reports*, CBS News, June 1964.
7. http://www.historyplace.com/speeches/reagan-d-day.htm.

8. *Daily Telegraph,* July 16, 2014.
9. *Daily Telegraph,* July 25, 2006.
10. *VSD* magazine, June 8, 1994.
11. *New York Times,* March 14, 2012.
12. *Baltimore Sun*, February 20, 2012.
13. *New York Times,* March 14, 2012.
14. News Broadcast, GMTV (UK), June 6, 1994.
15. Lovat, *March Past,* p. 360.
16. Lovat had been seriously wounded in Normandy but eventually made a full recovery. In early 1945, as undersecretary of state for foreign affairs, he was part of a parliamentary delegation sent to meet Stalin in Moscow. Winston Churchill wrote to Stalin before the visit, telling him that Lovat was "the mildest-mannered man that ever scuttled a ship or cut a throat." Lovat then served as minister of economic warfare. He resigned after Churchill's Conservative Party was heavily defeated by the Labour Party in July 1945. The swing to Labor was 12 percent, the largest in British parliamentary history. Lovat then returned to Scotland, where he managed his estate, but he did not entirely turn his back on politics, serving as a speaker on Highland affairs in the House of Lords. He was also a member of Inverness County Council for forty-two years. He died in 1995. Bull, *Commando Tactics,* p. 107.
17. *The Independent*, March 20, 1995.
18. Dan Farley, interview with author.
19. *The Independent*, December 21, 2013.
20. *The Independent*, December 21, 2013.
21. Mark Worthington, interview with author.
22. *Daily Mail*, December 26, 2012.
23. Morgan, *D-Day Hero,* p. 107.
24. *Darlington & Stockton Times,* June 3, 2014.
25. *Daily Mail*, December 26, 2012.
26. Léon Gautier, interview with author.

INDEX

ALEX KERSHAW is a journalist and a *New York Times* best-selling author of books on World War II. Born in York, England, he is a graduate of Oxford University and lives in Savannah, Georgia.